A Garland Series

THE ENGLISH BOOK TRADE
1660-1853

156 Titles relating to the early history of

English Publishing, Bookselling,

the Struggle for Copyright

and the Freedom of the Press

Reprinted in photo-facsimile in 42 volumes

edited, with bibliographical notes,
by
Stephen Parks
Curator, Osborn Collection
Beinecke Library, Yale University

Memoirs of the First Forty-five Years
of James Lackington

1794

Garland Publishing, Inc., New York & London

1974

Z
325
· L23 A35
1974 b

Library of Congress Cataloging in Publication Data

Lackington, James, 1746-1815.
    Memoirs of the first forty-five years of James
Lackington.

    (The English book trade, 1660-1853)
    Reprint of the 1794 ed. printed for the author,
London under title: Memoirs of the forty-five first
years of the life of James Lackington; with new pref.
    1. Lackington, James, 1746-1815. 2. Booksellers
and bookselling--London--Correspondence, reminiscences,
etc. I. Title. II. Series.
Z325.L23A35   1974b   686.2'092'4   74-23631
ISBN 0-8240-0979-7

Printed in the United States of America
Library
UNIVERSITY OF MIAMI

Preface

James Lackington made history in the book trade as well as a considerable fortune by his policies of selling for ready money only, at the lowest price, and by selling remainders at slight profit. His Temple of the Muses on Finsbury Square was one of the sights of London.* Lackington's *Memoirs* were first printed in 1791. The edition reprinted here is the seventh, 1794, "corrected and much enlarged," and the first to have an index. Lackington's *Confessions* are reprinted in another volume, and a satirical ode addressed to Lackington in *The Literary Property Debate: Eight Tracts, 1774-1775*, item I.

Brit. Mus. 10825.aa.11

April, 1974   *S.R.P.*

---

*An important source for the book trade of the late eighteenth century.

MEMOIRS

OF THE

FORTY-FIVE FIRST YEARS

OF

The LIFE

OF

JAMES LACKINGTON,

The prefent Bookfeller in Chifwell-ftreet, Finfbury-fquare,
LONDON.

Written by Himfelf.

In FORTY-SEVEN LETTERS to a FRIEND.

With a TRIPLE DEDICATION.

1. To the PUBLIC.
2. To RESPECTABLE } BOOKSELLERS.
3. To SORDID

SEVENTH EDITION.

Corrected and much enlarged; interfperfed with many *origina!
bumorous* Stories, and *droll* Anecdotes, to which is alfo added,
an INDEX.

Fair praife is fterling gold—all fhould defire it—
    Flatt'ry, bafe coin—a cheat upon the nation;
And yet, our vanity doth much admire it,
    And really gives it all its circulation.   PETER PINDAR.

As all Fanatics preach, fo all men write,
Out of the ftrength of Gifts, and inward Light,
In fpite of art; as horfes thorough pac'd
Were never taught, and therefore go more faft. BUTLER.

LONDON:

Printed for the AUTHOR, No. 46 and 47, Chifwell-Street;
and fold by all other Bookfellers.

MDCCXCIV.

[Price 2s. 6d. in boards—bound 3s.]

A TRIPLE DEDICATION.

―――――――――

I.

TO THE PUBLIC.

WORTHY PATRONS,

WERE I to address you in the
accustomed declamatory strain which has long been
adopted as the *universal language* of dedications, viz.
FLATTERY, I should not only merit your contempt,
for thus endeavouring to impose upon your understandings, but also render myself ridiculously conspicuous, by a feeble attempt to perform that, for
which, as well by nature, as long established habit,
I am totally disqualified.

On the other hand, I should esteem myself equally
meriting your censure, as being guilty of a flagrant
species of ingratitude, were I to omit availing myself of so favourable an opportunity as now presents
itself of expressing the respect and veneration I entertain for you, resulting from the very extensive
and ample encouragement with which you have
crowned my indefatigable exertions to obtain your
patronage, by largely contributing to the diffusion
of science and rational entertainment, on such moderate terms as were heretofore unknown.

Permit me to indulge the pleasing hope, that,
when I assert my mind is deeply impressed with the
most grateful sense of the obligation, I shall be honoured with credit. If this opinion be well founded,
to enlarge on the subject were superfluous—if otherwise, the strongest argument, the most splendid and

B

forcible language could convey, would not ensure conviction; I therefore desist, fully persuaded that the most satisfactory demonstration I can possibly exhibit of the sincerity of this declaration, will be, an inviolable adherence to that uniform line of conduct which has already secured your approbation to a degree eminent as unprecedented, and which is indeed daily rendered more evident, by a progressive increase in the number and extent of your commands; trusting, that so long as you find my practice invariably correspondent to those professions so frequently exhibited to your notice (from which to deviate would render me unworthy your protection) you will, in defiance of all malignant opposition, firmly persevere in the liberal support of him whose primary ambition it is, and during life shall be, to distinguish himself as,

WORTHY PATRONS,

Your much obliged,

Ever grateful,

And devoted humble servant,

Chiswell-Street,
October 1791.

JAMES LACKINGTON.

II.

To that part of the numerous body of BOOK-
SELLERS of Great Britain and Ireland, whose
conduct JUSTLY claims the additional title of
RESPECTABLE;

Whose candour and liberality he has in numerous instances
experienced, and feels a sensible pleasure in thus publicly
acknowledging:

And lastly, (though not least in *Fame*)

III.

To those sordid and malevolent BOOKSELLERS,
whether they resplendent dwell in stately mansions, or in wretched huts of dark and groveling
obscurity;

—" I'll give every one a smart lash in my way"—

To whose assiduous and unwearied labours to injure his reputation with their brethren and the public, he is in a considerable degree indebted for the confidence reposed in him, and
the success he has been honoured with, productive of his present prosperity,

THESE MEMOIRS,

are, with all due discrimination of the respective merits of each,

Inscribed by

THE AUTHOR.

P R E F A C E.

To print or not to print ?—this is the queftion ?
Whether 'tis better in a trunk to bury
The quirks and crotchets of outrageous fancy,
Or fend a well-wrote copy to the prefs,
And, by difclefing, end them ?——

For who would bear th' impatient thirft of fame,
The pride of confcious merit, and 'bove all,
The tedious importunity of friends——

To groan and fweat under a load of wit ?

'Tis Critics that makes cowards of us all.   JAGO.

CUSTOM, it has been repeatedly obferved by many of my worthy (and fome perhaps *unworthy*) predeceffors in authorfhip, has rendered a preface almoft indifpenfably neceffary; while others again have as frequently remarked, that "*cuftom is the law of fools.*" Thofe confiderations induced me to hefitate whether I fhould ufher my performance into the world with a preface, and thus hazard being claffed with the adherents to that law, or by omitting it, efcape the opprobrium, for "*who fhall deci e when doctors difagree ?*" Now, though I would not take upon me to decide in every point in which doctors difagree, yet, after giving the prefent fubject that mature confideration which fo important a concern required, I thought myfelf fully competent to decide, if not to general fatisfaction, at leaft fo as fully to fatisfy one particular perfon, for whom I profefs to have a very great regard, though perhaps few are to be found who would be equally condefcending to him; who that perfon is I do not wifh publicly to declare, as (being a very modeft man) it might offend him. I fhall only fay, the more you read the memoirs contained in the following pages, the better you will become acquainted with him. I ground my decifion on thefe arguments; I concluded, as moft of my brethren of the quill do of their labours, that my performance poffeffed fo much intrinfic merit, as would occafion it to be univerfally admired by all good judges, as a prodigious effort of human genius; and that this approbation muft naturally excite the envy of fome authors, who had not met with that high applaufe they deemed themfelves entitled to, and incline them to fearch for imperfections in my work; and though I was perfuaded of the impoffibility of their finding any, yet being thus foiled, they might catch at the want of a preface, and conftrue *that* into an omiffion, fo that in order to difarm them, I refolved to have one, efpecially as thofe who deem prefaces unneceffary may, if they choofe, decline reading it; whilft thofe on the other fide of the queftion, if there was none, might be difappointed, and have caufe for complaint; but to be feriou⁀ (if I can):

Almoft every author on producing the effufions of his pen (and his brain if he has any) thinks it prudent to introduce himfelf by a kind of *Prologue*, as it may be called, ftating his reafons with due precifion for intruding himfelf on his readers (whether true or otherwife, is not always material to enquire) befpeaking their candour towards his weakneffes and imperfections (which, by the bye, few are fo fenfible of as their readers) and not unfrequently endeavouring to foothe thofe GOLIAHS in literature, ycleped *critics*, (with whom not many little Davids are hardy enough to contend) hoping thus to coax them into good humour; or, perhaps, if his vanity preponderates, he throws the gauntlet of defiance, with a view of terrifying them either to hold their peace, or to do juftice to thofe mighty abilities *he* is confident he poffeffes in a degree eminently fuperior to moft of his brethren.

B 3

Among " true Parnaſſian bullies" De Scudery
ſtands one of the foremoſt ; he concludes his preface
to the works of his friend Theophile, with theſe remarkable words, " I do not heſitate to declare, that
amongſt all the dead and all the living, there is no
perſon who has any thing to ſhew, that approaches
the force of this vigorous genius ; but if amongſt the
latter, any one were ſo extravagant as to conſider
that I detract from his imaginary glory, to ſhew him
that I fear as little as I eſteem him, this is to inform
him that my name is DE SCUDERY." We have
another remarkable inſtance in Claude Terllon, a
poetical ſoldier, who begins his poems, by informing the critics, that " if any one attempts to cen-
ſure him, he will only condeſcend to anſwer him
ſword in hand."

For my own part, I diſclaim theſe modes : convinced, that in the firſt caſe, every reader, whatever
the author may plead, will judge for himſelf.—
To profeſſed critics I will repeat the following lines;

> " Think, at your bar, no old offender ſtands,
> " Us'd to diſpute and ſpurn at your commands ;—
> " No author bred in academic ſchools
> " To write by your's, or Ariſtotle's rules ;—

And were I ſo diſpoſed, neither my natural or acquired abilities enable me to *bully* thoſe who muſt be
very ill qualified for their taſk, if they were thus to
be intimidated from declaring their real ſentiments ;
and, on the other hand, to affect a degree of humi-
lity, and by flattery to aim at warping their minds,
is, in my opinion, paying them a very bad compliment ; ſo I will only quote for them four lines more
of poetry ;

> " Critics, forgive this firſt eſſay
> " Of one whoſe thoughts are plain,
> " Whoſe heart is full, who never means
> " To ſteal your time again."

Never ſhould I have ventured to appear in this
habit before the public, had not the following motives urged me thereto :

Many of my acquaintances have frequently expressed a desire of obtaining from myself such particulars as they could rely on, of my passage through life.

I have even been repeatedly threatened by some particular friends, that if I declined drawing up a narrative, they were determined to do it for me; one of the first mentioned gentlemen prevailed on me (as the most likely mode to bring it to a period) to devote now and then a spare hour in minuting down some of the most material occurrences of my life, and to send them to him in an epistolary form, intending to digest the whole into a regular narrative for publication: that gentleman, however, on perusal, was of opinion, that it would be additionally acceptable to the curious part of the public, if exhibited to them in the plain and simple manner in which these letters were written, as thus tending to display such traits and features of a somewhat original character, and give a more perfect idea of " I, great I, the little hero of each tale," than any other mode that could have been adopted; especially, as many *intelligent* persons were confident I could not write at all, while others *kindly* attributed to me what I never wrote.

> —————— " Then think,
> " That he who thus is forc'd to speak,
> " Unlefs commanded, would have died in silence."

If among the multitude of memoirs under which the press has groaned, and with which it still continues to be tortured, the following sheets should afford some degree of entertainment, as a relaxation from more grave and solid studies, to an inquisitive and candid reader (those of an opposite description are not to be pleased with the ablest performance) and he should deem it not the worst, nor the most expensive among the numerous tribe, I shall esteem myself amply rewarded; had I, however, been disposed to be more attentive to entertainment, and less to veracity, I might, to many, have rendered it much more agreeable, though less satisfactory to myself, as I believe the observation long since made to be just, that

B. 4.

few books are fo ill written, but that fomething may be gleaned from the perufal.

Should the infignificance of *my* life induce any perfon better qualified to prefent the world with *his*, big with interefting events, my difpofing of feveral large editions of that performance will afford me more *folid* fatisfaction as a *bookfeller*, than any fuccefs or emolument which can poffibly arife from this my firft, and moft probably laft, effay as an author.

If unfortunately any of my kind readers fhould find the book fo horridly dull and ftupid, that they cannot get through it, or if they do, and wifh not to travel the fame road again, I here declare my perfect readinefs to fupply them with abundance of books, much more witty, much more———whatever they pleafe, they never fhall want books while L. is able to affift them; and whether they prefer one of his writing, or that of any other author, he proteffs he will not be in the fmalleft degree offended: let every author make the fame declaration if he can.

Should my memoirs be attended with no other benefit to fociety, they will at leaft tend to fhew what may be effected by a perfevering habit of induftry, and an upright confcientious demeanor in trade towards the public, and probably infpire fome one of perhaps fuperior abilities, with a laudable ambition, to emerge from obfcurity, by a proper application of thofe talents with which Providence has favoured him, to his own credit and emolument, as well as the benefit of the community. To fuch an one I ever have, and ever fhall wifh every poffible fuccefs, as it has uniformly been my opinion, that whatever is thus acquired, is more honourable to the parties than the poffeffion of wealth obtained without any intrinfic merit or exertion, and which is too frequently confumed with rapidity in the purfuit of vice and diffipation.

One word to my old friends the bookfellers under No. III. of my dedication. This publication it is to be expected will tend to excite fome degree of mirth in them. Confcious that I have often been the caufe (however unintentional on my part) of ex-

citing less pleasing sensations in them, I will readily
allow them full scope; however, according to the
well known adage, " Let them laugh who win," I
hope they will indulge me in the same propensity of
laughing, if not *at* them, at least *with* them.

> ———such the vanity of great and small,
> Contempt goes round, and all men laugh at all.   YOUNG.

As a proof of my friendly disposition, I shall here
add a piece of advice, which I do not hesitate to pronounce will, if attended to, entitle them to promo-
tion amongst my *first* class of booksellers, and eventually prove more beneficial than a constant perseverance
in the mode of conduct they have hitherto pursued ;
and those who have children will, I hope, see the
propriety of inculcating the same doctrine to them
for their future benefit ; and I flatter myself my advice will prove equally productive of benefit to a great
number of the community at large, as well as to booksellers. It is this :

If they observe any person by industry and application endeavouring to obtain an honest livelihood in
that line for which his talents or disposition have
qualified him, never to attempt, by dark inuendoes,
sly hints, and false aspersions, to injure him, as, if
he happens to be a man of becoming spirit, such conduct will only tend to increase his exertions, and
render him still more cautious to obtain a good character; in so doing their weapons will recoil on themselves, and they will have the mortification to see
him flourish, whilst they become objects of contempt
in the eyes of the public, and will of course be
avoided by them. Here perhaps it will be remarked
that I have even presumed to differ in opinion from
the great Lord Bacon; that philosophical luminary
thought that the eye of an envious person darts a peculiar virulence, which wounds its objects: and thus
he accounts for persons in a triumph, or any exalted
prosperity, being more liable to be hurt by it than
others.

But I forget myself—from debating whether a preface was really necessary or not, if I proceed thus,

I shall produce one as long as my book, as indeed some of my seniors in authorship have done before me, though not altogether confistent with propriety.

I will therefore conclude with a wish that my readers may enjoy the feast with the same good humour with which I have prepared it; they will meet with some *solid* though not much *coarse* food, and the major part, I hope light and easy of digestion; those with keen appetites will partake of each dish, while others more delicate may select such dishes as are more light, and better adapted to their palates; they are all genuine British fare. But left they should be at a loss to know what the entertainment consists of, I beg leave to inform them, that it contains forty-seven dishes of various sizes, which (if they calculate the expence of their *admission tickets*) they will find does not amount to two-pence per dish; and what I hope they will consider as *immensely* valuable (in compliance with the precedent set by Mr. Farley, a gentleman eminent in the culinary science) a striking likeness of their *Cook* into the bargain.

I have also prepared a bill of fare at the end of the volume. Ladies and gentlemen, pray be seated; you are heartily welcome, and much good may it do you.

PREFACE

SECOND AND SUBSEQUENT EDITIONS.

'Tis nothing new, I'm sure you know,
For those who write, their works to shew;
And if they're praised, or render'd vain,
'Tis ten to one they write again:
And then they read it o'er with care,
Correcting here, and adding there.　　Mrs. SAVAGE.

THE first edition of my memoirs was no sooner published, than my old envious friends, mentioned in the third class of my dedication, found out that it was " d——n'd stuff! d——n'd low !" the production of a *cobler*, and only fit to amuse that honourable fraternity, or to line their garrets and stalls; and many gentlemen, who are my customers, have informed me, that when they asked for them at several shops, they received for answer, that they had already too much waste paper, and would not increase it by keeping Lackington's Memoirs; and some kindly added, " You need not be in haste to purchase, as in the course of the Christmas holidays, Mr. Birch, in Cornhill, will wrap up all his mince-pies with them, and distribute them through the town for the public good." Lord Bacon remarks, " that it was well said that envy has no holidays." And thus

" With all the eunuch's melancholy spite,
" They growl at you, because they cannot write;
" A gloomy silence, envy's pang imparts,
" Or some cold hint betrays their canker'd hearts."

B 6

But the rapid sale of this Life soon caused them to
alter their stories; and I was very much surprised to
hear that several of those gentlemen, who had scarce
done exclaiming, "Vile trash! beneath all criticism!"
&c. began to praise the composition; and on looking
into the English Review, I found that the editors had
filled seven pages in reviewing those Memoirs, and
had bestowed much praise on the author. I was then
ready to conclude, that their generous and manly
impartiality had, in a miraculous manner, effected
the conversion of others. But I was soon convinced,
that meanness can never be exchanged for generosity;
and that those that had been " unclean were unclean
still ;" as Churchill says,

> " That envy, which was woven in the frame
> " At first, will to the last remain the same.
> " Reason may drown, may die, but envy's rage,
> " Improves with time, and gathers strength from age."

It seems that several of those *liberal*-minded men,
being prodigiously mortified at the encreasing sale of
my Life, applied to different authors in order to get
one of them to father my book: but those authors,
either from principle, or from knowing that my manuscript was kept in my shop for the inspection of
the public, or from some other motive, refused to
adopt the poor bantling: and not only so, but laughed
at, and exposed the mean contrivance, to the very
great disappointment of those *kind and honest-hearted
friends of mine.*

> 'Tis hard to say, what mysteries of fate,
> What turns of fortune, on poor writers wait;
> The party slave will wound him as he can,
> And damn the merit, if he hates the man. **W. HARTE.**

That I might not be justly charged with ingratitude, I take this opportunity of thanking my friends,
customers, and the public, for their candid reception
of my volume; the sale of which, and the encomiums I have received on the subject, both by letter
and otherwise, have far exceeded my most sanguine
and self-flattering expectations; I very sensibly feel

the obligation! Their generosity has overwhelmed me! I am overpaid, and remain their debtor!

> " A truce with jefting ; what I here impart
> " Is the warm overflowings of a grateful heart;
> " Come good, come bad, while life or mem'ry laft,
> " My mind fhall treafure up your favours paft."

But, left I fhould be over vain, I muft at the fame time declare, that I have received fcurrilous and abufive letters from feveral of Mr. Wefley's people, merely becaufe I have expofed their ridiculous principles, and abfurd practices ; but more particularly, for having pulled off the hypocritical veil from *fome* of thofe *fanctified* deceivers which are amongft them.

The numerous letters of approbation which I have received from rational intelligent gentlemen, convinces me that I have not wronged the caufe of manly and rational Chriftianity, nor was it ever my intention fo to do:—

> But your philofophers will fay,
> Beft things grow worfe when they decay.
> If Phœbus' ray too fiercely burn,
> The richeft wines to foureft turn.   E. LLOYD.

I here alfo prefent my compliments and fincere thanks to my impartial friends, under the fecond clafs of my dedication, for the friendly difpofition they have fhewn, in freely diftributing my Memoirs among their cuftomers, and they may be affured, that I will not let flip any opportunity of making them proper returns for all their favours.

I cannot conclude this preface without faying fomething about this edition.

When I put the firft edition to the prefs, I really intended to print but a fmall number; fo that when I was prevailed on, by fome of my friends, to print a very large impreffion, I had not the leaft idea of ever being able to fell the whole ; and of courfe had not any intention of printing other editions. But the rapid fale of the work, and the many letters which I am continually receiving from gentlemen, in various parts of Great Britain and Ireland, who are pleafed to honour me with their approbation and thanks, encouraged me to read the whole over with more attention, to correct such typographical errors as had escaped my observation, and to improve the language in numberless places, and yet many errors still remain.

In executing this plan, I perceived that I had omitted to introduce many things which would have been an improvement to the work; and while inserting them, others occurred to my memory, so that most parts of the work is now very much enlarged. But although these additions have increased the expences of printing and paper, to near double, yet I have added but Sixpence to the price. Had profit been my motive, I could have divided the work into two volumes, and I may add that each volume would have been larger than some six shilling ones lately published. *

To such as ask why these additions were not printed separately, to the end that such as purchased the first edition, might have had them without purchasing the whole work over again? I answer, had that been practicable, I would have done it; but those additions being so many, and so various, rendered that method impossible, as every one who will take the trouble to compare the various editions, must readily acknowledge; nor can the purchasers of even the first edition complain with respect to the price, it being equal in size to most new publications which are sold at Six Shillings. And although some may think that the prefixed head is of no value, I can assure them, that I am of a very different opinion, *at least of the original*; and I have the pleasure to add, that a very great number of my customers have been highly pleased to have so striking a likeness of their old bookseller. Nor am I the first of the fraternity who has published his head; Mr. Nicholson (commonly called *Maps*) bookseller at Cambridge, two years since. had his head finely engraved; it is a good likeness, and is sold at 10s. 6d. Francis Kirk-

* This is only meant of the octavo edition.

man, partner with Richard Head (laſt century) prefixed his portrait to a book, entitled "The Wits,
or Sport upon Spoft." This Francis Kirkman alſo
publiſhed Memoirs of his own Life, and probably
led the way to John Dunton. See Granger's Biographical Hiſtory of England, vol. iv.

I could make many other apologies—

———— But why ſhould I diſtruſt,
My judges are as merciful as juſt;
I know them well, have oft their friendſhip try'd,
And their pretection is my boaſt—my pride.
                                    CUNNINGHAM.

V E R S E S,

Occasioned by reading

The LIFE of Mr. JAMES LACKINGTON.

Addreſſed to the ingenious AUTHOR,

By an *UNKNOWN FRIEND.*

SINCE your pen, Friend Unkown, ſuch improvement
    conveys,
'Tis but juſtice to you that this Tribute repays;
For when in the Boſom mild Gratitude burns,
'Tis a pleaſing relief which the Feeling returns:
For as dear as the Light to the thoughts of the Blind,
Is the Pen, or the Voice that enlightens the Mind;
And the more, as from Nature and Genius untaught
Your various adventures and humour are brought,
Which diſplay all the farce of the Methodiſt Plan,
The ſhame of Religion, of Reaſon, and Man;
While no Libertine Motives their Secrets diſpenſe,
But Propriety joins hand-in-hand with good Senſe,
Oh! with thee, could the Crowd view each ſanctified ſcene,
Where the Hypocrite oft wears Simplicity's mien;
Where youth, ſecond-childhood, and weakneſs of Sex,
Are objects they ever prefer to perplex;
Like thee, they'd contemn, or indignantly leave,
Whom Folly, and Knav'ry, combine to deceive;
And whoſe Newgate Converſions blaſphemouſly paint
The wretch moſt *deprav'd,* the moſt *excellent* Saint.
Go on; and diſcover each latent deſign,
And your rivals expoſe, who 'gainſt Learning combine:
O'er ſuch craft ſhall fair conduct, like thine, ſtill prevail,
And an envy'd ſuccefs lay them low in the Scale.
But as Time is too ſhort all your ſteps to retrace,
Let your LIFE ſpeak the reſt, and ſucceed in their place;
How Books mend the manners; and now ſo abound,
Where Rudeneſs and Ignorance lately were found.
But plain Truth, for itſelf, it muſt ſtill be confeſt,
Is the faithfulleſt advocate—therefore the beſt:
So I riſe from the Feaſt with a ſatisfied mind,
That the fame every Taſte, and each Temper, may find.
Still to drop all compariſon, Mental's the fare,
That needs only good taſte to invite us to ſhare;
Entertainment and Knowledge, the objects in view;
Then receive, as the Donor, the Praiſe that is due.

  BURY ST. EDMUND'S.   C. H——Sɥ

THE

LIFE

OF

J. LACKINGTON,

BOOKSELLER.

───────────

LETTER I.

Others with wishful eyes on Glory look,
When they have got their picture tow'rd a book,
Or pompous title, like a gaudy Sign
Meant to betray dull sots to wretched wine.
If at his title L——had dropt his quill,
L—— might have past for a great genius still:
But L——, alas! (excuse him if you can)
Is now a Scribbler, who was once a man.

YOUNG's Love of Fame.

DEAR FRIEND,

YOU have often requested me to
devote what few leisure moments I could spare, in
minuting down some of the principal occurrences of
my life, with a view, sooner or later, of exhibiting
the account to the public eye; who, as you were
pleased to say, could not but be somewhat curious to
learn some well-authenticated particulars of a man,
well known to have risen from an obscure origin to a
degree of notice, and to a participation of the favor
of the Public, in a particular line of business, I may
without vanity say, hitherto unprecedented. This
will appear more conspicuous if you consider, that I
was not only extremely poor, but laboured under
every other disadvantage; being a stranger in London,
and without friends, &c.

Ever willing to pay a becoming deference to the judgment of a perfon of your acknowledged merits, and whom I have the felicity of numbering among my firmeſt friends, yet being leſs anxious to appear as an adventurer among the numerous tribe of authors, than to continue a confiderable vender of the produce of their labours, I have continually delayed complying with your kind wiſhes.—By the bye, does the publication of a Catalogue of Books entitle the compiler to the name of *Author ?* If it does, many Bookſellers have long had a claim to that diſtinction, by the annual publication of their Catalogues, and myſelf, as *author* of a very voluminous one every fix months. The reaſon for my aſking this queſtion is, I laſt year obferved, that a certain bookſeller publiſhed his firſt Catalogue with this Introduction :—" As this is the firſt Catalogue ever the AUTHOR made, and is done in great haſte, he hopes inaccuracies will be treated with lenity."

But to return from this digreſſion. I ſhould probably have ſtill delayed compiling my narrative, if the editors of a certain periodical publication, who monthly labour to be witty, had not deemed me of ſufficient confequence to introduce into their work, what they are pleaſed to call a *Portrait* of me ! and though it was by them intended as a caricature, yet I am perſuaded it will appear to thoſe who beſt know me, as a daubing more characteriſtic of the heavy bruſh of a manufacturer of figns, than the delicate pencil of a true portrait-painter ; and on that account I ſhould moſt certainly have confidered it as unworthy of notice, had they not daubed me with falfe features. This at once determined my wavering refolution, and I am now fully refolved to minute down ſuch particulars of my paſſage through life, as, though not adorned with an elegance of ſtyle, will, I aſſure you, poſſeſs what to you, I flatter myſelf, will be a greater recommendation, viz, a ſtrict adherence to truth.

" To pomp or pathos I make no pretence,
" But range in the broad path of common fenſe,
" Nor ever burrow in the dark ſublime."

And though no doubt you will meet with some occurrences in which you may find caufe for cenfure,
yet I hope others will prefent themfelves, which your
candour will induce you to commend.

> Difdain not then thefe trifles to attend,
> Nor fear to blame, nor Study to commend.
>
> LORD HERVEY.

Should you be able to afford the whole a patient
perufal, and think the account meriting the public
eye, I fhall chearfully fubmit to your decifion, convinced that you will not,

> " With mean complacence e'er betray your truft,
> " Nor be fo civil as to prove unjuft."

John Dunton, a brother *Bibliopole*, long fince exhibited a whole volume of dulnefs, which he called
his " Life and *errors.*" The latter term I believe
might be a very proper appendage to the title page
of the innumerable lives which have been, and which
will be publifhed : For what man will dare to fay of
himfelf, his life has not been loaded with errors ?
That mine has been fuch I readily acknowledge ; and
fhould this narrative be publifhed, many perhaps may
deem that act another (poffibly the greateft) error.
To thofe I fhall only obferve, that,

> " To err is human, to forgive divine."

As an additional ftimulus, I can affure you as an
abfolute fact, that feveral gentlemen have at different periods (one very lately) intimated to me their
intentions of engaging in the tafk if I any longer
declined it.

Of my firft-mentioned *kind Biographers* I fhall take
my leave, with a couplet, many years fince written
by an eminent poet, and not inapplicable to the prefent ufe :

> " Let B—— charge low Grub-ftreet on my quill,
> " And write whate'er he pleafe, except—MY WILL."

And of you, for the prefent, atter informing you my
next fhall contain a faithful account of particulars re-

lative to the early part of my life, with affuring you that I am,

Dear Friend,

Your ever obliged

LETTER II.

Why fhould my birth keep down my mounting Spirit?
Are not all creatures fubject unto Time;
To time, who doth abufe the world,
And fills it full of hotch-podge baftardy?
There's legions now of beggars on the Earth,
That their original did fpring from Kings;
And many monarchs now, whofe fathers were
The riff-raff of their age; for time and fortune
Wears out a noble train to beggary;
And from the dunghill minions do advance
To ftate; and mark, in this admiring world,
This is but courfe, which in the name of fate
Is feen as often as it whirls about.
The river Thames that by our door doth pafs,
His firft beginning is but fmall and fhallow,
Yet keeping on his courfe grows to a fea."

SHAKSPEARE'S Cromwell.

DEAR FRIEND,

IN my laft I hinted that I fhould
confine myfelf to a plain narrative of facts, unembellifhed with the meretricious aid of lofty figures, or reprefentations of things which never had exiftence, but in the brain of the author. I fhall therefore not trouble you with a hiftory of predictions which foretold the future greatnefs of your humble fervant, nor with a minute account of the afpects of the planets at the very aufpicious and important crifis when firft I inhaled the air of this buftling orb:

Whatever ftar did at my birth prevail,
Whether my fate was weigh'd in Libra's fcale,
Or Scorpio reign'd, whofe gloomy pow'r
Rules dreadful o'er the natal hour,

Or Capricorn with angry rays,
Those tyrants of the western skies.   HORACE.

For extraordinary as it may appear, it has never yet
occurred to me, that any of the adepts in the astrolo-
gical science have made a calculation of my nativity;
'tis probable this high honor is by the planets destined
to adorn the sublime lucubrations of the very ingenious Mr. SIBLEY, in the next edition of his stup—
endous work! And here, for the honor of the craft,
let me remark, that this most sublime genius has,
with myself, to boast (and who would not boast of
their genealogy in having a prince for their an-
cestor?) in being a Son of the renowned PRINCE
CRISPIN.

A volume has been written with the title of "The
Honor of the Taylors; or, the History of Sir JOHN
HAWKWOOD." But were any learned writer to un-
dertake — The Honour of the Shoemakers, or the
History of ——, how insignificant a figure would the
poor Taylors make, when compared with the honor-
able craft!

" Coblers from Crispin boast their Public Spirit,
" And all are upright downright men of merit."

Should I live to see as many editions of my Memoirs published, as there have been of the Pilgrim's
Progress, I may be induced to present the world with
a Folio on that important subject; But Prior's line
occurs,

" Put off thy reflection and give us thy tale,"
               Derry down."

And so I will begin——

Were I inclined to pride myself in genealogical descent, I might here boast that the family were originally settled at White Lackington, in Somersetshire,
which obtained its name from one of my famous ancestors, and give you a long detail of their grandeur,
&c. but having as little leisure as inclination to boast
of what, if true, would add nothing to my merits,
I shall for the present only say, that I was born at

Wellington in Somersetshire, on the 31st of August, (old style) 1746. My father, George Lackington, was a Journeyman Shoemaker, who had incurred the displeasure of my grandfather for marrying my mother, whose maiden name was Joan Trott. She was the daughter of a poor weaver in Wellington; a good honest man, whose end was remarkable, though not very fortunate; in the road between Taunton and Wellington, he was found drowned in a ditch, where the water scarcely covered his face: He was, 'tis conjectured,

" —— Drunk when he died."

Alas, poor man! His drunkenness was not habitual; but having been separated from his wife and family a day or two, he was returning with his heart full of pleasure, and his pockets full of cakes and ginger-bread for his little ones; and while he was pleasing his imaginations with the pleasure he should have on his return, old Care quitted his hold, delightful sensations took place, and the brown jug went merrily round.

This happened some years before the marriage of my Father and Mother.

My grandfather, George Lackington, had been a Gentleman Farmer at Langford, a village two miles from Wellington, and acquired a pretty considerable property. But my father's mother dying when my father was about thirteen years of age, my grandfather, who had also two daughters, bound my father apprentice to a Mr. Hoadly, a master shoemaker in Wellington, with an intention of setting him up in that business at the expiration of his time. But my father worked a year or two as a journeyman, and then displeased his father by marrying a woman without a shilling, of a mean family, and who supported herself by spinning of wool into yarn, so that my mother was delivered of your friend and humble servant, her first-born, and hope of the family, in my grandmother Trott's poor cottage; and that good old woman carried me privately to church, unknown to my father, who was (nominally) a Quaker, that being the religion of his ancestors.

About the year 1750, my father having three or four children, and my mother proving an excellent wife, my grandfather's resentment had nearly subsided, so that he supplied him with money to open a shop for *himself*. But that which was intended to be of very great service to him and his family, eventually proved extremely unfortunate to himself and them; for, as soon as he found he was more at ease in his circumstances, he contracted a fatal habit of drinking, and of course his business was neglected; so that after several fruitless attempts of my grandfather to keep him in trade, he was, partly by a very large family, but more by his habitual drunkenness, reduced to his old state of a journeyman shoemaker: Yet so infatuated was he with the love of liquor, that the endearing ties of husband and father could not restrain him: by which baneful habit, himself and family were involved in the extremest poverty.

> To mortal men great loads allotted be;
> But of all packs, no pack like poverty."
>
> HERRICK.

So that neither myself, my Brothers, or Sisters, are indebted to a Father scarcely for any thing that can endear his memory, or cause us to reflect on him with pleasure.

> Children, the blind effects of love and chance,
> Bear from their birth the impression of a Slave.
>
> DRYDEN.

My father and mother might have said with Middleton,

> " How adverse runs the destiny of some creatures!
> " Some only can get riches and no children,
> " We only can get children and no riches;
> " Then 'tis the prudent part to check our will,
> " And, till our state rise, make our blood stand still."

But to our mother we are indebted for every thing. " She was a woman, take her for all in all, I shall not look upon her like again."

Let high birth triumph! what can be more great ?
Nothing——but merit in a low eftate.

                                   Dr. Young

Never did I know or hear of a woman who worked
and lived fo hard as fhe did to fupport Eleven children: and were I to relate the particulars, it would
not gain credit. I fhall only obferve, that for many
years together, fhe worked generally nineteen or
twenty hours out of every twenty-four; even when
very near her time, fometimes at one hour fhe was feen
walking backwards and forwards by her Spinning-
wheel, and her midwife fent for the next. Whenever
fhe was afked to drink a half pint of ale, at any fhop
where fhe had been laying out a trifling fum, fhe
afked leave to take it home to her hufband, who
was always fo mean and felfifh as to drink it.

Out of love to her family fhe totally abftained from
every kind of Liquor, water excepted; her food was
chiefly broth, (little better than water and oatmeal)
turnips, potatoes, cabbage, carrots, &c. her children
fared fomething better, but not much, as you may
well fuppofe. When I reflect on the aftonifhing
hardfhips and fufferings of fo worthy a woman, and
her helplefs infants, I find myfelf ready to curfe the
hufband and father that could thus invole them in
fuch a deplorable fcene of mifery and diftrefs. It is
dreadful to add, that his habitual drunkennefs
fhortened his days nearly one half, and that about
twenty years fince he died, unregretted by his own
children; nay more, while nature fhed tears over his
grave, reafon was thankful:

            " A parting tear to nature muft be paid,
            " Nature, in fpite of us, will be obey'd."

Thankful that the caufe of their poverty and mifery
was taken out of the way.

    The pious tear the fons and daughters fhed :
    Thus they, whom long he wrong'd, bewail'd him dead :
    With rev'rence they perform his obfequies,
    And bear their forrows as befeems the wife.

                                   Cooke.

Read this, ye inhuman parents, and shudder! Was a law made to banish all such fathers, would it not be a just, nay even a mild law? I have my doubts whether children should not be taught to despise and detest an unnatural brutal parent, as much as they are to love and revere a good one.

Here, sir, permit me to drop so gloomy a subject, and relate an uncommon circumstance that happened about this time.

Mr. James Knowland, who for many years kept the sign of the Eight Bells in Wellington, had a son weakly and infirm; when about nine years old, he was suddenly seized with illness, and soon after, to all appearance, died. He remained five days in this state; but those who were employed to remove the body down stairs in order to be interred, thought something moved in the coffin, and on opening it, they found him alive, and his eyes open. About two years after this, the boy was again taken ill, and in a day or two after, was to all appearance dead; but his father resolved not to have him interred, until he became offensive; he laid in this state six days, and again came to life, and I believe is now alive and well.

I am, Sir,

Yours.

c

L E T T E R   III.

" So have I wander'd ere thofe days were paft,
" That childhood calls her own. Ah ! happy days,
" That recollection loves, unftained with vice,
" Why are ye gone fo foon ?——   Village Curate.

For chiefly of himfelf his converfe ran,
As mem'ry well fupplied the narrative old man,
" His youthful feats with guiltlefs pride he told."
   In rural game what honours erft he won ;
How on the green he threw the wreftler bold ;
   How light he leap'd, and O ! how fwift he'd run ;
Then with a figh, he fondly turn'd his praife,
To rivals now no more, and friends of former days.
                              VERNON's Parifh Clerk.

DEAR FRIEND,

    A S I was the eldeft, and my father
for the firft few years a careful hard-working man, I
fared fomething better than my brothers and fifters.
I was put for two or three years to a day fchool,
kept by an old woman; and well remember how
proud I ufed to be to fee feveral ancient dames lift
up their hands and eyes with aftonifhment, while I
repeated by memory feveral chapters out of the
New Teftament, concluding me from this fpecimen
to be a prodigy of Science.   But my career of learning was foon at an end, when my mother became
fo poor that fhe could not afford the mighty fum of
two-pence per week for my fchooling.   Befides, I
was obliged to fupply the place of a nurfe to feveral
of my brothers and fifters.   The confequence of
which was, that what little I had learned was pre-
fently forgot; inftead of learning to read, &c. it
very early became my chief delight to excel in all
kinds of boyifh mifchiefs; and I foon arrived to be
the captain and leader of all the boys in the neighbourhood.

" The fprightlieft of the fprightly throng,
" The foremoft of the train."   Mifs BOWDLER.

So that if any old woman's lanthorn was kicked out of her hand, or drawn up a fign-poft; or if any thing was faftened to her tail, or if her door was nailed up, I was fure to be accufed as the author, whether I really were fo or not.

But one of my tricks had nearly proved fatal to me. I had obferved that *yawning* was infectious; and with a determination to have fome fport, I collected feveral boys together one market-day evening, and inftructed them to go amongft the butchers; whither I accompanied them. We placed ourfelves at proper diftances, and at a fignal given, all began to yawn as wide as we could, which immediately had the defired effect; the whole butcher-row was fet a yawning; on which I and my companions burft out into a hearty laugh, and took to our heels. The trick pleafed us fo well, that two or three weeks after, we attempted to renew it. But one of the butchers, who was half drunk, perceiving our intention, fnatched up his cleaver and threw it at me, which knocked off my hat without doing me any harm.

I was about ten years of age, when a man began to cry *apple-pies* about the ftreets, I took great notice of his methods of felling his pies, and thought I could do it much better than him. I communicated to a neighbouring baker my thoughts on the fubject in fuch a manner as gave him a very good opinion of my abilities for a pie-merchant, and he prevailed on my father to let me live with him. My manner of crying pies, and my activity in felling them, foon made me the favourite of all fuch as purchafed halfpenny apple-pies, and halfpenny plumb-puddings, fo that in a few weeks the old pie-merchant fhut up his fhop. You fee, friend, that I foon began to "make a noife in the world." I lived with this baker about twelve or fifteen months, in which time I fold fuch large quantities of pies, puddings, cakes, &c. that he often declared to his friends, in my hearing, that I had been the means of extricating him from the embarraffing circumftances in which he was known to be involved prior to my entering his fervice.

C 2

During the time I continued with this baker, many complaints were repeatedly made against me for the childish follies I had been guilty of, such as throwing snow-balls, frightening people by flinging serpents and crackers into their houses, &c. I also happened one day to overturn my master's son, a child about four years old, whom I had been driving in a wheel-barrow. Dreading the consequences, I immediately flew from my master's house, and (it being evening) went to a glazier's, and procured a parcel of broken glass; I also provided myself with a pocketful of peas; and thus equipped, made fine diversion for myself and my unlucky companions, by going to a number of houses, one after another, discharging a handful of peas at the windows, and throwing down another handful of glass in the street at the same instant, which made such a noise as very much frightened many people, who had no doubt of their windows being broken into a thousand pieces.

> By sports like these are all their care beguil'd,
> The sports of children satisfy the child.   TRAVELLER.

This adventure, together with throwing the child out of the wheel-barrow, produced such a clamour against me amongst the old women, that I would not return to my master, and not knowing what else to do, I went home to my father, who, you may easily conceive could not afford to keep me idle, so I was soon set down by his side to learn his own trade; and I continued with him several years, working when he worked, and while he was keeping *Saint Monday*, I was with boys of my own age, fighting, cudgel-playing, wrestling, &c. &c.

The following story has been variously stated; my father assured me that the origin of it was as follows; and that it happened nearly about this time.

He and some other frolicksome fellows being one Easter Sunday morning at the clerk's house at Langford, near Wellington, drinking (as it is called) clerk's ale, they overheard the old man rehearsing the verses of the Psalms which he was to read that morning at church: and in order to have some fun with the old clerk, one of the company set off early to church, and on the word *tree*, they stuck the word *horse*, so that when the old man came to that place, he read as follows, " And they shall flourish like a young bay horse. Horse! it should not be horse; but, by the Lord, it is horse!"

The above old man was called Red Cock for many years before his death, for having one Sunday slept in church, and dreaming that he was at a cock-fighting, he bawled out, " A shilling upon the red cock." And behold the family are called Red Cock unto this day.

The preceding reminds me of an odd circumstance that happened but a few years since at W————. As the good doctor was one Sunday morning going, through the street towards the cathedral, he heard a woman cry, " Mackerel, all alive, alive O!" And on his arrival at the church, he began the service as follows, " When the wicked man turneth away from his wickedness and doth that which is lawful and right, he shall save his soul alive, alive O!" These last words the doctor proclaimed aloud, in the true tone of the fish woman, to the great surprise of the congregation ; but the good doctor was so studious and absent, that he knew not what he had done.

Yours.

LETTER IV.

Who gather round, and wonder at the tale
Of horrid apparition, tall and ghastly,
That walks at dead of night, or takes his stand,
O'er some new-open'd grave : and (strange to tell!)
Evanishes at crowing of the cock.   Blair's Grave.

DEAR FRIEND,

I Must not forget an odd adventure
that happened when I was about twelve years of age,
as it tends to shew in part my dauntless disposition,
which discovered itself on many occasions in the very
early part of my life.

I had one day walked with my father to Holywell
ake, a village two miles from Wellington, where
meeting with some good ale, he could not find in his
heart to part from it until late at night. When we
were returning home by the way of Rockwell Green,
(commonly called *Rogue Green*, from a gang of rob-
bers and house-breakers who formerly lived there)
having just passed the bridge, we were met by several
men and women, who appeared to be very much
frightened, being in great agitation. They informed
us that they were returning back to Rogue Green,
in order to sleep there that night, having been prevented from going home to Wellington by a dreadful apparition, which they had all seen in the hollow way, about a quarter of a mile distant; adding,
that a person having been murdered there formerly,
the ghost had walked ever since; that they had never
before paid much attention to the well-known report :
but now they were obliged to credit it, having had
occular demonstration.

Aided by Fancy, Terror lifts his head,
And leaves the dreary mansions of the dead ;
In shapes more various mocks at human care,
Than e'er the fabled Proteus us'd to wear ;
Now, in the lonely way each traveller's dread,
He stalks a giant-shape without a head.

Now in the haunted house, his dread domain,
The curtain draws, and shakes the clinking chain;
Hence fabled ghosts arise, and spectres dire,
Theme of each ev'ning tale by winter's fire.
                                    PRALL's Superstition.

My father had drank too large a quantity of ale to
be much afraid of any thing, and I (who could not
let slip such an opportunity of shewing my courage)
seconded matters for the poor terrified people to return with us ; and as I offered to lead the van, they
were prevailed on to make the attempt once more ;
but said, that it was rather presumptuous, and hoped
that no dreadful consequence would ensue, as all the
company, they trusted, were honest hearted, and intended no harm to any person : they moreover added,
that " God certainly was above the devil." I then
advanced, and kept before the company about fifty
yards,

       " Whistling aloud to bear my courage up."

But when we had walked about a quarter of a mile,
I saw at some distance before us in the hedge, the
dreadful apparition that had so terrified our company.
Here it is! (said I). " Lord, have mercy upon us !"
replied some of the company, making a full stop ;
and would have gone back, but shame prevented
them. I still kept my distance before, and called out
to them to follow me, assuring them that I was still
determined to see what it was.

       " 'Tis a debt of honour, and must be paid."

They then fell one behind another, and advanced
in single files. As I proceeded I too was seized
with a timid apprehension, but durst not own it ;
still keeping on before, although I perceived my
hair to heave my hat from my head, and my teeth to
chatter in my mouth. In fact, I was greatly agitated at what I saw ; the object much resembled the
human figure as to shape, but the size was prodigious. However, I had promised to see what it was,
and for that purpose I obstinately ventured on about
thirty yards from the place where I first had sight of
                        C 4

it. I then perceived that it was only a very short tree, whofe limbs had been newly cut off, the doing of which had made it much refemble a giant. I then called the company, and informed them, with a hearty laugh, that they had been frightened at the ftump of a tree.

This ftory caufed excellent diverfion for a long time afterwards in Wellington, and I was mentioned as an hero.

The pleafure and fatisfaction I received from the difcovery, and the honour I acquired for the courage I poffeffed in making it, has, I believe, had much influence on me ever fince : as I cannot recollect that in any one inftance I have ever obferved the leaft fear of apparitions, fpirits, &c.

What education did at firft receive,
Our ripen'd age confirms us to believe. POMFRET.

Not that I have always fteadily difbelieved what has been related of fuch appearances, a few accounts of which feem fo well authenticated, as at leaft to make me doubt whether there might not exift in the fcale of beings fome of a more aerial fubftance than mankind, who may poffefs both the inclination and the power of affuming our fhape, and may perhaps take as much delight in teazing the human fpecies, as too many of our fpecies do in teazing and even tormenting thofe of the brute creation.

Some aftral forms I muft invoke by pray'r ;
Fram'd all of pureft atoms of the air :
In airy chariots they together ride,
And fip the dew, as thro' the clouds they glide ;
Vain fpirits, You, that fhunning heav'n's high noon,
Swarm here beneath the concave of the moon,
Hence to the tafk affign'd you here below !
Upon the ocean make loud tempefts blow ;
Into the wombs of hollow clouds repair,
And crafh out thunder from the bladder'd air ;
From pointed fun-beams take the mifts they drew ;
And fcatter them again in pearly dew ;
And of the bigger drops they drain below,
Some mould in hail, and others fift in fnow. DRYDEN.

While I am on this fubject, I cannot refift the temptation of relating a truly ridiculous affair that happened about this time at Taunton.

In the workhouse belonging to the parish of St. James, there lived a young woman who was an ideot. This poor creature had a great aversion to sleeping in a bed, and at bed-time would often run away to a field in the neighbourhood called the Priory, where she slept in the cowsheds.

In order to break her of this bad custom, two men agreed to try if they could not frighten her out of it. And one night, when they knew that she was there, they took a white sheet with them, and coming to the place, one of the men concealed himself to see the event, while the other wrapped himself up in the sheet, and walked backwards and forwards close before the cowshed in which she was laid. It was some time before Molly paid any attention to the apparition; but at last up she got, "Aha! (said she) a white devil!" and by her manner of expressing herself she thought it was very strange to see a *white* devil. And soon after she exclaimed, "A black devil too! a black devil too!" With that the man who had the sheet on, looked over his shoulder, and saw (or imagined he saw) a person all over black behind him; the sight of which made him take to his heels. Molly then clapped her hands as fast as she could, crying out at the same time, "Run, black devil, and catch white devil! Run, black devil, and catch white devil!" and was highly diverted. But this proved a serious adventure to the white devil, as he expired within a few minutes after he had reached his own house; and from that time poor Molly was left alone to sleep in peace.

About ten years after the above affair, at Wivelscombe, nine miles from Taunton, a gentleman farmer's house was alarmed every night between twelve and one o'clock. The chamber doors were thrown open, the bed-clothes pulled off the beds, and the kitchen furniture thrown with violence about the kitchen, to the great terror of the family, insomuch that the servants gave their master and mistress warning to leave their places, and some of them actually quitted their service. This dreadful affair had lasted about six weeks, when a young gentleman, who was there on a visit, being in bed one night, at the usual hour he heard his chamber door thrown open, and a very odd noise about his room. He was at first frightened, but the noise continuing a long time, he became calm, and laid still, revolving in his mind what he had best do. When on a sudden he heard the spirit creep under his bed, which was immediately lifted up, &c. This convinced him that there was some substance in the spirit; on which he leaped out of bed, secured the door, and with his oaken staff belaboured the ghost under bed as hard as he could, until he heard a female voice imploring mercy. On that he opened his chamber door, and called aloud for a light. The family all got up as fast as possible, and came to his room. He then informed them that he had got the spirit under the bed; on hearing which, most of them were terribly frightened, and would have run off faster than they came, but he assured them, they had nothing to fear: then out he dragged the half-murdered spirit from its scene of action. But how great was their surprise and shame, when they discovered that this tormenting devil was no other than one of their servant girls, about sixteen years of age, who had been confined to her bed several months by illness.

This ghost was no sooner laid, than two others alarmed the neighbourhood; one of which for a long time shook a house every night, and terribly distressed the family; at length they all resolved one night to go over the whole house in a body, and see what it was that so agitated the building. They examined every room, but in vain, as no cause could be discovered. So they very seriously as well as unanimously concluded, that it must be *the devil*.

But about a fortnight after this, one of the family being out late in the garden, saw a great boy get in at the window of an old house next door (part of which was in ruins), and soon after the house began to shake as usual, on which the family went out of their own habitation, and entered the old house where the boy was seen to get in; yet for a long time they could not discover any person, and were just turning to come out again, when one of the company obferved the boy fufpended above their heads, ftriding over the end of a large beam that ran acrofs both houfes.

It was then apparent, that the violent agitation of the adjoining houfe was occafioned by nothing more than his leaping up and down on the unfupported end of this beam.

Another apparition had for a long time ftolen many geefe, turkeys, &c. and altho' it had been feen by many, yet nobody would venture to go near it, until at length one perfon a little wifer than the reft of his neighbours, feeing the famous apparition, all over white, ftealing his fowls, was determined to be fully fatisfied what kind of fpirit it could be that had fo great a pedilection for poultry. He accordingly went round the yard, and as the apparition was coming over the wall, he knocked it down. This terrible ghoft then proved to be a neighbouring woman, who had put on her fhroud, in order to deter any perfons that fhould by chance fee her, from coming near her. Thus, though fhe had for a long time fuccefsfully practifed this ingenious way of procuring poultry, the old fox was caught at laft.

This is fo prolific a fubject, that I could fill many pages with relations of dreadful fpectres, which for a while reigned with tyrannic fway over weak minds, and at length when calm Reafon was fuffered to affume its power, have been difcovered to be no more objects of terror than thofe I have here noticed. But doubtlefs many fuch inftances muft have occurred to you.

> Chief o'er the fex he rules with tyrant fway,
> When vapours feiz'd them, or vain fears betray;
> With groans of diftant friends affrights the ear,
> Or, fits a phantom in the vacant chair;
> Fancy, like Macbeth, has murder'd fleep. PRALE.

It has indeed often aftonifhed me, that in this en-lightened age, there fhould yet remain numbers, not in the country only, but even in the metropolis, who fuffer themfelves to be made miferable by vain fears of preternatural occurrences, which generally owe their origin to the knavery of fome ill-difpofed perfon,

who has a finifter purpofe to anfwer thereby, or to the
foolifh defire of alarming the minds of weak people :
a practice fometimes (though intended as *fun*) productive of very ferious confequences. Now, and then,
indeed, thefe terrors are owing to accidental and ridiculous caufes. As an inftance, I fhall give you the
account of a terrible alarm which fome years fince
took place in a hofpital of this city, as related to me
by a gentleman, who at the time refided in the houfe,
for the purpofe of completing his medical education,
and on whofe veracity I can confidently rely.

For feveral nights fucceffively a noife had been
heard in the lower part of the building, like the continual tapping againft a window, which led the night
nurfes *wifely* to conclude it muft certainly be occafioned by the Spirit of one of the bodies depofited in
the dead-houfe endeavouring to efcape; as the found
feemed to proceed from that particular quarter. The
dread of thefe *fagacious ladies* at laft became fuch, as
totally to prevent their going from ward to ward to
do their duty, and determined my friend to attempt
to lay this perturbed fpirit; which however he ap-
prehended would more fpeedily, as well as effectually,
be performed by the affiftance of a good cudgel, than
by exorcifms; he therefore, inftead of confulting the
chaplain, gave orders the next night as foon as the
ufual *dreadful found* was heard, to give him notice.
This you may fuppofe they did not neglect doing,
though at the fame time they were fhocked at his temerity, and apprehenfive for the confequences. Impreffed with an idea of the alarm being occafioned by
fome fervant or patient in the houfe, he immediately
fallied forth, with a candle in one hand, and a good
tough twig in the other, accompanied by two of the
men fervants of the Hofpital, accoutred in the fame
manner, refolved that, if detected, the party fhould
meet with an ample reward. The dead-houfe was
paffed; the noife continued, though it evidently
procceded from a window at fome diftance in the
area. When the cavalcade came near the fcene of
action, the window fuddenly and violently broke,
without any thing being feen. This, my friend con-

feffed, for a moment occafioned his making a halt; but as nothing vifible had efcaped through the area, it occurred to him fomething might have made an entrance that way; accordingly he proceeded to the internal part of the building, and on opening the door, the apparition immediately not only appeared, but difappeared, and that fo inftantaneoufly as not to afford time to apply the remedy intended. And what think you, was this dreadful fpirit? That you may exercife your ingenuity at gueffing, I will here conclude with,

I am,

Dear Friend,

Yours,

LETTER V.

—— Were thy education ne'er fo mean,
Having thy limbs, a thoufand fair courfes
Offer themfelves to thy election.
BEN JOHNSON's Every Man in his Humour.

Laugh, if you are wife.   MARTIAL.

DEAR FRIEND,

A CAT!——An odd beginning of a Letter, by the bye—but here highly *important* and proper, as tending to relieve you from the anxious thoughts which (no doubt) muft have filled your mind on the fubject of the concluding part of my former letter. I muft give you a laughable inftance or two more, which lately happened. Mr. Higley, the bookfeller famous for felling odd volumes, or broken fets of books, lived next door to a public-houfe in Ruffell-court, Drury-lane; this public-houfe was feparated from his habitation only by a flight wainfcot partition, through which Mr. Higley caufed an hole to be cut, and a flider put over it, fo that when he wanted any beer, he always drew back the flider, and had it handed to him through this convenient aperture.

The night after Mr. Higley's death, which happened a few months fince, the man who was left to take care of the corps, about twelve o'clock hearing the landlord and his family going up ftairs to their beds, on a fudden drew back the flider and halloo'd through the hole, " Bring me a pint of beer." This order the landlord and his family heard, and were terribly alarmed, as they really thought it had proceeded from the ghoft of their neighbour Higley; the poor maid let fall the warming-pan, which came tumbling down the ftairs; the landlady being within the reach of her hufband's legs, caught faft hold of them, which in his fright he miftook for poor Higley. But the man burfting into a hearty laugh, reftored the fpirits of our hoft and his family.

About the year 1781, fix or feven mechanics having been drinking near the whole of the day at a public houfe in the Borough; they at night were at a lofs how to procure more liquor, their money being all gone, when two of the company obferving that an old wire-drawer in the room was dead drunk, they propofed to put him into a fack, and to carry him to Longbottom, the *refurrection-man*. This motion met with the approbation of the whole, and the two who propofed it took him away to Longbottom's houfe, as a dead fubject, and requefted a guinea, faying that they would call for the remainder in the morning. Their requeft was complied with, and the old wire-drawer was left in the fack in a room amongft dead bodies. About midnight the old man awaked, and made a terrible noife, which much alarmed Mr. Longbottom and his wife, as they really fuppofed that one of their dead fubjects was come to life again, durft not approach the room, but remained for a long time under a dreadful apprehenfion of what might be the confequences. The old fellow after a long ftruggle got out of the fack, and after tumbling about awhile

over the dead bodies, and skeletons, he at last found
his way down stairs, and off he set, leaving Mr.
Longbottom and his wife in the utmost consternation.
The old wire-drawer himself related this story to my
brother Philip Lackington.

Having now, I dare say, had enough of *Ghostesses,*
I will proceed with my narration.

During the time that I lived with the baker, my
name became so celebrated for selling a large number of pies, puddings, &c. that for several years
following, application was made to my father, for
him to permit me to sell Amanacks a few market days
before and after Christmas. In this employ I took
great delight, the country people being highly pleased
with me, and purchasing a great number of my Al-
manacks, which excited envy in the itinerant venders
of Moore, Wing, Poor Robin, &c. to such a degree,
that my father often expressed his anxiety lest they
should some way or other do me a mischief.   But I
had not the least concern, for possessing a light pair
of heels, I always kept at a proper distance.

O, my dear friend, little did I imagine at that
time, that I should ever excite the same poor mean
spirit in many of the booksellers of London and other
places ! but,

> *Envy* at last crawls forth, from hell's dire throng,
> Of all the direfull'st ! her black locks hung long,
> Attir'd with curling serpents ; her pale skin
> Was almost dropp'd from her sharp bones within,
> And at her breast stuck vipers, which did prey
> Upon her panting heart both night and day,
> Sucking black blood from thence ; which to repair,
> Both day and night, they left fresh poisons there ;
> Her garments were deep-stain'd with human gore,
> And torn by her own hands, in which she bore
> A knotted whip and bowl, which to the brim,
> Did green gall, and the juice of wormwood swim ;
> With which when she was drunk, she furious grew,
> And lash'd herself : thus from th' accursed crew,
> Envy, the worst of fiends, herself presents,
> Envy, good only when she herself torments.   COWLEY.

" ——— The true condition of Envy is,
" *Dolor alienæ felicitatis ;* to have

" Our eyes continually fix'd upon another
" Man's profperity, that is, his chief happinefs,
" And to grieve at that."

I was fourteen years and a half old, when I went
with my father to work at Taunton, feven miles from
Wellington. We had been there about a fortnight,
when my father informed our mafter, George Bowden,
that he would return to Wellington again. Mr.
Bowden was then pleafed to inform my father that he
had taken a liking to me, and propofed taking me
apprentice; I feconded Mr. Bowden's motion (having
a better profpect in continuing with Mr. Bowden than
in returning to Wellington with my father), as he
offered to take me without any premium, and to find
me in every thing. My father accepted his offer, and
I was immediately bound apprentice for feven years
to Mr. George and Mrs. Mary Bowden, as honeft
and worthy a couple as ever carried on a trade.

Religious, punctual, frugal, and fo forth;
Their word would pafs for more than they were worth.
POPE.

They carefully attended to their fhop fix days in the
week, and on the feventh went with their family twice
to an Anabaptift meeting: where little attention was
paid to fpeculative doctrines; but where found morality was conftantly inculcated.

" For modes of faith let gracelefs zealots fight,
" His can't be wrong whofe life is in the right."

But in this, as in many other places of worfhip, it
was performed in a dull fpiritlefs manner; fo that
the excellent morality taught there was not fo much
attended to as it would have been had it been enforced,
or re-inforced by the captivating powers of oratory.

I well remember, that although I conftantly attended this place, it was a year or two before I took
the leaft notice of the fermon, which was read; nor
had I any idea that I had the leaft concern in what
the minifter was (as 'tis called) preaching about.
For,

" Who a cold, dull, lifeless drawling keeps,
" One half his audience laughs, whilst t'other sleeps.

* * * * *

" Sermons, like plays, some please us at the ear,
" But never will a serious reading bear ;
" Some in the closet edify enough,
" That from the pulpit seem'd but sorry stuff.
" 'Tis thus there are who by ill reading spoil
" Young's pointed sense, or Atterbury's style !
" While others, by the force of eloquence,
" Make that seem fine, which scarce is common sense.
" But some will preach without the least pretence
" To virtue, learning, art, or eloquence.
" Why not ! you cry : they plainly see, no doubt—
" A priest may grow *right reverend* without."

Art of Preaching.

I am,

Dear Friend,

Yours.

LETTER VI.

Youth is the stock whence grafted superstition
Shoots with unbounded vigour.   MILLER's Mahomet.

—— All must lament that he's under such banners,
As evil community spoils our good manners.   SIMKIN.

DEAR FRIEND,

AT the time I was bound apprentice, my master had two sons, the eldest about seventeen years old, the youngest fourteen. The eldest had just been baptized, and introduced as a member of the arianistical dipping community where my master and his family attended. The boy was a very sober industrious youth, and gave his father and mother much pleasure. The youngest was also a good lad.

" Thus the firſt ſcene ended well,
" But at the next, ha ! what befell."——

Thus every thing continued well for ſome time after I had been added to the family. Both of the boys had very good natural parts, and had learned to read, write, keep accounts, &c. But they had been at ſchools where no variety of books had been introduced, ſo that all they had read was the Bible. My maſter's whole library conſiſted of a ſchool-ſized Bible, Watts's Pſalms and Hymns, Foot's Tract on Baptiſm, Culpepper's Herbal, the Hiſtory of the Gentle Craft, an old imperfect volume of Receipts in Phyſic, Surgery, &c. and the Ready Reckoner. The ideas of the family were as circumſcribed as their library. My maſter called attention to buſineſs and working hard, " *minding the main chance.*" On Sundays all went to meeting ; my maſter on that day ſaid a ſhort grace before dinner, and the boys read a few chapters in the Bible, took a walk for an hour or two, then read a chapter or two more.

" What right, what true, what fit we juſtly call,
" And this was all our care—for this is all."

They then ſupped, and went early to bed, perfectly ſatisfied with having done their duty ; and each having a quiet conſcience, ſoon fell into the arms of Nature's ſoft nurſe! ſweet ſleep.

And thus whatever be our ſtation,
Our hearts in ſpite of us declare
We feel peculiar conſolation,
And taſte of happineſs a ſhare.   HORACE Imitated.

I cannot here omit mentioning a very ſingular cuſtom of my maſter's : Every morning, at all ſeaſons of the year, and in all weathers, he roſe about three o'clock, took a walk by the river-ſide round Frenchware-fields, ſtopt at an alehouſe that was early open to drink half a pint of ale, came back before ſix o'clock, then called up his people to work, and went to bed again about ſeven.

Thus was the good man's family jogging eaſily and quietly on, no one doubting but he ſhould go to

heaven when he died, and every one hoping it would
be a good while firſt.

"A man ſhould be religious, not ſuperſtitious."

But, alas! the dreadful criſis was at hand that put
an end to the happineſs and peace of this little family.
I had been an apprentice about twelve or fifteen
months, when my maſter's eldeſt ſon George happened to go and hear a ſermon by one of Mr. Weſley's preachers, who had left the plough-tail to preach
the *pure* and *unadulterated* Goſpel of Chriſt. By this
ſermon the fallow ground of poor George's heart
was ploughed up, he was now perſuaded that the innocent and good life he had led would only ſink him
deeper into hell: in ſhort, he found out that he had
never been converted, and of courſe was in a ſtate of
damnation, without benefit of Clergy. But he did
not long continue in this damnable ſtate, but ſoon
became one of

―――――――― The ſanctified band,
Who all holy myſteries well underſtand.   SIMKIN.

He perſuaded himſelf that he had paſſed through the
New Birth, and was quite ſure that his name was re-
giſtered in the Book of Life, and (to the great grief
of his parents) he was in reality become a *new creature*.

'Twas methodiſtic grace that made him toſs and tumble,
Which in his entrails did like jalap rumble.
                              OVID's Epiſt. Burleſqued.

George had no ſooner made things ſure for himſelf,
than he began to extend his concern to his father,
mother, brother, and me; and very kindly gave us
to underſtand, that he was ſure we were in a very
deplorable ſtate, "without hope, and without God
in the world," being under the curſe of the Law.

For all enthuſiaſts when the fit is ſtrong,
Indulge a volubility of tongue.   FENTON.

In the long winter nights, as we ſat at work together, he proved (in his way) that every man had
original ſin enough to damn a thouſand ſouls; and a

deal was faid on that fubject. A paffage was quoted
from the wife determination of the doctors of the
Sorbonne, where they fay that children inclofed in
their mother's womb, are liable to damnation, if they
die there unbaptized. Quotations were alfo made
from fome *deep* author who had afferted, that there
were " infants in hell but a fpan long ;" and that
" hell was paved with infant fculls," &c.

 " Thus feigning to adore, make thee,
 " A tyrant God of cruelty !
 " As if thy right-hand did contain
 " Only an univerfe of pain ;
 " Hell and damnation in thy left,
 " Of ev'ry gracious gift bereft :
 " Hence reigning floods of grief and woes,
 " On thofe that never were thy foes,
 " Ordaining torments."

As to morality, George affured us it was of no avail;
that as for good works, they were only fplendid fins;
and that in the beft good work that any creature
could perform, there was fin enough to fink the doer
to the nethermoft hell; that it was *faith* alone that
did every thing, without a grain of morality; but
that no man could have one particle of this myfterious
faith, before he was juftified; and *juftification* was a
fudden operation on the foul, by which the moft
execrable wretch that ever lived might inftantaneoufly
be affured of all his fins being pardoned; that his
body from that very moment became the living temple of the Holy Ghoft; that he had fellowfhip with
the Father, Son, and Holy Spirit; and, that Spirit
was to be their conftant and infallible guide:

 " Whate'er men fpeak by this new light,
 " Still they were fure to be i'the right.
 " This dark lanthorn of the Spirit,
 " Which none fee by but thofe that bear it ;
 " A light that falls down from on high,
 " For fpiritual trades to cozen by ;
 " An *ignis fatuus*, that bewitches,
 " And leads men into pools and ditches.
 " This light infpires and plays upon
 " The noife of Saint, like bagpipe drone,
 " And fpeaks through hollow empty foul,
 " As through a trunk, or whifpering hole.

" Such language as no mortal ear
" But fpiritu'l eaves-droppers can hear."

My mafter very feldom heard any of thefe curious
converfations ; but my good miftrefs would fit down
for hours together, with her Bible in her lap, from
which fhe would read fuch fcriptures as proved the
neceffity of living a good life, performing good works,
&c. fhe alfo did her beft to confute the tenets of
Original Sin, Imputed Righteoufnefs, Doctrine of the
Trinity, &c. &c. Unfortunately the good woman
had no great talents for controverfy ; however,
George had a very tenacious memory, and employed
all his thoughts on thefe fubjects ; fo that John his
younger brother, and I alfo (two compctent judges no
doubt) thought that he had the beft of the arguments
on thefe edifying fubjects. Nothing, fays Montaigne,
is fo firmly believed as that which we leaft know, for
which reafon Plato faid, " that it was more eafy to
fatisfy his hearers with difcourfes about the nature
of the Gods than of men." About five months after
George's converfion, John went to hear thofe only
true Ambaffadors from Heaven,

> Who ftroll and teach from town to town
> The good old Caufe : which fome believe
> To be the devil that tempted Eve
> With knowledge, and do ftill invite
> The world to mifchief with new light.   BUTLER.

Thefe devil-dodgers happened to be fo very *powerful* (that is very *noify*) that they foon fent John home,
crying out, he fhould be damn'd! he fhould be
damn'd for ever !

But John foon got out of the damnable ftate, and
affured us that all his fins were forgiven, merely by
believing, that he had paffed from death into life, and
had union and communion with God. He now became as merry as before he had been forrowful, and
fung in Mr. Wefley's ftrain,

> " Not a doubt fhall arife
> " To darken the fkies,
> " Nor hide for a moment my God from my Eyes."

John fung to me, and faid to me a great deal in this
wonderful ftrain; of which I did not comprehend one
fyllable.

> " —————— His words were loofe
> " As heaps of fand, and fcatter'd wide from fenfe.
> " So high he mounted in his airy throne,
> " That when the wind had got into his head,
> " It turn'd his brains to frenzy."

But thefe extraordinary accounts and difcourfes, together with the controverfies between the mother and
the fons, made me think they knew many matters of
which I was totally ignorant. This created in me a
defire for knowledge, that I might know who was
right and who was wrong. But to my great mortification, I could not read. I knew moft of the letters,
and a few eafy words, and I fet about learning with
all my might. My miftrefs would fometimes inftruct
me ; and having three-halfpence per week allowed me
by my mother, this money I gave to John (my mafter's youngeft fon) and for every three-halfpence he
taught me to fpell one hour; this was done in the
dark, as we were not allowed a candle after we were
fent up ftairs to bed.

> " No youth did I in education wafte ;
> " Happily I'd an intuitive *Tafte:*
> " Writing ne'er cramp'd the finews of my thumb,
> " No barb'rous birch did ever brufh my b——
> " My guts ne'er fuffer'd from a college cook,
> " My name ne'er enter'd in a buttery book.
> " Grammar in vain the fons of Prifcian teach ;
> " Good parts are better than eight parts of fpeech.
> " Since thefe declin'd, thofe undeclin'd they call ;
> " I thank my ftars, that I declin'd them all.
> " To Greek or Latin tongues without pretence,
> " I truft to Mother Wit and Father Senfe.
> " Nature's my guide ; all pedantry I fcorn ;
> " Pains I abhor, I was an Author born."

I foon made a little progrefs in reading ; in the
mean time I alfo went to the Methodift meeting.
There, as " enthufiafm is the child of melancholy,"
I caught the infection. The firft that I heard was
one Thomas Bryant, known in Taunton by the name
of the *damnation preacher* (he had juft left off cobbling
foles of another kind.) His fermon frightened me

moſt terribly. I ſoon after went to hear an old Scotchman, and he aſſured his congregation, that they
would be damn'd, and double damn'd, and treble
damn'd, and damn'd for ever, if they died without
what he called *faith*.

> " Conj'rers like, on fire and brimſtone dwell,
> " And draw each moving argument from hell."
> SOAME JENYNS.

This marvellous doctrine and noiſy rant and enthuſiaſm ſoon worked on my paſſions, and made me
believe myſelf to be really in the damnable condition
that they repreſented; and in this miſerable ſtate I
continued for about a month, being all that time unable to work myſelf up to the proper key.

At laſt, by ſinging and repeating enthuſiaſtic
amorous hymns, and ignorantly applying particular
texts of ſcripture, I got my imagination to the proper
pitch, and thus was I born again in an inſtant, and
became a very great favourite of heaven:

> And with my new invented patent eyes,
> Saw Heav'n and all the angels in the ſkies.
> PETER PINDAR.

I had angels to attend all my ſteps, and was as familiar with the Father, Son, and Holy Ghoſt, as any
old woman in Mr. Weſley's connection; which, by
the bye, is ſaying a great deal. Thus,

> Remote from liberty and truth,
> By fortune's crime, my early youth
> Drank error's poiſon'd ſprings.
> Taught by dark creeds and myſtic law,
> Wrapt up in *ſuperſtitious* awe.——
> Earl NUGENT.

I am,

Deer Sir,

Yours.

LETTER VII.

No fleep, no peace, no reft
Their wand'ring and afflicted minds poffefs'd ;
Upon their fouls and eyes
Hell and eternal horror lies,
Unufual fhapes and images,
Dark pictures, and refemblances
Of things to come, and of the worlds below,
O'er their diftemper'd fancies go :
Sometimes they curfe, fometimes they pray unto
The gods above, the gods beneath ;
No fleep, but waking now was fifter unto death.

BP. SPRAT.

DEAR FRIEND,

IT is perhaps worth remarking, that what the methodifts call conviction of fin, being awakened, &c. is often a moft dreadful ftate, and has the very fame effect on fuch as have lived a very innocent life as it has upon the moft notorious of-fenders; this conviction (as they call it) is brought about by the preachers heaping all the curfes in the Bible on the heads of the moft virtuous as well as moft vicious; for, fay they, he who keepeth the whole law and offendeth but in one point, is as much in a ftate of damnation, as he that hath broken every one of the commandments, or committed robbery, murder, &c. fo that they pour out every awful de-nunciation found in the Bible, and many not found there, againft all who have not the methodiftical faith: this they call fhaking the people over the mouth of hell, and they in reality believe,

That cruel God, who form'd us in his wrath,
To plague, opprefs, and torture us to death,
Who takes delight to fee us in defpair,
And is more happy, the more curs'd we are.
In vain all nature fmiles, but man alone,
He's form'd more perfect, and was made to groan.

YOUNG's Soldier's Trifles.

Thus are many who before poffeffed " confciences void of offence towards God and mankind," tricked out of their peace of mind, by the ignorant application of texts of fcripture. Their fears being once fo dreadfully alarmed, they often become infupportable to themfelves and all around them; many in this ftate have put a period to their exiftence, others run mad, &c.

Permit me, Sir, to addrefs you in the words of Alonza, in Columbus: "Does thy exalted mind, which owns the nobleft energies of reafon, does it approve that ftructure reared by miftaken zeal, to glorify the Diety, by the dire facrifice of all his deareft bleffings?"

> Oh! would mankind but make great truths their guide,
> And force the helm from prejudice and pride;
> Were once thefe maxims fix'd, that God's our friend,
> Virtue our good, and happinefs our end;
> How foon muft reafon o'er the world prevail,
> And error, fraud, and fuperftition fail!
> None would hereafter, then, with groundlefs fear,
> Defcribe th' Almighty cruel and fevere.
>   SOAME JENYNS's Epiftle to Hon. P. YORK.

If the above terror of confcience was only to take place in knaves and rafcals, there would be no reafon for blaming the methodifts on that head; "the wretch deferves the hell he feels." A terrible inftance of this kind happened near London-bridge about two years fince: a perfon in a lucrative branch of bufinefs had put unbounded confidence in his head fhopman, and well rewarded him for his fuppofed fidelity. One morning, this young man not coming down ftairs fo foon as ufual, the fevant-maid went up to call him, and found him hanging up to the bed-poft; fhe had the prefence of mind to cut him down, but he being nearly dead, it was fome days before he perfectly recovered.

On his mafter coming to town, he was informed of what had happened to his favourite fhopman; he heard the relation with the utmoft aftonifhment, and took great pains to difcover the caufe of fo fatal a refolution, but to no purpofe. However, he endeavoured to reconcile this unhappy man to life, was very tender towards him, and gave him more encouragement than ever; but the more the mafter did to en-

D

courage and make him happy, the more the poor
wretch appeared to be dejected; in this unhappy state
of mind he lived about six months; when, one morning, not appearing at his usual time, the servant-
maid went to see if he was well, and found him very
weak in bed, a day or two after, his master came to
town, and being told of his situation, went up to see
him, and finding him in bed, and apparently very
ill, proposed sending for a physician, but the poor
devil refused to take any thing, and rejected every
assistance, saying, his time was nearly come. Soon
after this the servant informed her master that he
would not have the bed made, and that she had just
observed some blood on one corner of the sheet.
The master then went up stairs again, and by lifting
up the bed-clothes found that he had stabbed himself
in several places, and that in this state he had lain
three or four days.

> When innocence and peace are gone,
> How sad, how teasable to live!   SECUNDUS.

On the surgeon's appearance, he refused to have the
wounds inspected, and the surgeon being of opinion
that it was too late to render him any kind of service,
they let him lie still. The master soon after this
pressed him much to know the mysterious cause of so
much misery, and so unnatural an end. The dying
wretch exclaimed, " a wounded conscience, who can
bear." The master then endeavoured to comfort
him, and assured him that his conscience ought not
to wound him. " I know you (continued he) to be a
good man, and the best of servants." "Hold! hold!"
exclaimed the wretch, "your words are daggers to my
soul! I am a villain, I have robbed you of hundreds,
and have long suffered the tortures of the damned for
being thus a concealed villain; every act of kindness
shewn to me by you has been long like vultures tear-
ing my vitals. Go, sir, leave me; the sight of you
causes me to suffer excruciating tortures." He then
shrunk under the bed-clothes, and the same night
expired in a state of mind unhappy beyond all description.

Hope gone! the guilty never reft!
. Difmay is always near;
There is a midnight in the breaft,
    No morn can ever cheer.   Night Scenes.

    Terrible as the above relation is, I affure you that I
have not heightened it: when an ungrateful villain is
punifhed by his own reflections, we acknowledge it to
be but juft. In Morton's Hiftory of Apparitions are
feveral fhocking ftories of perfons who, by their abandoned practices, have brought on themfelves all the
horrors of a guilty confcience.

O treacherous confcience; while fhe feems to fleep
On rofe and myrtle, lull'd with fyren fong:
While fhe feems nodding o'er her charge, to drop
On headlong appetite the flacken'd rein,
And gives up to licence unrecall'd,
Unmarked; fee from behind her fecret ftand,
The fly informer minutes every fault,
And her dread diary with horror fills.
A watchful foe! the formidable fpy,
Lift'ning, o'rhears the whifpers of our camp:
Our dawning purpofes of heart explores,
And fteals our embryos of iniquity.
As all rapacious ufurers conceal
Their doomfday-book from all confuming heirs;
Thus with indulgence moft fevere fhe treats,
Writes down our whole hiftory, which death fhall read,
In ev'ry pale delinquent's private ear.   Night Thoughts.

But the cafe is otherwife amongft the methodifts, they
work on the fears of the moft virtuous; youth and
innocence fall victims daily before their threats of hell
and damnation, and the poor feeble-minded, inftead
of being comforted and encouraged, are often by
them funk into an irrecoverable ftate of gloomy def-
pondence and horrible defpair.

    If they hear of any who are on a fick-bed, they en-
deavour, if poffible, to gain admittance, and often difturb many very innocent people in their laft moments.
And I believe that I may fafely add they fometimes
haften thofe moments. For only think of three or
four of thefe Spiritual Quixotes, or Dons of the Woe-
ful Countenances, ftalking into a room and furround-
ing a bed in which a perfon lays very ill. To fee
their difmal faces, and to hear their terrifying dif-

courses, their gloomy and superstitious prayers, must greatly alarm even persons whose lives were not before in any great danger; and I have no doubt but some are by these means frightened out of their existence.

It is true that many of their hearers are not only methodistically convinced, or alarmed, but are also *hocus pocusly converted*; for as some of their preachers employ all their art and rhetoric, to alarm and terrify, so others of them use their utmost skill, to give them assurance of their sins being pardoned; which remind us of the law-suit, where one party sued for a forged debt, and the other produced a forged receipt. But with thousands that is not the case, even with those who join their society, where so much divine love, assurance, and extasies are talked of, where enthusiastic, rapturous, intoxicating hymns are sung; and besides the unhappy mortals in their own community, thousands there are who have lost their peace of mind by occasionally hearing their sermons.

> " The gulph of hell wide op'ning to his eyes,
> " Gone! gone for ever! to himself he cries,
> " Rack'd with despair; wastes silently within
> " His friend, *himself*, unconscious of what sin."

And even those among them who have arrived to the highest pitch of enthusiasm, and who at times talk of their foretaste of heaven, and of their full assurance of sins forgiven, and of talking to the Deity, as familiarly as they will to one another; (all which, and much more, I have heard a thousand times) yet even those very pretended favourites of heaven are (if we believe themselves) miserable for the greatest part of their time, having doubts, fears, horrors of mind, &c. continually haunting them wherever they are.

> See superstition trembling at the noise
> Of rushing torrents, or the thunder's voice;
> The moon's ecclipse, the flashing meteor's glare,
> And each vicissitude of earth and air;
> Involv'd in Guilt's or Ignorance's shade,
> Each vain or cruel practice call in aid,
> Maintain with reason a perpetual fight,
> And virtue barter for the empty right.

Obferve the entrails, mark the fly ing bird,
Hang on the crafty augur's doubtful word,
Hollow the pavement with the midnight pray'r,
Or to the cutting fcourge the fhoulders bare.

Effay on Senfibility.

Cicero has faid the fame in profe: "The fuperftitious man, (fays he) is miferable in every fcene,
in every incident in life: even fleep itfelf, which
banifhes all other cares of unhappy mortals, affords
to him matter of new terror, while he examines
his dreams, and finds in thofe vifions of the night,
prognoftication of future calamities." Between
twenty and thirty years fince, fome thoufands of
them in London took it into their heads that the
world would be at end on fuch a night, and for fome
days previous to this fatal night, nothing was attended
to but fafting and praying, and when it came, they
made a watch-night of it, and fpent it in prayer, &c.
expecting every moment to be the laft; and it is remarkable, that thoufands who were not methodifts
gave credit to this ridiculous prophecy, and were
terribly alarmed; but the next morning they were
afhamed to look at one another, and many durft not
appear in their fhops for fome time afterwards. But
others of them faid that God had heard the prayers
of the righteous, and fo fpared the world a little
longer.

What numbers floth with gloomy horror fills!
Racking their brains with vifionary ills.
Hence what loud outcries, and well meaning rage,
What endlefs quarrels at the prefent age!
How many blame! how often may we hear,
"Such vice!—well, fure, the Laft day muft be near!"
T'avoid fuch wild, imaginary pains,
The fad creation of diftemper'd brains,
Difpatch, dear friend! move, labour, fweat, run, fly!
Do ought—but think the day of judgment nigh.

E. Rolle.

Some years after that, Mr. Wefley alarmed his
people all over England, with the tail of a comet;
great numbers were dreadfully apprehenfive left this
comet fhould fcorch the earth to a cinder; but the

D 3

faints by prayer made the comet keep a proper diftance.

Charnock, of the laſt century, in his Diſcourſe on
Providence, has proved (in his way) that the univerſe
was created and is kept agoing for the ſake of the
elect, and that as ſoon as their number is complete,
the whole will be deſtroyed. This is genuine Calviniſm.

> But theſe our more enlighten'd days,
>   Confeſs the native force of truth,
> Feel the full luſtre of her rays,
>   And bow to her eternal truth.   **Beloe.**

The fanatics in every age have found their account
in making their followers believe the end of the
world was at hand. In ſome of the wills and deeds,
by which eſtates have been given to monaſteries, &c.
in France, they have expreſſed their belief of the
world's being nearly at an end, as a reaſon for making ſuch liberal donations to the church. But it is
happy for us that in England ſuch wills would be ſet
aſide. A caſe of this nature occurred while Lord
Northington was at the head of the law department.
Reilly the preacher, had wheedled, or frightened, an
old woman (Mrs. Norton) out of a deed or gift of
fifty pounds a year, but after the old woman's panic
and fear of damnation was over, ſhe had recourſe to
Chancery, and his Lordſhip annulled the deed of
gift. His Lordſhip's remarks on ſuch kinds of impo-
ſition are very curious, and worth your reading. See
Collectanea Juridica, vol. i. p. 458.

In fact, the very beſt of the methodiſts are like
children, elated or depreſſed by mere trifles; and
many who joined them while young and ignorant,
quit their ſociety as they attain to years of diſcretion,
or as their judgment is better informed.

> Reaſon, ariſe and vindicate thy claim,
> Flaſh on our minds the joy-infuſing flame;
> Pour forth the fount of light, whoſe endleſs ſtore
> Thought drinks inſatiate, while it thirſts for more.
>   Earl **Nugent.**

Love or anger, ambition or avarice (ſays a great
man) have their root in the temper and affections,

which the foundeft reafon is fcarce able fully to correct; but fuperftition, being founded on falfe opinion, muft immediately vanifh, when true philofophy
has infpired jufter fentiments of fuperior powers.

> Thus the fair order, mark'd on all around,
> In the clear mirror of his foul is found,
> Which fhows each object in its native dyes,
> Not thofe diftorting prejudice applies.
>
> Effay on Senfibility.

I am,

Dear Friend,

Yours.

LETTER VIII.

> Religion's luftre is, by native innocence,
> Divinely fair, pure, and fimple from all arts;
> You daub and drefs her like a common miftrefs,
> The harlot of your fancies; and by adding
> Falfe beauties, which fhe wants not, make the world
> Sufpect her angel face is foul within.   Rowe's Tamerlane.

> Be careful to deftroy the book of James,
> Subftantial virtues that vile papift claims;
> Fergetting Paul, he fpurns at faith alone,
> And bids our faintfhip by our lives be known:
> All Cato's virtue was not worth a pin,
> And Phocion's exit but a fhining fin.

DEAR FRIEND,

THE enthufiaftic notions which I
had imbibed, and the defire I had to be talking about
religious myfteries, &c. anfwered one valuable purpofe; as it caufed me to embrace every opportunity
to learn to read, fo that I could foon read the eafy
parts of the Bible, Mr. Wefley's Hymns, &c. and
every leifure minute was fo employed.

D 4

In the winter I was obliged to attend my work from fix in the morning until ten at night. In the fummer half-year, I only worked as long as we could fee without candle; but notwithftanding the clofe attention I was obliged to pay to my trade, yet for a long time I read ten chapters in the Bible every day: I alfo read and learned many hymns, and as foon as I could procure fome of Mr. Wefley's Tracts, Sermons, &c. I read them alfo; many of them I perufed in *Cloacina's* Temple (the place where my Lord Chefterfield advifed his fon to read the claffics) but I did not apply them after reading to the farther ufe that his Lordfhip hints at.

I had fuch good eyes, that I often read by the light of the moon, as my mafter would not permit me to take a candle into my room, and that prohibition I looked upon as a kind of perfecution, but I always comforted myfelf with the thoughts of my being a dear child of God; and as fuch, that it was impoffible for me to efcape perfecution from the children of the devil, which epithets I very *pioufly* applied to my good mafter and miftrefs. And fo ignorantly and imprudently zealous (being a real methodift) was I for the good of their precious fouls, as fometimes to give them broad hints of it, and of the dangerous ftate they were in.

> To wanton whim and prejudice we owe,
> Opinion is the only God we know.
> Where's the foundation of religion plac'd;
> On every individual's fickle tafte.
> The narrow way fantic mortals tread,
> By fuperftitious prejudice mifled——
> This paffage leads to heaven—yet ftrange to tell!
> Another's confcience finds it leads to hell. CHATTERTON.

Their pious good old minifter, the Reverend Mr. Harrifon, I called "*a blind leader of the blind*;" and I more than once affured my miftrefs, that both he and his whole flock were in a ftate of damnation; being without the affurance of their fins being pardoned, they muft be "ftrangers to the hope of Ifrael, and without God in the world." My good miftrefs wifely thought that a good ftick was the beft way of arguing with such an ignorant infatuated boy as I was, and had often recourse to it; but I took care to give her a deal of trouble; for whenever I was ordered in my turn to read in the Bible, I always selected such chapters as I thought militated against Arians, Socinians, &c. and such verses as I deemed favourable to the doctrine of Original Sin, Justification by Faith, Imputed Righteousness, the Doctrine of the Trinity, &c. On such parts I always placed a particular emphasis, which puzzled and teazed the old lady a good deal.

Among other places I thought (having so been taught by the methodists) that the sixteenth chapter of Ezekiel very much favoured the doctrines of original sin, imputed righteousness, &c. that chapter I often selected and read to her, and she has often read the eighteenth chapter of the same prophecy, for the sake of the parable of the Father's eating *four grapes*.

Whenever I read in St. Paul's Epistles on justification by faith alone, my good mistress would read in the Epistle of St. James, such passages as say that a man is not justified by faith alone, but by faith and works, which often embarrassed me not a little. However, I comforted myself with the conceit of having more texts of Scripture on my side of the question than she had on her side. As to St. James, I was almost ready to conclude, that he was not quite orthodox, and so at last I did not much mind what he said.

" —— False opinions rooted in the mind,
" Hood-wink the soul and keep our reason blind.
" In controverted points can reason sway,
" When passion or conceit hurries us away."

Hitherto I had not frequented the methodist meetings by the consent or knowledge of my master and mistress; nor had my zeal been so great as to make me openly violate their commands. But as my zeal increased much faster than my knowledge, I soon disregarded their orders, and without hesitation ran away to hear a methodistical sermon as often as I could find opportunity. One Sunday morning, at eight o'clock, my mistress seeing her sons set off, and knowing that they were gone to a methodist meeting, determined to prevent me from doing the fame by locking the door, which fhe accordingly did; on which in a fuperftitious mood, I opened the Bible for direction what to do (ignorant methodifts often practife the fame fuperftitious method) and the firft words I read were thefe, " He has given his angels charge concerning thee, left at any time thou fhouldeft dafh thy foot againft a ftone." This was enough for me; fo without a moment's hefitation, I ran up two pair of ftairs to my own room, and out of the window I leaped, to the great terror of my poor miftrefs. I got up immediately, and ran about two or three hundred yards, towards the meeting-houfe; but alas! I could run no farther; my feet and ancles were moft intolerably bruifed, fo that I was obliged to be carried back and put to bed: and it was more than a month before I recovered the ufe of my limbs. I was ignorant enough to think that the Lord had not ufed me very well, and refolved not to put fo much truft in him for the future, which reminds me of the following ftories: Dr. Moore in his Travels through France, Switzerland and Germany, informs us that a certain Frenchman, purchafed a fmall filver figure of our Saviour on the Crofs, and having bought fome tickets in the lottery, he prayed to his crucifix that they may come up prizes; and having alfo a great fhare in the cargo of a fhip, he would not infure it, but committed it to the care of his filver god: And his cargo being loft at fea; and his tickets come up blanks, he fold his crucifix in great anger. And Suetonius informs us, that the fleet of Auguftus having been difperfed by a ftorm, and many of the fhips loft, the Emperor gave orders that the ftatue of Neptune fhould not be carried in proceffion with thofe of the other gods.

My above rafh adventure made a great noife in the town, and was talked of many miles round. Some few admired my amazing ftrength of faith, but the major part pitied me, as a poor ignorant, deluded and infatuated boy.

The neighbours ftar'd, and figh'd, yet blefs'd the lad;
Some deem'd him wond'rous wife, and fome believ'd him mad.

DR. BEATTIE.

I am, dear Friend, yours.

LETTER IX.

One makes the rugged paths fo fmooth and even,
None but an ill-bred man can mifs of heaven.
Another quits his ftockings, breeches, fhirt,
Becaufe he fancies virtue dwells in dirt:
While all concur to take away the ftrefs,
From weightier points, and lay it on the lefs.
STILLINGFLEET, on Converfation.

'Gad! I've a thriving traffic in my eye.
Near the mad manfions of Moorfield's I'll bawl;
Friends, fathers, mothers, fifters, fons and all,
Shut up your fhops, and liften to my call,   FOOTE.

DEAR FRIEND,

IN the fourth year of my apprenticefhip, my mafter died; now although he was a
good hufband, a good father, and a good mafter, &c.
yet as he had not the methodiftical faith, and could
not pronounce the *Shibboleth* of that fect, I *pioufly*
feared that he was gone to hell.

My miftrefs thought that his death was haftened by
his uneafy reflections on the bad behaviour of his fons,
after they commenced methodifts, as before they were
converted each was dutiful and attended to his trade,
but after they became *faints* they attended fo much to
their fpiritual concerns, that they acted as though they
fuppofed they were to be fed and cloathed by miracles, like Mr. Huntingdon, who informs us, in his
book called " The Bank of Faith," that the Lord
fent him a pair of breeches, that a dog brought him
mutton to eat, fifh died at night in a pond on purpofe to be eaten by him in the morning; money, and
in fhort every thing he could defire, he obtained by
prayer. Mr. Wefley ufed to cure a violent pain in
his head the fame way, as he relates in his Journals.
Thus, as Foote fays,

" With labour, toil, all fecond means difpenfe,
" And live a rent-charge upon providence."

D 6

To give you a better idea of methodiftical ignorance and neglect of ordinary means of living, &c. I will
relate one inftance more. Mary Hubbard (an old woman of Mr. Wefley's fociety) would often wafh her
linen, hang it out to dry, and go away to work in
the fields, or to Taunton-market, four miles from her
houfe; and when blamed, fhe would anfwer " that
the Lord watched over her, and all that fhe had, and
that he would prevent any perfon from ftealing her
two old fmocks, or if he permitted them to be ftolen,
he would fend her two new in their ftead." And I
ferioufly affure you, fir, that there are many thoufand Mary Hubbards amongft the methodifts.

As I had been bound to my miftrefs as well as my
mafter, I was of courfe an apprentice ftill. But after
my mafter's death I obtained more liberty of confcience (as I called it,) fo that I not only went to
hear the methodift fermons, but was alfo admitted
into their fociety; and I believe they never had a
more devout enthufiaftical member; for feveral years
I regularly attended every fermon and all their private meetings.

> " I, like an hackney-coachman, knew
> " Short way to heav'n by a clew,
> " Cou'd cut acrofs, and fave the road,
> " That guided to the blefs'd abode."

As you are probably unacquainted with the nature
of thefe *private meetings*, a fhort account of them may
perhaps afford you fome amufement.

Mr. Wefley inftituted amongft his people, befides
the public preachings, feveral kinds of private meetings; and as the *prayer-meeting* is the leaft private of
any of them, I will firft take notice of that.

To the prayer-meetings, which were in general
held in private houfes, they often invited people who
were not of their fociety. An hymn was firft fung,
then they all knelt, and the firft perfon who felt a
motion, made an extempory prayer; when he had
done, another began, and fo on, for about two hours.

> There every foul a face of forrow wears,
> And not one fign of happinefs appears;

But looks of terror and dejected eyes,
Defpairing murmurs, and heart-rending fighs;
No eye doth wander, and no lip doth fmile,
But holy horrors chill us all the while.

YOUNG SOLDIER.

It fo happened fometimes, that one of the brethren began to pray without having *the gift* of prayer
(as they call it), and then he often ftuck faft, like
fome of the young orators at Coach-maker's Hall, &c.
Prayer-meetings were held in fuch high efteem a-
mongft them that they afferted, more were " *born*
" *again*," and more " *made free* from all the remains
of fin," or in other words of their own, " made *perfect* as God is perfect," in thefe kinds of meetings,
than at public preaching, &c. Thus, as Pomfret
fays,

" The fpirits heated will ftrange things produce."

But it is impoffible for you, my friend, to form
any juft idea of thefe affemblies, except you had been
prefent at them: one wheedles and coaxes the Divine
Being, in his addreffes; another is amorous and luf-
cious; and a third fo rude and commanding, he will
even tell the Deity that he muft be *a liar* if he does
not grant all they afk. In this manner will they mag-
netize, or work up one another's imaginations, until
they may actually be faid to be in a ftate of intoxica-
tion; and whilft in this intoxicated or magnetized
ftate, it often happens that fome of them recollect a
text of fcripture, fuch as, " thy fins are forgiven
thee," or " go and fin no more," &c. and then they
declare themfelves to be born again, or to be fanctified, &c.

They have another kind of private meeting after
the public preaching on Sunday evenings, in which
the preacher meets all the members of the fociety,
who ftay behind after the general congregation is difmiffed. To this fociety the preacher gave fuch advice as he deemed better fuited to a godly few than
to a promifcuous multitude of " *outward-court* wor-
fhippers."

Their *love-feaft* is alfo a private meeting of as
many members of the community as pleafe to attend;

and they generally come from all parts, within several
miles of the place where love-feasts are held.

> " Those holy knaves whose hypocritic zeal,
> " In warmest strains their transports now reveal,
> " Strives the fond rabble's ign'rant souls to move,
> " Then fly with rapture to their feast of love."

When all are met they alternately sing and pray;
and such amongst them as think that their *experience*
(as they call it) is remarkable, stand up in their place,
and relate all the transactions between God, the devil,
and their souls:

> Discussing evils, which begin,
> In every soul, that tastes of sin!
> As head of chosen, doth foreknow,
> How far the devil means to go.   Pious Incendiary.

At such seasons as this I have heard many of them
declare they had just received the pardon of all
their sins while Brother such a-one was in prayer;
another would then get up and assert that he was just
at that instant made perfectly free from sin.

At these times the Spirit is supposed to be very
powerfully at work amongst them; and such an *unison*
of sighing and *groaning* succeeds, that you would
think they had all lost their senses. In this frantic
state, many apply to themselves such texts of scripture as happen to come into their heads.

In the love-feast they have *buns* to eat, which are
mutually broken between each brother and sister; and
they have also *water* to drink, which they hand from
one to another. These meetings begin about seven
o'clock, and last until nine or ten.

In London, Bristol, and other large places, they
have some *private* meetings, unknown to the community at large. These meetings consist of all married
men at one time: young and unmarried men at another time: the married women by themselves, and
the single women by themselves; and to each of these
classes Mr. Wesley went, and gave such advice or ex-
hortations as he thought suitable to their situation in
life, seldom failing to speak much in praise of celi-
bacy, to the *Maids* and *Bachelors*, under his pastoral

care. I will in my next give you an account of their watch-nights, clafs-meetings, bands, and other particulars.

I am,

Dear Friend,

Yours.

LETTER X.

——————— Here, Gamaliel fage
Trains up his babes of grace, inftructed well.
In all the —— difcipline of prayer ;
To point the holy leer : by juft degrees
To clofe the twinkling eye ; expand the palms,
To expofe the whites, and with the fightlefs balls
To glare upon the crowd ; to rife, to fink
The docile voice ; now murmur'ng foft and flow,
With inward accent calm, and then again,
In foaming floods of rapt'rous eloquence
Let loofe the ftorm, and thunder, thro' the nofe
The threatened vengeance.   SOMERVILLE.

DEAR FRIEND,

THE *Watch-night* begins about feven o'clock. They fing hymns, pray, preach, fing, and pray again ; then exhort, fing and pray alternately, until twelve o'clock. The hymns which they fing on thofe nights, are wrote for fuch occafions, and abound with gloomy ideas, which are increafed by the time of night ; and it muft be remarked, that the major part of thofe who attend thefe nocturnal meetings, having fafted the whole of the day (according to Mr. Wefley's orders) are in a very proper ftate of mind to entertain the moft extravagant whims or enthufiaftic notions that can poffibly enter the heads of any vifionaries. So that fuch nights are often very prolific, as numbers are faid to be born again, and become the temples of the Holy Ghoft on watch-nights, which makes thofe nights efteemed by them.

Mr. Wefley, in every place where his people were numerous, had divided them into *claffes*, confifting of twelve or fourteen brothers or fifters. Sometimes men and women met together in the fame *clafs* (as they called it) and other claffes confifted of all men or all women. Each of thefe claffes had one in it who was called the leader. In fuch claffes where men and women meet together, the leader was always a bro-ther : and fo of courfe when the clafs confifted of men alone. But in the women's claffes a fifter was always the leader.

When they met together, the leader firft gave out a hymn, which they all fang; after the hymn they all knelt, and their leader made an extemporary prayer; after which they were feated ; and when the leader had informed them of the ftate of his own mind, he enquired of all prefent, one after another, how they found the ftate of their fouls. Some he found were full of faith and *affurance*, others had dreadful doubts and fears; fome had horrid temp-tations.

> It doth affect my inward man,
> To think of Satan's wicked plan ;
> Ah ! me, how doth that fiend confpire,
> To drag each faint to lafting fire. Fanaticifm Difplayed

Others complained of a lukewarm ftate, &c. In thefe meetings, fome of the members fpoke of them-felves, as though they were as pure as angels are in heaven, but with the generality of them, it was far otherwife ; and nothing was more common among them than to hear the major part exclaiming againft themfelves, and declaring that they were the moft vile abandoned wretches on this fide hell, that they won-dered why the earth did not open and fwallow them up alive. But they generally added, that " the blood of Chrift cleanfes them from all fin," and that " where fin abounded there would grace much more abound." Indeed it was eafy to remark that the reafon why they painted themfelves in fuch odious co-lours, was only to boaft of an aftonifhing quantity.

of grace that God had bestowed on them, in thus
pardoning all their abominations, and numbering
them with the household of faith, who ought to have
been shut up in the nethermost hell. The greater
the sinner (say they) the greater the saint. To each
of these the leader gave a word of comfort, or of cor-
rection in the best manner he was able. They then
sang and prayed again. This lasted about one hour.
And every one in Mr. Wesley's connexion did, or
was expected to meet, each in his own class once in
a week. In these classes each made a weekly contri-
bution towards the general support of the preachers,
&c. Such as were very poor continued a penny per
week, others two-pence, and some who could afford
it sixpence. This money was entered in a book kept
for that purpose, and one in every class called the
steward, had the care of the cash.

I now come to speak of the *Bands*, which consisted
only of *justified* persons; that is, such as had received
the *assurance* of their sins being pardoned. In the
classes, both the *awakened* (as they call them) and
the justified, and even those that were made *perfect*,
met all together, as did the married and the single,
and often men and women. But none were admitted
into any *band* but such as were at least in a justified
state, and the married of each sex met by themselves,
and the single by themselves. About ten was the
number generally put in one band; all these must
belong to and meet in some class, once a week, when
not hindered by sickness, &c. and they were also to
meet weekly in their band. When met, they first
sung, then made a short prayer; that done, the *band-
leader* informed them of the state of his mind, during
the last week, &c. He then made inquiry into the
state of all present, and each related what had passed
since they last met; as what visitations they had received from God, what temptations from the devil,
the flesh, &c. And it is a maxim amongst them that
exposing to one another what the devil has particularly
tempted them to commit will make the old fellow
more careful how he tempts, when he knows that all
his secrets will be told the next meeting. This they

call shaming the devil. In the classes they only confessed in general terms, that they have been tempted
by the world, the flesh, and the devil. But in the
bands they confessed the particular sins which they
had been tempted to commit, or had actually com-
mited.

The last time I met in band was in London, where
an old man (near seventy years of age) informed us
that he had for several weeks together laboured under
a very grievous temptation of the devil, who all this
time had been constantly tempting him to commit
adultery; he further informed us, that having let
too much of his house to lodgers, they were obliged
to put the maid's bed in the room where he and his
wife slept; and that one morning he had seen the
maid lying asleep, nearly or quite uncovered, and he
again assured us, that ever since that time the devil
had been every day tempting him to do that which
was nought with the maid. I could not help thinking the old gentleman was right in charging it on *the
devil*, as there was little reason to think it was any
temptation of *the flesh*. Permit me to add, that this
old buck had a wife about half his own age. I have
been informed, that some young men of the brother-
hood have at times disguised themselves in women's
clothes, and have so got into the women's bands;
it may be very curious to hear the confessions of the
holy sisters. By this time I suppose you have had
enough of *band-meetings*.

Mr. Wesley instituted another kind of private
meeting for the highest order of his people, called
the *select bands*; to which none were admitt d but
such as were sanctified, or made *perfect* in love, and
freed from all the remains of sin. But as I never
professed *perfection*, I was not permitted to enter into
this holy of holies. But I have known a great number of these perfect saints, of both sexes; and I also
lived in the same house a whole year with one of
those entire holy sisters. A few days before I came to
live in Chiswell-Street, one of these perfect sisters was
detected in stealing coals out of the shed of one of
the sanctified brothers; but she, like the old fellow

above mentioned, said it was the devil that tempted her to do it.

Four times every year new *tickets* are distributed to all Mr. Wesley's people throughout the three kingdoms. Their ticket is a very small slip of paper, with a text of scripture on it, which is exchanged every quarter for some other text. Such as are only in a *class*, have a different text from such as are in a *band*, so that no one can be admitted into a general meeting of the bands, appointed by any of the preachers when he intends to give them an exhortation, nor into any particular band, by a common society ticket. On the common tickets are such texts as these: " Now is the accepted time." " Awake, thou that sleepest,"—and such like. But those for the *bands* are in a higher strain; as, " Be ye perfect as your heavenly Father is perfect."— " Go on unto perfection."—" Ye are children of the light."—" Your bodies are temples of the Holy Ghost;" and other texts of a similar tendency. For these tickets, each poor person paid one shilling, such as were rich paid more; indeed the money seemed to be the principal end of issuing tickets, at least in country places, the members in the community being so well known to each other, that they scarce ever shewed their tickets in order to gain admittance. I forgot to inform you that prayer-meetings, class-meetings, band-meetings, &c. were in general held in private houses, belonging to some of the brethren.

I am,

Dear Friend,

Yours.

LETTER XI.

" Stiff in opinions, always in the wrong;
" Was every thing by starts, and nothing long."

*   *   *   *   *   *

" Then all for women, panting, rhiming, drinking,
" Besides ten thousand freaks that died in thinking."

DEAR FRIEND,

YOU now see what sort of a society I was got into. In country places particularly, they consist of farmers, husbandmen, shoemakers, woolcombers, weavers, their wives, &c. I have heard Mr. Wesley remark that more women are converted than men; and I believe that by far the greatest part of his people are females; and not a few of them four, disappointed old maids, with some others of a a less prudish disposition ;

" Who grown unfit for carnal bliss,
" Long to taste how Spirits kiss."

Lavater, in his Essay on Physiognomy, says, " Women sink into the most incurable melancholy, as they also rise to the most enraptured heights." In another place he says, " By the irritability of their nerves, their incapability for deep enquiry and firm decision, they may easily, from their extreme sensibility, become the most irreclaimable, the most rapturous enthusiasts."

" There is (says Mr. Hume) only one subject on which I am apt to distrust the judgment of females : and that is, concerning books of gallantry and devotion, which they commonly affect as high-flown as possible; and most of them seem more delighted with the warmth, than with the justness of the passion. I mention gallantry and devotion as the same subject : because, in reality, they become the same when treated in this manner; and we may observe, that they both depend on the very same complection, as

the fair fex have a great fhare of the tender and amorous difpofition, it perverts their judgment on this
occafion, and 'makes them be eafily affected, even in
what has no propriety in the expreffions, nor nature
in the fentiment. Mr. Addifon's elegant difcourfes
of religion have no relifh with them, in comparifon
to books of myftic devotion: and Otway's fine tra-
gedies are rejected for the rant of Mr. Dryden."

There are thoufands in this fociety who will never
read any thing befides the Bible, and books publifhed
by Mr. Wefley. For feveral years I read very little
elfe, nor would I go (at leaft very feldom) to any
other place of worfhip; fo that inftead of hearing the
fenfible and learned minifters at Taunton, I would
often go four, five, or fix miles, to fome country village, to hear an infpired hufbandman, fhoemaker,
blackfmith, or woolcomber; and frequently in froft
and fnow have I rofe a little after midnight (not
knowing what time of night it was) and have wandered about the town until five o'clock, when the
preaching began; where I have often heard a fermon
preached to not more than ten or a dozen people.
But fuch of us as did attend at this early hour, ufed
afterwards to congratulate each other on the great
privilege we enjoyed, then off we went to our work,
fhivering with cold.

I was firft converted to methodifm when I was
about fixteen years of age ; from that time until I was
twenty-one I was a fincere enthufiaft, and every fpare
hour I enjoyed I dedicated to the ftudy of the Bible,
reading methodiftical books, learning hymns, hearing fermons, meeting in focieties, &c. My memory
was very tenacious, fo that every thing I read I made
my own. I could have repeated feveral volumes of
hymns; when I heard a fermon; I could have preached
it again, and nearly in the fame words; my Bible
had hundreds of leaves folded down, and thoufands
of marks againfts fuch texts as I thought favoured
the doctrines (or whims) which I had imbibed. So
that I ftood forth as the champion of methodifm
wherever I came.

But alas! my godly strict life at length suffered interruption. I will give you a farther account of the methodists when I come to the time when I finally left their society.

The election for two members of parliament was strongly contested at Taunton, just as I attained my twenty-first year; and being now of age, the six or seven months, which I had to serve of my apprenticeship were purchased of my mistress by some friends of two of the contending candidates: so that I was at once set free in the midst of a scene of riot and dissipation.

> Present example gets within our guard,
> And acts with double force, by few repell'd.   YOUNG.

> " Nor shame, nor honour could prevail,
> " To keep me thus from turning tail."

As I had a vote, and was also possessed of a few ideas above those of my rank and situation, my company was courted by some who were in a much higher sphere; and (probably what they partly intended) in such company I soon forgot my godly or methodistical connections, and ran into the opposite extreme: so that for several months most of my spare hours were devoted to the

> Young-ey'd God of Wine! Parent of joys!
> Frolic and full of thee, while the cold sons
> Of temperance, the fools of thought and care,
> Lay stretch'd in sober slumbers.   MALLET's Eurydice.

Here I nearly sunk for ever into meanness, obscurity, and vice; for when the election was over, I had no longer open houses to eat and drink in at free cost. And, having refused bribes, I was nearly out of cash.

I began the world with an unsuspecting heart, was tricked out of about three pounds (every shilling I was possessed of) and part of my cloaths, by some country sharpers. Having one coat and two waistcoats left, I lent my best waistcoat to an acquaintance, who left the town, and forgot to return it.

Whate'er or fages teach, or bards reveal,
Men ftill are men, and learn but when they feel.
                                    J. H. BROWNE.

However, I did not fink quite fo low as the com-
monality of journeyman fhoemakers, but in general
worked very hard, and fpent my money in better
company.

To know good, preferring fpecious ill,
Reafon becomes a cully to the will ;
Thus men, perverfely fond to roam aftray,
Hood-winks the guide affigned to fhew the way;
And in life's voyage, like the pilot fares,
Who breaks the compafs, and contemns the ftars.
                                    FENTON.

Notwithftanding, at times, I was very uneafy, and
although I had not been at any methodiftical meeting
during the time that I had lived this diffipated life,
yet my mind was not freed entirely from the fuperftitious fears I had there imbibed ; fo that whenever
any perfon afked me, what would become of me (that
had lived fuch an holy life) if I fhould die in the ftate
of *backfliding* from " the good old way ?" I always
acknowledged that I fhould be eternally damn'd,
were that to be the cafe. But I muft confefs that I
was not much afraid of dying in fuch a ftate, as I
was too much prepoffeffed with the methodiftical notions of *free-grace*, that would not let me be finally
loft, prefuming that I muft wait, as it were, for a *fecond call* to repentance, juftification, &c. which I had
been taught to believe might take place inftantaneoufly,
and put the devil to flight in a hurry, and fo matters
would be all right again. And I have known many
who having thefe ideas, have continued to live very
profligate lives to the end of the chapter.

There is a curious paffage in the confeffions of St.
Auguftin, in which he owns that in his youth he was
exceffively addicted to women, and that he made ufe
of a prayer, in which he defired God to make him
change, but not too foon.

I often privately took the Bible to bed with me,
and in the long fummer mornings read for hours
together in bed, but this did not in the leaft influence

my conduct. As you know great events often arise from little causes, I am now going to relate a circumstance, trivial in itself, though productive of a more considerable change in my situation, than any I had yet experienced.

I was twenty-one years of age the 11th of September 1767, the election was over the latter end of March 1768. It was in this year that my new master's wife insisted on my purchasing milk of a milk-maid who was a customer at the shop; which command I refused to comply with, as I had a smart little milk-maid of my own. But as my mistress *wore the breeches*, my master was obliged, by his wife's order, to inform me, that I must comply with her mandate, or get another master. I left him without hesitation; and the same afternoon went to Wellington, took leave of my father and mother, and informed them of my intention to go to Bristol. After two or three days, I returned back to Taunton, where I stayed a day or two more. In which time I became enamoured with, or infatuated by, the beautiful *Nancy Trott*:

> ——In sweet words that breath delight and joy,
> She fix'd the attention of the heart-struck boy.
> ——Beauty triumphs and the joys of love !
>
> Rape of HELEN.

And although I saw the impropriety of the measure, yet I could not resist the fair temper, who prevailed with me to permit her to accompany me in my journey.

> Reason was given to curb our headstrong will,
> And yet but shews a weak physician's skill;
> Gives nothing while the raging fit does last,
> But stays to cure it when the worst is past.
> Reason's a staff for age, when Nature's gone;
> But youth is strong enough to walk alone.
>
> DRYDEN's Con. of Gran.

We rested a week in Bridgewater, where I worked hard and got money to convey us to Exbridge, seventeen miles on this side Bristol; and there I saw my conduct in such a point of view as made me resolve to leave her.

In well-feign'd accents, now they hail my ear,
My life, my love, my charmer, or my dear,
As if these sounds, these joyless sounds could prove
The smallest particle of genuine love;
O! purchas'd love, retail'd through half the town,
Where each may share on paying half-a crown;
Where every air of tenderness is art,
And not one word the language of the heart;
Where all is mockery of Cupid's reign,
End in remorse, in wretchedness and pain.

Art of Living in London.

My finances amounted to three shilllings and one penny, out of which I gave her half-a-crown, and with the remaining seven-pence, without informing her of my purpose, I set off for Bristol; where I arrived in a few hours, and got work the same evening.

A few days after, I went to the inn where the Taunton carrier put up, to enquire after *Miss Trott*, as I wanted to know if she had returned safe to Taunton. I was informed that she was in Bristol nearly as soon as I was. Knowing but little of the world, and still less of women of her description, I was quite unhappy on her account, for fear that being in a strange place she might be in want and distress; which thought induced me to offer to several of my countrymen five shillings to the first who should bring me an account where I might find her; but I did not see her until several weeks after that.

Some foe to his upright intent,
Finds out his weaker part,
Virtue engages his assent,
But pleasure wins the heart.
'Tis here the folly of the wise,
Through all his arts we view,
And while his tongue the charge denies,
His conscience owns it true.

COWPER.

The Taunton carrier gave me a letter from my good Mistress Bowden (who, by marrying again, had changed her name to Dingle). The contents of this letter very much surprised me. It informed me that a day or two before I fell out with my last mistress (which was the trifling cause of my leaving Taunton) *Betty Tucker*, a common lass, had sworn a child to

E

me; that the parish officers had been to my master's shop within an hour after I had left it to go to Wellington, and that they had been at Wellington just as I had left that place, and afterwards hearing that I was in Bridgewater, they had pursued me thither. But the morning on which they arrived, I had set off for Exbridge; and believing that I had intentionally fled before them, they had given over this chase for the present.

Reflecting on this affair, although my conduct was very far from entitling me to entertain such a supposition, yet I was then weak enough to imagine, that being a particular favourite of heaven, a kind of miracle had been wrought to save me from a prison, or from marrying a woman I could not bear the idea of living with a single week; and as I had not any knowledge of her being with child (not having seen her for three months before) I had not taken any measure to avoid the consequence, but put myself in the way of the officers: for, as I have just told you, after I had taken leave of my father and mother, I went back to Taunton, and walked about publicly one whole day, and part of another.

This girl was delivered about two months afterwards of a still-born child, so that I was never troubled for expences. Methinks you are ready to say with Pomfret,

" 'Tis easy to descend into the snare,
" By the pernicious conduct of the fair:
" But safely to return from their abode,
" Requires the wit, the prudence of a God."

I am,

Dear Friend,

Yours.

LETTER XII.

Terror in dreams the anxious mother moves,
Or bids fond virgins mourn their absent loves.
Sylvia in vain her wearied eyes would close,
Hark! the sad death watch clicks—adieu, repose;
The distant owl, or yelling mastiff near,
Terror still vibrates on the list'ning ear,
And bids th' affrighted Sylvia vigils keep,
For Fancy, like Macbeth, has murder'd sleep.

Mr. PRALL.

DEAR FRIEND,

THE subject of my last recalls to my mind a ridiculous affair, which excited much mirth in that part of the country.

During the election at Taunton, a gentleman one day came in a post-chaise to the White-hart Inn, kept by Mr. Baldwin, and after having refreshed himself, strolled into the yard, and seeing the hostler, asked him if he could inform him where they took in the *news?* The hostier understanding him in a literal sense, directed him to a bookseller's shop on the opposite side of the way; this shop was kept by Miss A—d—n, a beautiful young lady of irreproachable character, and one whose fine understanding and polished taste did honour to the profession; which profession she only adopted for an amusement, as she possessed an independent fortune.

Our gentleman on entering the shop, enquired of the shopmaid for her mistress, but the maid being used to serve in the shop, and knowing that her mistress had some ladies with her, informed the gentleman that she could help him to any thing that he wanted. But on his saying he had some private business with her mistress, he was shewn into a back parlour, and the mistress being informed a gentleman wanted to speak to her, she went directly to him. The moment she entered the room, he clasped her in his arms, called her a divine creature, &c. This so alarmed Miss A—d—n, that she screamed aloud; on hearing

E 2

which, the ladies, preceded by the housemaid and shop-maid, repaired to the parlour, where they found Miss A—d—n almost in fits. The gentleman thinking that it was only a trick to raise her price, took but little notice, on which one of the maids ran out and called in several of the neighbours, who, on coming into the parlour, saw with astonishment our Sir Harry Wildair taking improper liberties with Miss A—d—n, and desired him to desist. But he desired them not to attempt to put tricks on travellers, and ordered them to leave the room. Instead of obeying his injunctions they in a resolute tone ordered our spark to go instantly about his business. However, he still kept his ground, until the mayor of the town, who happened to live just by, was called in. Mr. Mayor demanded why he took such freedom with the lady. Our gentleman, seeing that the affair began to look very serious, now became calm, and informed the company that having an inclination for a frolic, he had enquired for a bad house, and had been directed there; adding, that if there had been any mistake, he was very sorry for it, and would beg the lady's pardon. On hearing this the company was more surprized than before, and demanded of the gentleman, who had informed him that that house was a bawdy-house? He, without hesitation, replied, the hostler at the White-hart Upon this the hostler was sent for, and on his being asked, if he had directed that gentleman. to Miss A—d—n's as a bawdy-house? The poor fellow, with marks of terror and surprise, answered, No. The Gentleman never asked me for a bawdy-house, he only asked me for a house where they took in the news. So that the hostler's understanding him in a literal sense, caused all the confusion. The affair, however, had got so much air, that our spark was glad to leave the town immediately.

A very strange unaccountable circumstance happened in this Inn about the same time; one of those occurrences that puzzle the philosopher, and strengthen superstition in weak minds. Three or four gentlemen of the neighbourhood were drinking wine in one of the rooms, when the landlord of the Inn (as it appeared to them) walked into the room, and coming up to the table, around which they were seated, they addressed him with " Mr. Baldwin how do you do ? sit down and take a glass of wine with us ;" but instead of doing as requested, the supposed Innkeeper walked out, without making any reply; which not only surprized, but offended the company, who rung the bell violently, and on the waiter's appearance, they ordered him to send in his master. The waiter informed them that his master was not at home. The gentlemen replied, that he was at home a few minutes since, and therefore they insisted on seeing him; but the man assured them they were mistaken, as his master was in Bristol, and had been there several days. They then ordered the waiter to send in Mrs. Baldwin, who immediately appearing, the gentlemen asked her where Mr. Baldwin was, and she informed them, as the waiter had already done, that he was at Bristol, and had been there several days ; on which the gentlemen grow very angry, and swore that Mr. Baldwin had just before come into the room, and on their requesting him to partake of their wine, had insulted them by going out of the room, without deigning to give them answer. Mrs. Baldwin then drew out of her pocket a letter she had that morning received from Mr. Baldwin, by which it was apparent, that he really was at Bristol. The story was then told round the neighbourhood, and all the old women certainly concluded that Mr. Baldwin must certainly be dead, and that he died at the very instant that the gentlemen saw him come into the room; but Mr. Baldwin, returning two days after, rendered it necessary for them to vary their story ; they then asserted that it was a token, or some warning of his death, and had no doubt but it would very soon happen. It was generally thought that Mr. Baldwin was weak enough to pay such attention to the story and inference, as to hurt his health, as he really died within a year after, and the old women were not a little pleased at the event, as it tended to justify the truth of their prediction.

E 3

A more ridiculous affair happened about ten years since, at the Two Bells, opposite Whitechapel-church. The landlord was sitting one night with some jovial company, one of whom happening to say, that he prayed to God, that such a thing should not come to pass; the landlord replied in a good humoured manner, your prayers will neither do good nor harm; upon which the other said a deal to persuade the host that his prayers would do great things; but the more he said in praise of his prayers, the more the landlord laughed at, and ridiculed him. The man at last insisted that he could pray the landlord to death in two months time, and offered to bet him a crown bowl of punch to the truth of it, which the landlord accepting, the wager was laid, and almost every night after this, the man came to the house, and constantly laughed at the landlord, and assured him that he would lose his wager; and however strange it may appear, our host did die within the time, and his widow paid the wager. I think there cannot remain a doubt but that the ridiculous talk of the fellow actually affected the landlord's mind, and hastened his death; and the following instances tend also to shew how easily the lives of some are shortened:

Joseph Scales, Esq. about five years since, in turning short one day in one o. the streets of London, met a man whom he had not seen for some time, and innocently addressed him with, Ha! what are you alive yet! which had such an effect on the poor man, that he died a few hours after.

Being at Bristol about four years since, I enquired after a worthy leather-seller whom I had formerly known, and was informed that he was lately dead, and that his death was supposed to have been hastened by a famous fortune-teller, who, having cast his nativity, declared that he would die within six months, which affected his mind so as to accomplish his prediction.

> Live to day, the now is ours,
> Who can trust the future hours?
> Now the rapt'rous moments roll;
> This is the sun-shine of the soul.

        Fawkes.

The following lines of Pope, being so much to my purpose, I must quote them also:

Heav'n from all creatures hides the book of fate,
All but the title page, prescrib'd their present state;
From brutes what men, from men what spirits know:
Or who could suffer being here below?
The lamb thy riot dooms to bleed to day,
Had he thy reason, would he skip and play?
Pleased to the last, he crops the flow'ry food,
And licks the hand just rais'd to shed his blood.
Oh, blindness to the future kindly given,
That each may fill the circle mark'd by heav'n.

Dr. Moore in his travels through France, Switzerland and Germany, relates the following remarkable account which is to the point: Being at Berlin, he went to see a man executed for the murder of a child. His motives for this horrid deed were much more extraordinary than the action itself. He had accompanied some of his companions to the house of a fellow, who assumed the character of a fortune-teller; and having disobliged him, by expressing a contempt for his art, the fellow, out of revenge, prophesied, that this man should die on a scaffold. This seemed to make but little impression at the time, but afterwards recurred often to this unhappy creature's memory, and became every day more troublesome to his imagination. At length the idea haunted his mind so incessantly, that he was rendered perfectly miserable, and could no longer endure life.

He would have put himself to death with his own hands, had he not been deterred by the notion that God never forgives suicide; though, upon repentance, he pardons every other crime. He resolved, therefore, to commit murder; and thinking that if he murdered a grown person, he might possibly send a soul to hell, he in consequence of those ideas murdered a child of his master's, of whom he was exceedingly fond; and thus the random prophesy proved its own completion.

About a week after my Life had been published, Mr. Heyden sent to me to know the day, hour, and minute of my birth, in order that he might cast my nativity; and at the fame time politely informed me, that being fo celebrated a character, he meant not to charge me any thing for doing it. But I did not choofe to have it done, as I thought it was poffible he might predict fomething or other, that in a time of ficknefs or weaknefs of body might hurt my mind. As no man can at all times call in reafon to his affiftance, and as we often fee that even the moft rational part of mankind are fometimes hurt or mifled by extravagant whims and idle chimeras. And could I learn for certain, what is to be my fortune in future, I cannot think that knowledge would be of any real benefit to me. If I am to be always profperous and happy, it will be fome addition to me, fhould it overtake me unexpectedly; and fhould it be my fate once more to fee a fcene fhift, and a gloomy profpect prefent itfelf, I would not wifh to forbode it, and thus prevent me from making the moft of the prefent moment. Anacreon was alfo of the fame way of thinking.

The ftory of the late Dr. Pitcairn, of Edinburgh, and the collier, is well known. This ftrong healthy man was, on his way to Edinburgh, made to believe by the doctor's ftudents, although in perfect health, that he was really very ill, and went home to bed and died.

I have fet down the above inftances, in order to fhew how eafy it is to trifle away the lives of our fellow creatures, and furely fuch who wantonly do it, muft afterwards have very gloomy reflections.

I am,

Dear Friend,

Yours.

LETTER XIII.

I had a friend that lov'd me :
I was his foul : : he liv'd not but in me.
We were fo clofe link'd in each other's breaft,
The rivets were not found that join'd us firft.
                                    DRYDEN's All for Love.

The wretch to fenfe and felf-confin'd,
    Knows not the dear delight ;
For generous friendfhip wings the mind,
    To reach an Angels flight: MRS. CHANDLER.

DEAR FRIEND,

IN my laft I mentioned my arrival at Briftol, where I took a lodging in a ftreet, called (I think) Queen-Street, in Caftle-Street, at the houfe of a Mr. *James*; a much more decent refidence, than commonly falls to the lot of journeymen fhoemakers.

In this houfe I found a Mr. John Jones, a genteel young man, juft turned of twenty-one years of age : He was alfo a fon of *Crifpin*, and made women's ftuff fhoes : which he fold by the dozen to warehoufes. This Mr. Jones and I were foon very intimate ; we kept ourfelves neatly dreffed, and in general worked hard, fpending our money chiefly in the company of women. As,

All men have follies, which they blindly trace
Thro' the dark turnings of a dubious maze.
But happy thofe, who by a prudent care,
Retreat betimes from the fallacious fnare.   POMFRET.

We followed this courfe about four months. During this time, Mr. Jones once perfuaded me to go with him to the Playhoufe, where we faw Shake-fpear's fine comedy of "As you like it." This was a feaft indeed to me, who had never before feen nor even read any theatrical production. 'Tis impoffible for me to defcribe my fenfations on the occafion.

E 5

No folio inftruction like the drama conveys;
Perifh, perifh the wretches who would cenfure all plays,
When that vile, abject race firft exifted below,
A heart nature in them forgot to beftow.

FRANCKLIN's Voltaire.

Between the play and the entertainment (which was the Mayor of Garrat) Mr. Edward Shuter performed a fhort piece called " The Drunken man." This was the only time that I ever faw that extraordinary genius; but he made fuch an impreffion on my mind, that it is impoffible I ever fhould forget him. I believe it is not generally known, as few would ever have fufpected, that this child of Momus was alfo a child of grace.

Since the publication of the firft edition of thefe Memoirs, I have read " The Memoirs of Mr. Tate Wilkinfon," patentee of the Theatres Royal of York and Hull, and was much furprized to learn that the the famous Ned Shuter was a *gracious foul.* I will give you a paffage or two out of Mr. Wilkinfon's Memoirs, vol. iii. page 27, &c. " My imitation of Mr. Whitefield was beyond compare. Mr. Foote was ftruck by ftepping in by chance, and once hearing Whitefield ; the mixture of whofe abfurdity, whim, confequence, and extravagance, pleafed his fancy, and entertained him highly, as Whitefield was that day dealing out damnation, fire and brimftone, as cheerfully as if they were fo many bleffings. What pity it is that our fears only, and not our reafon, will bring conviction ; but reafon handed by unaffected pure piety and religion would be a day of woe to methodifm.

" Mr. Foote was only a fpy at Whitefield's academy, while I (fays Mr. Wilkinfon) had been a zealot for fome feafons before my encounter at Covent-garden with Mr. Foote, my attendance had been conftant with my friend Shuter, and as he actually was one of the new-born, and paid large fums to Whitefield, I was always permitted to ftay with him, for he was really bewildered in his brains, more by his wifhing to acquire imaginary grace, than by all his drinking ; and whenever he was warm with the bottle, and with

a friend or two, like Maw-worm, he could not mind
his shop, because he thought it a sin, and wished to
go a preaching; for Shuter like Maw-worm believed he had a call. I have gone with Shuter at six
in the morning of a Sunday at Tottenham-Court-
Road, then before ten to Mr. Wesley's in Long-
Acre; at eleven again at Tottenham-Court-Road
Tabernacle, dined near Bedlam (a very proper place
for us both) with a party of the holy ones; went at
three to Mr. Wesley's theatre; then from that to
Whitefield's till eight, and then shut up, to commune
with the family compact, page 29. I having had so
much practice (while a zealot) I really obtained and
exhibited a much stronger likeness of Whitefield than
Mr. Foote did. The week before my Covent-Garden
exhibition, I met Shuter at the Tabernacle; a great
coolness had continued for some time, as we had not
spoke, or even looked at each other since the breach
between us in 1758; but as we were met together in
a place of charity and forgiveness to all who sub-
scribed to the preacher, we became very sociable;
and before Whitefield's lecture was done we were
perfectly reconciled: *we adjourned to the Rose, and by
three the next morning were sworn friends*, and continued
so until his death. Ned Shuter was a lively, spirited, shrewd companion; a superior in natural whim
and humour surely never inhabited a human breast,
for what he said and did was all his own, as it was
with difficulty he could read the parts he had to play,
and could not write at all; he had attained to sign
an order, but no more. Nature could not here bestow her gifts to greater advantage, than on poor
Ned, as what she gave he made shine, not only conspicuously, but brilliantly, and to the delight of all
who knew him on or off the stage; he might truly
be dubbed the child of nature. He was no man's
enemy but his own; peace, rest, and happiness, I
hope he now possesses; for, the poor, the friendless,
and the stranger he often comforted, and when sometimes reduced by his follies, he never could see a real
object in misery and resist giving at least half he was
worth to his distressed-fellow creatures." Page 5, vol.

iii. " But, O ye saints of your own creating! I will preach to you: Mark! *judge not of plays and players, left you be judged*; those who are the most censorious on the infirmities of others, are usually most notoriously guilty of far greater failings themselves, *and sanctified methodistical slander* is of all the *most severe, bitter, and cruel.*"

Page 6. " In the comedy of the Hypocrite, the Colonel says, he supposes they go to the play for the benefit of the brethren. Cantwell answers, " the charity covereth the sin ;" which was actually the case, for in 1757, *as Shuter was bountiful to the Tabernacle, Mr. Whitefield not only permitted, but advised his hearers to attend Shuter's benefit*; but for that night only." Alas, poor Shuter !

It is singular enough that about this time, although I could not write, yet I composed several songs, one of which was sold for a guinea ; some were given to the Bristol printers, who printed them, and the ballad-singers sung them about the streets ; on which occasions I was as proud as though I had composed an opera.

> ———— Yet this, so small a gift,
> Proves nature did not turn him quite adrift. **E. ROLLE.**

And I will even presume to quote the following lines of the celebrated Mrs. Robinson.

> " Obscurely born—No generous friend he found,
> " To lend his trembling steps o'er classic ground ;
> " No Patron fill'd his heart with flatt'ring hope,
> " No tutor'd lesson gave his genius scope ;
> " And yet he soar'd beyond the spells that bind
> " The slow perception of the vulgar mind."

My friend Mr. Jones was my secretary, who before I came to live with him had not the least relish for books, and I had only read a few enthusiastic authors, together with Pomfret's poems ; these last I could almost repeat by memory; however, I made the most of my little stock of literature, and strongly recommended the purchasing of Books to Mr. Jones. But so ignorant were we on the subject, that neither of us knew what books were fit for our perusal, nor what to enquire for, as we had scarce ever heard or seen even any *title pages*, except a few of the religious sort, which at that time we had no relish for. So that we were at a loss how to increase our small stock of science. And here I cannot help thinking that had Fortune thrown proper books in our way, we should have imbibed a just taste for literature, and soon made some tolerable progress; but such was our obscurity, that it was next to impossible for us ever to emerge from it.

> The mind untaught in vain,
> Her powers, thro' blooming vigour nourish,
> Hopes in perfect pride to flourish;
> Culture must her might maintain.   Mr. PINKERTON.

As we could not tell what to enquire for, we were ashamed to go into the booksellers shops; and I assure you, my friend, that there are thousands now in England in the very same situation: many, very many have come to my shop, who have discovered an enquiring mind, but were totally at a loss what to ask for, and who had no friend to direct them.

> ———— Reason grows apace, and calls
> For the kind hand of an assiduous care.
> Delightful task! to rear the tender thought,
> To teach the young idea how to shoot,
> To pour the fresh instruction o'er the mind,
> To breathe th' enlivening spirit, and to fix
> The gen'rous purpose in the glowing breast.
>   THOMSON.

One day as my friend Jones and I were strolling about the fair that is annually held in and near St. James's church-yard, we saw a stall of books, and in looking over the title-pages, I met with Hobbs's Translation of Homer's Iliad and Odyssey. I had somehow heard that Homer was a great poet, but unfortunately I had never heard of Pope's translation of him, so we very eagerly purchased that by Hobbs. At this stall I also purchased Walker's Poetical Pharaphrase of Epictetus's Morals: and home we went, perfectly well pleased with our bargains.

We that evening began with Hobbs's Homer; but found it very difficult for us to read, owing to the obfcurity of the tranflation, which together with the indifferent language, and want of poetical merit in the tranflator, fomewhat difappointed us: however, we had from time to time, many a hard puzzling hour with him.

But as to Walker's Epictetus, although that had not much poetical merit, yet it was very eafy to be read, and as eafily underftood. The principles of of the *ftoics* charmed me fo much, that I made the book my companion wherever I went, and read it over and over in raptures, thinking that my mind was fecured againft all the fmiles or frowns of fortune.

> When foes revil'd, or friends betray'd,
>   Our hearts have wrung, perhaps with forrow;
> But a firm effort always made
>   Complete refources for to-morrow.
>
> Then why repine at vice elate,
>   For injur'd worth our courage drown;
> Let us, who cannot alter fate,
>   Mind no men's bufinefs but our own.
>
>   J. ROBERTSON's Martial.

I now grew weary of diffipating my time, and began to think of employing my fpare hours in fomething more fatisfactory. For want of fomething elfe to do, I went one evening to hear Mr. John Wefley preach in Broadmead, and being completely tired of the way of life that I had lived (more or lefs) ever fince I had been out of my apprenticefhip, and happening to have no other purfuit or hobby horfe, there was a kind of vacuity in my mind; in this ftate I was very fufceptible of any impreffions, fo that when I came to hear Mr. Wefley, my old fanatical notions returned full upon me, and I was once more carried away by the tide of enthufiafm. So the following lines by Mr. S. Rogers, might then have been applied to me with great propriety:

> His humour once o'er, with a grave contrite face
> To the mead he repairs, that rich fountain of grace,
> Where in fpiritual fervour he turn'd up his eyes,
> True-mechanical-faint! and in unifon fighs;
> With every true godly exterior indu'd,
> As if from his cradle this line he'd purfu'd.

My friend Mr. Jones soon saw with grief and indignation the wonderful alteration in me; who, from a gay, volatile, dissipated young fellow, was at once metamorphosed into a dull, moping, praying, psalm-singing fanatic, continually reprehending all about me for their harmless mirth and gaiety.

> For saints themselves will often be,
> Of gifts that cost them nothing, free.   HUDIBRAS.

Nothing is more common than to see mankind run from one extreme to another: which was my case once more.

> Whate'er the leading passion be,
> That works the soul's anxiety,
> In each extreme th' effect is bad,
> Sense grows diseas'd, and reason mad.   E. LLOYD.

About this time we left our habitation in Queenstreet, and took lodgings of Mr. Jones's mother, on St. Philip's Plain, where lived a brother of Mr. Jones, who was about seventeen years of age. Soon after we had removed to this place, the brother, whose name was Richard Jones, was permitted to work in the same room with my friend and me. They had also a sister about twenty years of age, who frequently joined our company.

Our room over-looked the church-yard, which contributed to increase my gloomy ideas; and I had so much of the spiritual quixotism in me, that I soon began to think that it was not enough for me to save my own soul, but I ought in conscience to attempt the conversion of my companions, who (I really believed) were in the high road to hell, and every moment liable to eternal damnation. Of this charitable disposition are almost all the methodists; who, as Hudibras says,

> " Compound for sins they are inclin'd to,
> " By damning those they have no mind to."

The frequency of newly opened graves, which we saw from our windows, furnished me with opportunities for descanting on the uncertainty of life and all sublunary enjoyments; I assured them that nothing deferved attention but what related to our everlafting ftate, and that they might, on their repentance, receive in one moment the pardon of all their fins, have a foretafte of the joys of heaven, and know that their names were enrolled in the book of life. I farther protefted that they had no time to lofe; that they all ftood on the very verge of hell, and the breaking-brink of eternal torments; with a great deal more of fuch edifying ftuff.

The youngeft brother foon became a convert; and Mifs Betfy was *born again* foon after.

> " Lo! in the twinkling of an eye,
> " Their fouls were frank'd for kingdom come."

But I had a tight job to convert my friend John; he held out, and often curfed me heartily, and fung prophane fongs all day long.

But about four or five weeks after my re-converfion, John alfo was converted, and became a favourite of heaven, fo that we confidered ourfelves as a holy community:

> Who knew the feat of Paradife,
> Could tell in what degree it lies;
> Could deepeft myfteries unriddle,
> As eafily as thread a needle.
>
> HUDIBRAS.

A laughable affair happened during my refidence here. A captain of a fhip one day brought a parrot as a prefent to a family, the miftrefs of which being a methodift, happened to have one of the preachers call in juft as the dinner was putting on the table, fo that the captain and the preacher were both afked to ftay. As foon as the table was covered, the preacher began a long grace, in the midft of which *Poll*, who had been put up in a corner of a room, cried out, " *D—n your eyes, tip us none of your jaw.*" This, with the immoderate laughter of the captain, entirely difconcerted the pious chaplain; at laft he began his grace again, but he had not got to the end before Poll again interrupted him with, " *You d— a canting fon of a b—h.*" By the above it appeared that the captain had tutored Poll on purpose to have fome fun.

in this canting family; however, the good lady of the house made it a point of conscience to have Polly converted, but found it utterly impossible to effect so great a change in the methodistical way, that is, *instantaneously*; as after she had scolded her six months for speaking bad words, and had actually taught her a part of the Lord's prayer, yet Poll would not entirely leave off her sea language; so that it often happened, while the good lady was teaching her to pray, Poll would out with, " *D——n your eyes, tumble up, you lubbers*;" and even after she had preached to her several years, she would not venture to say that Poll was in a state of grace; but be that as it will, Poll obtained a good name, being called by the neighbours, the Methodist Parrot.

I must inform you also that the poor preacher above-mentioned being just come out of Wales, understood English but very imperfectly, and in the course of his sermon one day he had forgot the English for the word lamb, and after hammering a good while about it, he out with " Goddymighty's little Mutton, that took away the sins of the world," which caused a good deal of diversion among the ungodly.

I am,

Dear Friend,

Yours,

LETTER XIV.

—— He was a shrewd philosopher,
And had read every text and glofs over;
Whate'er the crabbed'ft author hath,
He underftood b'implicit faith;
Whatever fceptic could enquire for,
For every why he had a wherefore;
Knew more than forty of them do,
As far as words and terms could go:
All which he underftood by rote,
And as occafion ferv'd would quote:
No matter whether right or wrong,
They might be either faid or fung.

HUDIBRAS.

DEAR FRIEND,

MR. John Jones and myfelf were now greater friends than ever, fo that one would on no account ftir out of the houfe without the other.

Mr. Jones had the advantage of me in temporals, he could get more money than I could: but as to grace, and fpiritual gifts, I had much the fuperiority of all our community; fo that I was their fpiritual director, and if they thought that any of their acquaintance held any opinions that were not quite found and orthodox, fuch were introduced to me, in order that I might convince them of their errors. In fact, being looked upon as an apoftle, whatever I afferted was received as pure gofpel: nor was any thing undertaken without my advice.

We all worked very hard, particularly Mr. John Jones and me, in order to get money to purchafe books; and for fome months every fhilling we could fpare was laid out at old book-fhops, ftalls, &c. infomuch that in a fhort time we had what we called a very good library. This choice collection confifted of Polhill on precious Faith, Polhil on the Decrees; Shepherd's found Believer; Bunyan's Pilgrim's Progrefs; Bunyan's Good News for the vileft of Sinners; his Heavenly Footman; his Grace abounding to the chief of Sinners; his Life and Death of Mr. Badman;

his Holy War in the town of *Manfoul*; Hervey's Meditations; Hervey's Dialogues; Roger's Seven Helps to Heaven; Hall's Jacob's Ladder; Divine Breathings of a devout Soul; Adams on the Second Epiftle of Peter; Adams's Sermons on the *black* Devil, the *white* Devil, &c. &c. Colling's Divine Cordial for the Soul; Pearfe's Soul's Efpoufal to Chrift; Erfkine's Gofpel Sonnets; the Death of Abel; the Faith of God's Elect; Manton on the Epiftle to St. James; Pamble's Works; Baxter's Shove for a *heavy-arfed* Chriftian; his Call to the Unconverted; Mary Magdalen's Funeral Tears; Mrs. Moore's Evidences of Heaven; Mead's Almoft a Chriftian; the Sure Guide to Heaven; Brooks on Affurance; God's Revenge againft Murder; Brooks's Heaven upon Earth; the Pathway to Heaven; Wilcox's Guide to eternal Glory; Derham's Unfearchable Riches of Chrift; his Expofition of Revelations; Alleine's Sure Guide to Heaven; the Sincere Convert; Watfon's Heaven taken by Storm; Heaven's Vengeance; Wall's None but Chrift; Ariftotle's Mafterpiece; Coles on God's Sovereignty; Charnock on Providence; Young's Short and Sure Guide to Salvation; Wefley's Sermons, Journals, Tracts, &c. and others of the fame defcription.

We had indeed a few of a better fort, as Gay's Fables, Pomfret's Poems; Milton's Paradife Loft; befides Hobbs's Homer, and Walker's Epictetus, mentioned in my laft letter.

But what we wanted in judgment in choofing our library, we made up in application; fo anxious were we to read a great deal, that we allowed ourfelves but about three hours fleep in twenty-four.

> In fearch of knowledge cheerfully employ'd,
> No minute loft, no feafon unenjoy'd;
> Each hour of leifure innocently fpent,
> And every moment gilded with content.   ARLEY.

For fome months together we never were all in bed at the fame time (Sunday nights excepted.) But left we fhould overfleep the time allowed, one of us

fat up to work until the time appointed for the others
to rife, and when all were up, my friend John and
your humble fervant took it by turns to read aloud to
the reft, while they were at their work.

> Such there are, deny'd, by ftars unkind,
> The feafons to exert the noble mind,
> Should watch occafions, and attend the hours,
> And catch the moments, to indulge the pow'rs.   Cooke.

But this mad fcheme of ours had nearly been attended with very ferious confequences. One night,
it being my turn to watch, I removed to the fire-fide,
to read fome particular paffage, and the candleftick
which we worked by not being convenient to move
about, and there being no other at that time in the
room, I fet up the candle againft the handle of a
pewter pot, and was fo extremely heavy (owing to
much watchfulnefs) that I fell faft afleep, and had
like never to have waked again; for the candle burned
down to the handle of the pot, melted it off, and then
fell on the chair on which it ftood; fo that Mr. Jones
found me in the morning, faft afleep, and part of the
chair confumed; which alarmed us all very much,
and made us more cautious.

But ftill we continued our plan of living, fo that
we made a rapid progrefs in what we called fpiritual
and divine knowledge; and were foon mafters of the
various arguments made ufe of by moft polemical divines, &c.

And the better to guard my pupils from what I
called *falfe doctrines*, I ufed often to engage them in
various controverfies, in which I fometimes took one
fide the queftion, fometimes the other, in order to
make them well verfed in controverfy, and acquainted
with the ftrength of their adverfaries. So that I was,
by turns, a Calvinift, an Arminian, an Arian, a So-
cinian, a Deift, and even an Atheift. And after they
had faid all they could to confute me, I would point
out where they had failed, and added fuch arguments
as I was mafter of, and in general we were all fatisfied.
But when any doubts occurred, we had recourfe to
the Bible and commentators of our own fide of the

question; and I assure you, my dear friend, this was a very fine hobby-horse, which, like Aaron's serpent, swallowed up all the other hobby-horses.

Light minds are pleased with trifles.   OVID.

I am,

Dear Friend,

Yours.

LETTER XV.

Laugh where you must; be candid where you can. POPE.

Know then, that always when you come,
  You'll find me sitting on my bum;
Or lying on a couch, surrounded
With tables, pens, and books, confounded;
Warpt up in lofty speculation,
As if on the safety of the nation.   HUMBY

Go to the stoic, hear the ancient sage,
And draw pure wisdom from the moral page;
Wisdom, that conquers pains, and toil, and strife,
And tow'rs above the accidents of life.   MURPHY.

DEAR FRIEND,

IN the course of my reading, I learnt that there had been various sects of philosophers amongst the Greeks, Romans, &c. and I remembered the names of the most eminent of them. At an old book-shop I purchased Plato on the Immortality of the Soul, Plutarch's Morals, Seneca's Morals, Epicurus's Morals, the Morals of Confucius the Chinese Philosopher, and a few others. I now can scarce help thinking that I received more real benefit from reading and studying them and Epictetus, than from all other books that I had read before, or have ever read since that time.

> These, these, are joys alone, I cry;
> 'Tis here divine Philosophy,
>   Thou deign'st to fix thy throne!
> Here, Contemplation points the road
> Thro' Nature's charms to Nature's God!
>   These, these, are joys alone.
>
> Adieu, ye vain low-thoughted cares,
> Ye human hopes, and human fears,
>   Ye pleasures and ye pains!—
> While thus I spake, o'er all my soul
> A philosophic calmness stole,
>   A stoic stillness reigns.
>
> The tyrant passions all subside,
> Fear, anger, pity, shame, and pride,
>   No more my bosom move;
> Yet still I felt, or seem'd to feel
> A kind of visionary zeal
>   Of universal love.   W. WHITEHEAD.

I was but about twenty-two years of age, when I first began to read those fine moral productions; and I assure you, my friend, that they made a very deep and lasting impression on my mind. By reading them, I was taught to bear the unavoidable evils attending humanity, and to supply all my wants by contracting or restraining my desires.

> To mend my virtues, and exalt my ought,
> What the bright sons of Greece and Rome have wrote,
> O'er day and night I turn; in them we find
> A rich repast for the luxurious mind.   COOKE.

It is now twenty-three years since I first perused them; during which time I do not recollect that I have ever felt one *anxious* painful wish to get money, estates, or any way to better my condition:

> " Indeed, my friend, were I to find
>   " That wealth could e'er my real wishes gain;
> " Had e'er disturbed my thoughtful mind
>   " Or cost one serious moment's pain;
> " I should have said, that all the rules,
> " I learn'd of moralists and schools,
>   " Were very useless, very vain."

And yet I have never since that time let slip any fair opportunity of doing it. " Be contented (says Isocrates) with what you have, and seek at the same to make the best improvement of it you can." So that all I mean is, that I have not been over *solicitous* to obtain any thing that I did not possess; but could at all times say, with St. Paul, that I have learned to be contented in all situations, although at times they have been very gloomy indeed.

Regard the world with cautious eye,
Nor raise your expectations high.
See that the balanc'd scale be such
You neither fear nor hope too much.
For disappointment's not the thing,
'Tis pride and passion points the sting.
Life is a sea, where storms must rise,
'Tis folly talks of cloudless skies;
He who contracts his swelling sail,
Eludes the fury of the gale.   CONTENT.

Mr. Dryden has said nearly as much in two lines.

We to ourselves may all our wishes grant,
For, nothing coveting, we nothing want
                    DRYDEN's Indian Emperor.

And in another place he says,

They cannot want who wish not to have more:
Who ever said an anchoret was poor?
                    DRYDEN's Secret Love.

The pleasures of eating and drinking I entirely despised; for some time I carried this disposition to an extreme, and even to the present time I feel a very great indifference about these matters: when in company I frequently dine off one dish, when there are twenty on the table.

Gryle, big and bloated with one endless feast,
Sues with long life and vigour to be blest.
Grave fool! thy sauces and soups resign;
Or know, the lot of PARR will ne'er be thine. NEVILLE.

The account of Epicurus living in his garden, at the expence of about a halfpenny per day, and that when he added a little cheese to his bread on particu-

lar occasions, he considered it as a luxury, filled me
with raptures.

> He talk'd of virtue, and of human bliss,
>   What else so fit for man to settle well?
> And still his long researches met in this,
>   This *truth* of *truths*, which nothing can repel.
> From virtue's fount the purest joys out-well
>   Sweet rills of thought that chear the conscious soul,
> While vice pours forth the troubled streams of hell,
>   Which, howe'er disguis'd, at last will dole;
> Will through the tortur'd breast their fiery torrents roll.
>
> THOMPSON.

From that moment I began to live on bread and
tea, and for a considerable time did not partake of any
other viands, but in those I indulged myself three or
four times a day. My reasons for living in this abstemious manner were in order to save money to purchase books, to wean myself from the gross pleasures
of eating and drinking, &c. and to purge my mind,
and to make it more susceptible of intellectual pleasures. Here I cannot help remarking, that the term
Epicure, when applied to one who makes the pleasures of the table his chief good, casts an unjust reflection on *Epicurus*, and conveys a wrong idea of that
contemplative and very abstemious philosopher: for
although he asserted that pleasure was the chief or su-
preme good, yet he also as strongly asserted, that it
was the tranquillity of the mind, and intellectual pleasure, that he so extolled and recommended- " This
pleasure (says he) that is the very centre of our happiness, consists in nothing else than having our mind
free from disturbance, and our body free from pain ;
drunkenness, excessive eating, niceness in our liquors,
and all that seasons good cheer, have nothing in them
that can make life happy ; there is nothing but frugali-
ty and tranquility of mind that can establish this happy
state ; it is this calm that facilitates our distinguishing
betwixt those things that ought to be our choice, and
those ought to shun ; and it is by the means thereof,
that we discard those notions that discompose this first
mover of our life."

When Epicurus to the world had taught,
  That pleasure was the chiefest good,
(And was perhaps in the right, if rightly underſtood)
  His life he to his doctrine brought,
And in a garden's ſhade, that ſovereign pleaſure ſought ;
  Whoever a true Epicure would be,
May there find cheap and virtuous luxury.

                                        COWLEY's Garden.

St. Evremont in his vindication of Epicurus ſays,
" Ignorant men know not his worth. Wiſe men
have given large and honourable teſtimonies of his
exalted virtue and ſublime precepts. They have
fully proved his pleaſures to be as ſevere as the ſtoicks
virtue ; that to be debauched like Epicurus, a man
muſt be as ſober as Zeno.—His temperance was ſo
great that his ordinary diet was nothing but bread
and water. The ſtoics and all other philoſophers
agree with *Epicurus* in this ; that the true felicity of
life is to be free from perturbations, to underſtand our
duty towards God and man, and to enjoy the preſent without any anxious dependance upon the
future ; not to amuſe ourſelves either with hope or
fear ; to curb and reſtrain our unruly appetites, to
reſt ſatisfied with what we have, which is abundantly
ſufficient ; for he that is content wants nothing."

  Some place the bliſs in action, ſome in eaſe ;
  Thoſe call it pleaſure, and contentment theſe ;
  Some ſunk to beaſts, find pleaſure end in pain ;
  Some ſwelled to Gods, confeſs e'en virtue vain.   POPE.

I continued the above ſelf-denying life until I left
Briſtol, which was on Whitſunday in 1769. Having
for ſome time before been pointing out to my friend
John Jones, the pleaſures and advantages of travelling, I eaſily prevailed on him to accompany me towards the Weſt of England ; and in the evening we
arrived at Bridgewater, where Mr. Jones got work.
He was employed by Mr. Caſh, with whom he continued near twelve months, and in the end married
Mr. Caſh's daughter, a very pretty and very amiable
little woman, with ſome fortune. When my friend
was offered work by Mr. Caſh, I prevailed on him to
accept of it, aſſuring him that I had no doubt of my

F

being able to get work at Taunton: but in that I was
difappointed, nor could I get a conftant feat of work
until I came to Exeter, and of that place I was foon
tired; but being informed that a Mr. John Taylor of
Kingfbridge (forty miles below Exeter) wanted fuch
a hand, I went down, and was gladly received by
Mr. Taylor, whofe name infpires me with gratitude,
as he never treated me as a journeyman, but made
me his companion. Nor was any part of my time
ever fpent in a more agreeable pleafing manner, than
that which I paffed in this retired place, or I believe
more profitable to a mafter. I was the firft man he
ever had that was able to make ftuff and filk fhoes,
and it being alfo known that I came from Briftol,
this had great weight with the country ladies, and
procured my mafter cuftomers, who generally fent for
me to take meafure of their feet, and I was looked
upon by all to be the beft workman in the town,
altho' I had not been brought up to ftuff-work, nor
had ever entirely made one ftuff or filk fhoe before.
Nor fhould I have prefumed to proclaim myfelf a
ftuff-man, had there been any fuch workmen in the
place; but as there were none, I boldly ventured,
and fucceeded very well; nor did any one in the town
ever know that it was my firft attempt in that branch.

During the time that I lived here, I as ufual was
obliged to employ one or other of my acquaintance
to write my letters for me; this procured me much
praife among the young men as a good inditer of letters (I need not inform you that they were not good
judges). My mafter faid to me one day, he was furprized that I did not learn to write my own letters;
adding, he was fure that I could learn to do it in a
very fhort time. The thought pleafed me much, and
without any delay I fet about it, by taking up any
pieces of paper that had writing on them, and imi-
tating the letters as well as I could. I employed my
leifure hours in this way for near two months, after
which time I wrote my own love-letters, a bad hand,
you may be fure; but it was plain and eafy to read,
which was all I cared for.

Heav'n firſt taught letters for ſome wretch's aid,
Some baniſh'd lover, or ſome captive maid;
They live, they ſpeak, they breathe what love inſpires,
Warm from the ſoul, and faithful to its fires.

ELOISA to ABELARD.

Nor to the preſent moment can I write much better, as I never would have any perſon to teach me,
nor was I ever poſſeſſed of patience enough to employ time ſufficient to learn to write well; and yet as
ſoon as I was able to ſcribble, I wrote verſes on ſome
trifle or other every day for years together.

Out of ſome thouſands I at preſent recollect the
following, which I placed by the ſide of the figure of
a clergyman in his robes, with his hands and eyes
lifted up; this image ſtood over the fire-place in my
room.

Here's a ſhoemaker's chaplain has negative merit,
As his vice he ne'er flatters or ruffles his ſpirit;
No wages receiving, his conſcience is clear;
Not prone to deceiving, he's nothing to fear.
'Tis true he is ſilent—but that's nothing new;
And if you'd repent, his attitude view;
With uplifted hands all vice to reprove,
How ſolemn he ſtands, his eyes fix'd above!

As a kind of contraſt I will inſert an epigram that
I wrote but a few days ſince on an ignorant methodiſt
preacher:

A ſtupid fellow told me t'other day,
That by the ſpirit he could preach and pray;
Let none then ſay that miracles have ceas'd,
As God ſtill opes the mouth of beaſt?
And aſſes now can ſpeak as plain
As e'er they could in Balaam's reign.

But I always wrote as faſt as I could, without endeavouring to write well, and that this is my preſent
practice I need not inform you.

I came to this place in but a weak ſtate of body;
however, the healthy ſituation of the town, together
with bathing in the ſalt water, ſoon reſtored me to
perfect health. I paſſed thirteen months here in a very
happy manner.

F 2

———————— Ye kind few,
With whom the morning of my life I pafs'd,
May every blifs, your generous bofoms knew
In early days, attend you to the laft.   W. WHITEHEAD.

But the wages for work being very low, and as I
had fpent much time in writing hymns to every fong-
tune that I knew, befides a number of love-verfes,
letters, &c. I was very poor. To complete all, I began to keep a deal of company, in which I gave a
loofe to my natural gaiety of difpofition, much more
than was confiftent with the grave, fedate ideas which
I had formed of a religious character; all which made
me refolve to leave Kingfbridge, which I did in
1770.

I travelled as far as Exeter the firft day, where I
worked about a fortnight, and faved fufficient to carry
me to Bridgewater, where I worked two or three
weeks more. Before I arrived there, Mr. John Jones
had gone back to refide at Briftol, but as foon as he
heard of my being in Bridgewater, he and his brother
Richard fent me an invitation to come to Briftol again
and live with them. Finding that I did not immediately comply, they both came to Bridgewater, and
declared their intentions of not returning to Briftol
without me; fo that after a day or two I yielded to
their folicitations, and again lived very comfortably
with them, their mother and fifter.

But where is the bofom untainted by art,
   The judgment fo modeft and ftay'd,
That union fo rare of the head and the heart;
   Which fixes the friends it has made.   W. W.

I think it was about this period, that I went feveral
times to the Tabernacle, and heard Mr. George
Whitfield; and of all the preachers that I ever attended, never did I meet with one that had fuch a
perfect command over the paffions of his audience.
In every fermon that I heard him preach, he would
fometimes make them ready to burft with laughter,
and the next moment drown them in tears; indeed it
was fcarce poffible for the moft guarded to efcape the
effect.

He had something 'twas thought still more horrid to say,
When his tongue lost its powers, and he fainted away;
Some say 'twas his conscience that gave him a stroke,
But those who best knew him treat that as a joke;
'Tis a trick which stage orators use in their need,
The passions to raise and the judgment mislead.   SIMKIN.

In one of my excursions I passed many agreeable
hours with the late Mr. La Bute, at Cambridge, who
was well known, he having taught French in that
university upwards of forty years.   He informed me
that near forty years since, Mr. Whitefield having
advertised himself to preach at Gog-Magog-Hill,
several thousand people collected together from many
miles round. While he was preaching, he was elevated on the highest ground, and his audience stood
all round on the declivity; during his sermon, a
young countrywoman, who had come some miles to
hear him, and waited several hours, being very faint,
owing to the violent heat of the sun, the breaths of
the multitude; as well as the want of refreshment;
and it is very likely much agitated in her mind by the
extraordinary doctrines of the preacher, she fell backwards, just under the orator, and there lay kicking
up her heels. On seeing the poor girl lie in a kind
of convulsion, some of the company moved to assist
her, and the women began to draw down her apron
and petticoats over her feet, but Mr. Whitfield
cry'd out, " *Let her alone! Let her alone! A glorious
fight! A glorious fight!*" No doubt the holy man meant
that it was a glorious fight to see a sinner fall before
the power of the word; but the young college bucks
and wits construed his meaning differently, and put
the audience into such immoderate fits of laughing,
that even Mr. Whitfield's utmost efforts were not
able to restore their gravity, but he was obliged to
dismiss his congregation abruptly.

For a long time after this happened, the Cantabs
as they reeled homewards in the night-time, disturbed
the sober inhabitants, by loudly exclaiming, " A
glorious fight! A glorious fight! As Dr. Squintum
says."

F 3

Here Prior's couplet naturally occurs:

" Like other myft'ries men adore,
" Be hid, to be rever'd the more."

I am,

Dear Friend,

Yours.

LETTER XVI.

Love the moft generous paffion of the mind,
The fofteft refuge innocence can find;
The foft director of unguided youth,
Fraught with kind wifhes, and fecured by truth;
The cordial drop heav'n in our cup has thrown,
To make the naufeous draught of life go down:
On which one only bleffing God might raife,
In lands of atheifts fubfidies of praife;
For none did e'er fo dull and ftupid prove,
But felt a God, and blefs'd his pow'r, in love.

MONRARES.

DEAR FRIEND,

I Muft now requeft you to go back with me a few years, as I have not yet made you acquainted with my principal amours. If we believe the Platonifts, the paffion of love is produced after the following manner: " A perfon is prefented to my fight; the image of this perfon, after having paffed through the organ of vifion, comes to offer itfelf to the foul. The foul contemplates it, and compares it to that which it has received from the Deity by infufion. If this external image proves to refemble the internal infufed image, the foul is immediately in love with it."

Aristotle tells us, that the love of the beautiful is an instinct implanted in us by nature; and to obviate all objections, he establishes two sorts of nature: namely, specific, which inspires mankind in general; and the individual, which inspires each man in particular; and that it is by the last we love this or that beauty in particular.

Descartes gravely asserts, that nature has made certain impressions upon the brain, which, at a particular age, makes a man consider himself as defective, and as it were one half of a whole, which is to be completed by a person of the other sex; and that this blessing when attained we call love; we find in Plato this opinion; as according to this philosopher's fable, man and woman were not always two distinct beings as they are at present.

But here is still another hypothesis respecting the god-like passion of love.

Lewenhoeck, by the help of the microscope, has discovered in the skin 125,000 minute pores, or transpiring vessels, in a space small enough to be covered by a grain of sand. Sanctorius, by balancing himself in his elbow-chair, discovered that after eating and drinking, he always lost some of his weight; concluded that something must have escaped through those pores in the skin. From these and other experiments, some late philosophers have concluded, that these minute pores could not answer any other end, but to transmit the most refined particles of sympathetic matter! Heister, in his anatomy, thinks that it is by the transpiring fluid, that fathers have sometimes felt pleasure in beholding their children when they did not know them. But the grand end of this sympathetic matter is discovered (it seems) in the passion of love. So that when a man and a woman happens to fall in love with each other, it is occasioned by the sympathetic matter acting reciprocally in its full force on both of them. As Dryden says,

> " Their twisted rays together met."

I will not attempt to determine which of all these systems, or hypothesis is the true one. But whether my "Soul had the fair image stamped on it," or if I considered "Myself but an half of a whole;" or whether the hitherto dormant "Sympathetic matter" began to operate, certain it is I was about seventeen years of age when an adventure discovered, that although I was so very spiritual, as I before informed you, I was notwithstanding susceptible of another kind of impression.

> Oh, let me still enjoy the cheerful day,
> Till many years unheeded o'er me roll;
> Pleas'd in my age I trifle life away,
> And tell how much I lov'd ere I grew old.
>
> HAMMOND's Love Elegies.

Being at farmer Gamlin's at Charlton, four miles from Taunton, to hear a methodist sermon, I fell desperately in love with the farmer's handsome dairy-maid.

> Her home-spun dress in simple neatness lies,
> And for no glaring equipage she sighs.
> She gratefully receives what heav'n has sent,
> And, rich in poverty, enjoys content.
> Her reputation which is all her boast,
> In a malicious visit ne'er was lost.
> No midnight masquerade her beauty wears,
> And health, not paint, the fading bloom repairs,
> If Love's soft passions in her bosom reign,
> An equal passion warms her happy swain.   GAY.

At that time I abounded in *spiritual gifts*, which induced this honest rustic maid to be very kind to me, and to walk several fields with me in my road back to Taunton, talking all the way of her spiritual distress and godly concerns; while I poured heavenly comfort into her soul, and talked so long of *divine* love, until I found that my affection for her was not altogether of that *spiritual* nature.   And yet,

> We lov'd without transgressing Virtue's bounds:
> We fixt the limits of our tenderest thoughts,
> Came to the verge of honour, and there stopp'd;
> We warm'd us by the fire, but were not scorch'd.
> If this be sin, Angels might live with more;
> And mingle rays of mind less pure than ours.
>
> DRYDEN's Love Triumphant.

After this you may be sure that I did not let slip any opportunity of hearing sermons at farmer Gamlin's; and I generally prevailed with Nancy Smith, my charming spiritual dairy-maid, to accompany me part of the way home, and at every gate I accompanied my spiritual advice with a kiss.

> —— Oh then the longest summer's day
> Seem'd too, too much in haste ; still the full heart
> Had not imparted half: 'twas happiness
> Too exquisite to last. Of joys departed
> Never to return, how painful the remembrance !
> BLAIR's Grave.

But alas! these comfortable Sunday walks were soon at an end ; as my charming Nancy Smith, for some reason or other (I have forgot what) left her place, and went to live as dairy-maid with a farmer in the marsh country, between Bridgewater and Bristol, seventeen miles from Taunton ; so that I did not see her for near two years afterwards ; during which time I gave spiritual advice to another holy sister, whose name was Hannah Allen.

> Sure philosophy, reason, and coldness must prove
> Defences unequal to shield us from Love.   C. J. Fox.

I prevailed on this lovely maid to attend the methodist preaching at five o'clock on Monday mornings, and as we often met at three or four ; we had an hour or two to spend in walking and conversation on spiritual affairs. Had you seen and heard us on the cold frosty mornings, it would have put you in mind of Milton's *Devils*, whom he represents as at times starving with cold :

> Others apart, sat on a hill, retir'd,
> In thoughts more elevate, and reason'd high
> Of Providence, foreknowledge, will, and fate;
> Fix'd fate, free-will, fore-knowledge absolute ;
> And found no end, in wandering mazes lost.
> Paradise Lost.

But I assure you, my friend, that we were sometimes like the Galatians of old ; we began in the *spirit*, and ended in the *flesh*.

F 5

Now on the mofs-bank, beneath the fhade,
For hours of love, or mediation, made ;
To the foft paffion I my heart refign,
To make the long obdurate maiden mine.   COOKE.

With this dear girl I fpent all my leifure time, for two or three years; fo that we enjoyed together hundreds of happy, and I can truly add, *innocent* hours.

O days of blifs !
To equal this
Olympus ftrives in vain ;
O happy pair,
O happy fair !
O happy, happy fwain !   JOANNES SECUNDUS.

But ftill I never could entirely forget my charming innocent *Dairy-maid*. In fact, I had love enough for both, to have taken either for better or worfe ; but my being an apprentice, prevented me from marrying at that time.

Abfence, fays Rochefoucault, leffens moderate paffions, but increafes great ones ; like the wind which blows out tapers, but kindles fire.

It is true, I had the greateft love for Nancy Smith ; but Hannah Allen had the advantage of Nancy, as I could fee Hannah almoft every day, and Nancy only once or twice in about three years. However, I at laft fell out with Hannah (on what occafion I cannot recollect) and I fent Nancy a letter, which made up matters with her ; for, like Sterne, I was " always in love with one goddefs or other ;" and Xenophon in his banquet, informs us, that the divine Socrates faid, that he never remembered that he was ever without being in love, nor would he part from the company without faying fomething on " the attributes of that great power ; he refembles but a child, fays he, who by his power is mafter of all things, and is grafted into the very effence and conftitution of the foul of man."

And rather than not be in love at all, I would prefer falling in love with a toothlefs old woman, as we are told the great philofopher Plato actually did ; for agreeable to his fable, and the fyftem of Defcartes, I always thought myfelf but one half ; and fo was always looking out for my other half, or as a Cartesian would express himself, I always found a tendency to make a complete system.

Soon after Nancy Smith came to live for a little time at her father's house at Petherton near Bridge-water, seven miles from Taunton. This happened during the election at Taunton, when I was changed from a strict methodist to a rake; and although the wedding-ring was purchased, and we were to have been married in a few days, yet the marriage was put off on account of my dissipated character.

> With wine, I strove to sooth my love-sick soul,
> But vengeful Cupid dash'd with tears the bowl:
> All mad with rage, to kinder nymphs I flow.
>   GRAINGER'S TIBULLUS.

I soon after set off for Bristol, as I before informed you: nor did I see her after that, until my return from Kingsbridge, when I saw her several times prior to my setting off for Bristol with my friend Jones, and his brother Richard.

I am,

Dear Friend,

Yours.

LETTER XVII.

Hail, nuptial felicity! rapturous station!
That forms the best prop in the strength of a nation.
Blest source, from whence ev'ry happiness flows,
That subjugates passion, or conquer our woes!
The connubial twain, whom sweet virtue impresses,
Can draw forth the arrow from human distresses;
Their mutual strife is to banish despair,
And hide the shorn heart from the pressure of care;
Like the dreams of an angel, to transport resign'd,
The finger of peace smoothes the springs of the mind.
As the kindred tie of soft sympathy moves,
And the organs are tun'd by confederate loves;
A commerce empyreal the senses unite,
To barter for blisses, and feed on delight;
Till the mind so high charged, it can treasure no more,
But, fill'd with the balm of enjoyment, runs o'er.
                              Children of THESPIS.

If you will use the little that you have,
More has not heav'n to give, or you to crave,
Cease to complain. He never can be poor
Who has sufficient, and who wants no more.
If but from cold, and pining hunger free,
The richest monarch can but equal thee.
                              HORACE Imitated.

DEAR FRIEND,

I Had not long resided a second time with my good Bristol friends, before I renewed my correspondence with my old sweetheart Nancy Smith. I informed her that my attachment to books, together with my travelling from place to place, and also my total disregard for money, had prevented me from saving any; and that while I remained in a single unsettled state, I was never likely to accumulate it. I also pressed her very much to come to Bristol to be married, which she soon complied with: and married we were at St. Peter's Church, towards the end of the year 1770; near seven years after my first making love to her.

When join'd in hand and heart, to church we went,
Mutual in vows, and pris'ners by consent.
My Nancy's heart beat high, with mix'd alarms,
But trembling beauty glow'd with double charms.
In her soft breast a modest struggle rose,
How she should seem to like the lot she chose:
A smile she thought would dress her looks too gay;
A frown might seem too sad, and blast the day.
But while nor this, nor that, her will could bow,
She walk'd, and look'd, and charm'd, and knew not how.
Our hands at length th' unchanging fiat bound,
And our glad souls sprung out to meet the sound.
Joys meeting joys unite, and stronger shine:
For passion purified is half divine:
Now Nancy thou art mine, I cry'd—and she
'Sigh'd soft—now Jemmy thou art Lord of me! A. Hill.

We kept our wedding at the house of my friends
the Messrs. Jones's, and at bed-time retired to ready-
furnished lodgings, which we had before provided,
at half-a-crown per week. Our finances were but
just sufficient to pay the expences of the day, for the
next morning, on searching our pockets (which we
did not do in a careless manner) we discovered that
we had but one halfpenny to begin the world with.
But—

> "The hearth was clean, the fire clear,
> "The kettle on for tea;
> "Palemon, in his elbow-chair,
> "As bless'd as man could be.
> "Clarinda, who his heart possess'd,
> "And was his new-made bride,
> "With head reclin'd upon his breast,
> "Sat toying by his side.
> "Palemon with heart elate,
> "Pray'd to Almighty Jove,
> "That it might ever be his fate,
> "Just so to live and love."

It is true, we had laid in eatables sufficient for a
day or two, in which time we knew we could by our
work procure more, which we very cheerfully set
about, singing together the following lines of Dr.
Cotton:

> "Our portion is not large, indeed,
> "But then how little do we need?

" For Nature's cal's are few;
" In this the art of living lies,
" To want no more than may fuffice,
" And make that little do."

The above, and the following ode by Mr. Fitzgerald,
did we fcores of times repeat, even with raptures!

" No glory I covet, ro riches I want,
" Ambition is nothing to me :
" The one thing I beg of kind heaven to grant,
"Is, a mind independent and free.

" By paffion unruffled, untainted by pride,
" By Reafon my life let me fquare;
" The wants of my nature are cheaply fupplied,
" And the reft are but folly and care.

" Thofe bleffings which Providence kindly has lent,
" I'll juftly and gratefully prize:
" While fweet meditation and cheerful content,
" Shall make me both healthy and wife.

" In the pleafures the great man's poffeffions difplay,
" Unenvy'd I'll challenge my part;
" For every fair object my eyes can furvey,
" Contributes to gladden my heart.

" How vainly thro' infinite trouble and ftrife,
" The many their labours employ;
" When all that is truly delightful in life,
" Is what all, if they will, may enjoy."

After having worked on ftuff-work in the country,
I could not bear the idea of returning to the leather-
branch; I therefore attempted and obtained a feat of
Stuff in Briftol. But better work being required
there than in Kingfbridge, &c. I was obliged to take
fo much care to pleafe my mafter, that at firft I could
not get more than nine fhillings a week, and my wife
could earn but very little, as fhe was learning to bind
ftuff-fhoes, and had never been much ufed to her
needle; fo confequently what with the expence of
ready-furnifhed lodging, fire, candles, &c. we had
but little left for purchafing provifions.

To increafe our ftraits, my old friend being fomewhat difpleafed at our leaving him and his relations,
took an early opportunity to tell me that I was indebted to him nearly forty fhillings, of two years
ftanding. " It is more difhonourable (fays Roche-

foucault) to diftruft our friends, than to be deceived by them.

> ———— Prudence, I thought with fcorn,
> Thy miferable maxims quaint,
> Were but of four fufpicion born:
> " Let felfifh fouls, I madly cry'd,
> " Submit to fuch a coward guide." DELLA CRUSCA.

I was not convinced of the juftice of the claim, but to avoid difpute, I paid him in about two months.

> But if friends prove unfaithful, and fortune's a whore,
> Still may I be virtuous, although I am poor. A. BOURNE.

I wifh that the above had been the only or laft inftance, or proof of his being a poor felfifh being, and as fuch incapable of real friendfhip. The author of the following lines has expreffed fome of my ideas and feelings:

> O Friendfhip! am I doom'd to find
> Thou art a Phantom of the mind,
> A glitt'ring fhade, an empty name,
> An air-born Vifion's vap'rifh flame?
> And yet the *dear deceit* fo long
> Has wak'd with joy my matin fong;
> Has bid my tears forget to flow,
> Chas'd ev'ry pain, footh'd ev'ry woe;
> That *truth*, unwelcome to my ear,
> Swells the deep figh, recals the tear,
> Gives to the fenfe the keeneft fmart,
> Checks the warm pulfes of the heart,
> Darkens my fate, and fteals away
> Each gleam of joy thro' life's fad day. LAURA.

During nearly the whole of which time it was extremely fevere weather, and yet we made four fhillings and fixpence per week pay for the whole of what we confumed in eating and drinking. Strong beer we had none, nor any other liquor (the pure element excepted), and inftead of tea, or rather coffee, we toafted a piece of bread; at other times we fried fome wheat, which when boiled in water made a tolerable fubftitute for coffee; as to animal food, we made ufe of but little, and that little we boiled and made broth of.

> The recollection of paft toils is fweet. EURIP.

During the whole of this time we never once wished for any thing that we had not got; but were quite contented, and with a good grace, in reality made a virtue of necessity. We

> Trembled not with vain desires,
> Few the things which life requires.   FRANCIS's Hor.

And the subject of our prayer was,

> " This day be bread and peace our lot,
> " All else beneath the sun,
> " Thou know'st, if best bestow'd or not ;
> " And let thy will be done."

I am,

Dear Sir,

Yours.

LETTER XVIII.

> To temper thus the stronger fires,
> Of youth he strove, for well he knew,
> Boundless as thought tho' man's desires,
> The real wants of life are few.   CARTWRIGHT.

> In adverse hours an equal mind maintain.
>   FRANCIS's Horace.

DEAR FRIEND,

IN a few days after we had paid the last five shillings of the debt claimed by my friend Mr. Jones, we were both together taken so ill as to be confined to our bed, but the good woman of the house, our landlady, came to our room and did a few trifles for us. She seemed very much alarmed at our situation, or rather for her own, I suppose, as thinking we might in some measure become burthensome to her. We had in cash two shillings and ninepence, half-a-crown of which we had carefully locked up in a box, to be saved as a resource on any extraordinary emergence. This money supported us two or three days, in which time I recovered without the help of medicine: but my wife continued ill near six months, and was confined to her bed the greatest part of the time; which illness may very easily be accounted for.

Before she came to Bristol, she had ever been used to a very active life, and had always lived in the country; but in coming to dwell in a populous city, she had exchanged much exercise and good air for a sedentary life and very bad air; this I presume was the cause of all her illness, from time to time, which at length, as unfortunately as effectually, underminded her constitution. During her first six months illness, I lived many days solely on water-gruel. "What nature requires, (says Montaigne,) is so small a matter, that by its littleness it escapes the gripes of fortune;" for as I could not afford to pay a nurse, much of my time was taken up in attendance on her, and most of my money was expended in procuring medicines, together with such trifles as she could eat and drink.

> " Yet tho' his lot was low, his fortune hard,
> " Serene he smil'd contented with his fate;
> " Nor look'd with envy on the rich and great."

But what added extremely to my calamity was the being within the hearing of her groans, which were caused by the excruciating pains in her head, which for months together defied the power of medicine.

It is impossible for words to describe the keenness of my sensations during this long term; yet, as to *myself*, my poverty and being obliged to live upon water-gruel gave me not the least uneasiness.

> In ruffling seasons I was calm,
> And smil'd when fortune frown'd.   Young.

But the necessity of being continually in the sight and hearing of my beloved object, a young, charming, handsome, innocent wife,

> Who sick in bed lay gasping for her breath;
> Her eyes, like dying lamps, sunk in their sockets,
> Now glar'd, and now drew back their feeble light;

> Faintly her fpeech fell from her fault'ring tongue
> In interrupted accents, as fhe ftrove
> With ftrong agonies that fhook her limbs,
> And writh'd her tortur'd features into forms
> Hideous to fight.   BELLER's Injur'd Innocence.

How I fupported this long dreary fcene, I know
not; the bare recollection of which is exceedingly
painful, even at this diftance of time.

> Lo, from amidft affliction's night,
> Hope burft all radiant on the fight;
> Her words the troubled bofom footh,
> Why thus difmay'd?
> Hope ne'er is wanting to their aid,
> Who tread the path of truth.
> 'Tis I, who footh the rugged way,
> I, who clofe the eyes of forrow,
> And with glad vifions of to-morrow,
> Repair the weary foul's decay.   BEATTIE's Ode to Hope.

At laft, when every thing that feemed to promife
relief had been tried in vain, fome old woman recommended *cephalic* fnuff. I own I had not much faith
in it; however, I procured it, and in a fhort time
after fhe was much relieved from the intolerable pain
in her head, but yet continued in a very bad ftate of
health; her conftitution having fuffered fuch a dreadful fhock, I thought that no means could be ufed fo
likely to reftore it, as a removal to her native air.
Accordingly I left my feat of work at Briftol, and
returned with her to Taunton, which is about feven
miles from Petherton, her native place. But in
Taunton I could not procure fo much work as I could
do; therefore as foon as I thought fhe could bear the
air of Briftol, we returned thither, where fhe foon
relapfed, and we again went back to Taunton.

> Faft bound in penury's relentlefs chain,
> Attempts to rife, but ftill attempts in vain.   SWAIN.

This removing to Taunton was repeated about five
times in little more than two years and a half.

> Of chance or change, O let not man complain,
> Elfe fhall he never ceafe to wail!
> For, from the imperial dome, to where the fwain
> Rears the lone cottage in the filent dale,
> All feel th' affault of Fortune's fickle gale.   MINSTREL.

But at laft, finding that fhe had long fits of illnefs at Taunton alfo, as well as at Briftol, with a view of having a better price for my work I refolved to vifit London. Not having money fufficient to bear the expences of both to town, I left her all the money I could fpare, took a place on the outfide of the ftage-coach, and the fecond day arrived at the metropolis, in Auguft 1773, with two fhillings and fixpence in my pocket; and recollecting the addrefs of an old townfman, who was alfo a fpiritual brother,

Whofe hair in greafy locks hung down,
As ftrait as candles from his crown,
To fhade the borders of his face,
Whofe outward fign of inward grace
Were only vifible in fpiteful
Grimaces, very ftern and frightful.

                                        BUTLER's Pofth. Works

This holy bother was alfo a journeyman fhoe-ma-ker, who had arrived at the fummit of his expecta-tions, being able to keep a houfe over his head (as he chofe to exprefs himfelf), that is, by letting nearly the whole of it out in lodgings, he was enabled to pay the rent. This houfe was in Whitecrofs-ftreet, which I found out the morning after my arrival, where I procured a lodging, and Mr. Heath, in Fore-ftreet, fupplied me with plenty of work.

I laugh'd then and whiftl'd, and fung too moft fweet,
Saying, juft to a hair I've made both ends to meet.
                                        Derry-down.

I am,

Dear Friend,

Yours.

LETTER XIX.

I'll travel no more—I'll try a London audience—
Who knows but what I may get an engagement.

Wild Oats.

When fuperftition (bane of manly virtues!)
Strikes root within the foul; it over-runs
And kills the power of Reafon.

PHILIPS' Duke of GLOUCESTER.

DEAR FRIEND,

A T this time I was as vifionary
and fuperftitious as ever I had been at any preceding
period, for although I had read fome fenfible books,
and had thereby acquired a few rational ideas, yet
having had a methodiftical wife for near three years,
and my keeping methodiftical company, together with
the gloomy notions which in fpite of reafon and philofophy I had imbibed during the frequent, long, and
indeed almoft conftant illnefs of my wife, the confequence was, that thofe few rational or liberal ideas
which I had before treafured up, were at my coming
to London in a dormant ftate, or borne down by the
torrent of enthufiaftic whims, and fanatical chimeras:

——— Oh! what a reafonlefs machine
Can fuperftition make the reas'ner man!

MILLET's Mahomet.

Therefore as foon as I had procured a lodging and
work, my next enquiry was for Mr. Wefley's *Gofpel-
fhops:* on producing my *clafs* and *band* tickets from
Taunton, I was put into a clafs, and a week or two
after admitted into a band.

But it was feveral weeks before I could firmly refolve to continue in London; being really ftruck with
horror for the fate of it; more particularly on Sundays, as I found fo few went to church, and fo many
were walking and riding about for pleafure, and the
lower clafs getting drunk, quarrelling, fighting,
working, buying, felling, &c. I had feen fo much

of the fame kind in Briftol, that I often wondered
how God permitted it to ftand; but London I found
infinitely worfe, and ferioufly trembled for fear the
meafure of iniquity was quite full, and that every
hour would be its laft.   However, I at length concluded, that if London was a fecond *Sodom*, I was a
fecond *Lot*; and thefe comfortable ideas reconciled
me to the thought of living in it.

> I faid it was a wretched place,
> Unfit for any child of grace ;
> 'Tis ripe for judgment: Satan's feat,
> The fink of fin, and hell complete ;
> In ev'ry ftreet of trulls a troop,
> And ev'ry cook-maid wears a hoop.   SOMERVILLE.

Some of Mr. Wefley's people gave me great comfort by affuring me, that " the Lord had much people in this city:" which I foon difcovered to be true,
as I got acquainted with many of thofe righteous
chofen faints, who modeftly arrogate to themfelves
that they are the peculiar favourites of heaven, and
confequently that any place they refide in muft be
fafe.

In a month I faved money fufficient to bring up
my wife, and fhe had a pretty tolerable ftate of health ;
of my mafter I obtained fome ftuff-fhoes for her to
bind, and nearly as much as fhe could do.   Having
now plenty of work and higher wages, we were tolerably eafy in our circumftances, more fo than we
had ever been, and we were foon enabled to procure
a few cloaths.   My wife had all her life before done
very well with a fuperfine broad cloath cloak, but
now I prevailed on her to have one of filk.

> The man who by his labour gets
>   His bread in independent ftate ;
> Who never begs, and feldom eats,
>   Himfelf can fix, or change his fate.   PRIOR.

Until this winter I had never found out that I
wanted a *great coat*, but now I made that important
difcovery.

> A winter garment now demands your care,
> To guard the body from the inclement air ;

Soft be the inward veſt, the outward ſtrong,
And large to wrap you warm, down reaching long.
                                     Cookː's Heſiod.

My landlord ſhewed me one made of a coarſe kind
of Bath-coating, which he purchaſed new at a ſhop
in Roſemary-lane, for ten ſhillings and ſixpence; ſo
that the next half-guinea I had to ſpare, away I went
to Roſemary-lane (and to my great ſurpriſe), was
hauled into a ſhop by a fellow who was walking up
and down before the door of a ſlopſeller, where I
was ſoon fitted with a great coat of the ſame ſort as
that of my landlord. I aſked the price; but was
greatly aſtoniſhed when the honeſt ſlopman told me,
that he was ſo taken with my clean, honeſt, induſtrious looks, that he would let me have it cheaper
than he would his own brother, ſo in one word he
would oblige me with it for five and twenty ſhillings,
which was the very money it coſt him. On hearing
this, I croſſed the ſhop in a trice, in order to ſet off
home again, but the door had a faſtening to it beyond
my comprehenſion, nor would the good man let me
out before I had made him an offer. I told him, I
had ſo little money about me that I could not offer
any thing, and again deſired that he would let me
out. But he perſiſted, and at laſt I told him that my
landlord had informed me that he had purchaſed ſuch
another coat for ten ſhillings and ſixpence; on which
he began to give himſelf airs, and aſſured me, that
however ſome people came by their goods, for his
part, he always paid for his. I heartily wiſhed myſelf out of the ſhop, but in vain; as he ſeemed determined not to part with me until I had made ſome
offer. I then told him that I had but ten ſhillings
and ſixpence, and of courſe could not offer him any
more than I had got. I now expected more abuſe
from him, but inſtead of that the patient good man
told me, that as he perhaps might get ſomething by
me another time, I ſhould have the coat for my half-
guinea, although it was worth more than double the
money.

About the end of November I received an account
of the death of my grandfather.

" The good old gentleman expir'd,
" And decently to heaven retir'd."

I was also informed that he had left a will in favour of my grandmother-in-law's relations, who became possessed of all his effects, except a small freehold estate, which he left to my youngest brother,
because he happened to be called George (which was
the name of my grandfather,) and ten pounds a piece
to each of his other grand-children.

So totally unacquainted was I with the modes of
transacting business, that I could not point out any
method of having my ten pounds sent up to London,
at least, no mode that the executor of the will would
approve of; for being such a *prodigious* sum, that the
greatest caution was used on both sides, so that it cost
me about half the money in going down for it, and
in returning to town again. This was in extremely
hard frosty weather (I think some time in December;)
and being on the outside of a stage-coach, I was so
very cold, that when I came to the inn where the
passengers dined, I went directly to the fire, which
struck the cold inward, and I had but a very narrow
escape from instant death. This happened in going
down. In returning back to town, I had other misfortunes to encounter. The cold weather still continuing, I thought the basket warmer than the roof,
and about six miles from Salisbury, I went back in
it. But on getting out of it, in the inn-yard at Salisbury, I heard some money jingle, and on searching
my pockets, I discovered that I had lost about sixteen
shillings, two or three of which I found in the basket,
the rest had fallen through on the road; and no doubt
the whole of what I had left of my ten pounds would
have gone the same way, had I not (for fear of highwaymen) sewed it up in my cloaths. I recollected
that Seneca had said, " A wise and good man is proof
against all accidents of fate; and that a brave man is
a match for fortune; and knowing myself to be both
wise, good, and *brave*, I bore the loss of my silver
with the temper of a stoic, and like Epictetus reasoned,
that I could not have lost it, if I had not first had it;

and that as I had loft it, why it was all the fame as
though it had never been in my poffeffion.

But a more dreadful misfortune befel me the next
morning; the extreme fevere weather ftill continuing,
in order to keep me from dying with cold, I drank
fome purl and gin, which (not being ufed to drink
any thing ftrong) made me fo drunk, that the coachman put me infide the carriage for fear I fhould fall
off the roof. I there met with fome of the jovial fort,
who having alfo drank to keep out the cold, were in
high glee; being afked to fing them a fong, I immediately complied, and forgetting that I was one of
the holy brethren, I fung fong for fong with the mer-
rieft of them; only feveral times between the acts, I
turned up the whites of my eyes, and uttered a few
ejaculations, as " Lord, forgive me!" " O Chrift!
What am I doing?" and a few more of the fame
pious fort.

> The verrieft hermit in the nation,
> May yield, God knows, to ftrong temptation.   SWIFT.

However, after eating a good dinner, and refrain-
ing from liquor, I became nearly fober, and by the
time I arrived in town, quite fo; though in a terrible
agitation of mind, by reflecting on what I had done,
and was fo afhamed of the affair, that I concealed it
from my wife, that I might not grieve her righteous
foul with the knowledge of fo dreadful a fall: fo
that fhe with great pleafure ripped open the places in
my clothes, which contained my treafure, and with
an heart full of gratitude, pioufly thanked Providence
for affording us fuch a fupply, and hoped that the
Lord would enable us to make a good ufe of it.

> Whate'er can good or ill befall,
> Faithful partner fhe of all.   WESLEY's Meliffa.

Here perhaps I may with great propriety quote the
following lines of Gray:

> " Let not ambition mock their ufeful toil,
> " Their homely joys, and deftiny obfcure;
> " Nor grandeur hear with a difdainful fmile,
> " The fhort and fimple annals of the poor."

I am, dear friend, yours.

LETTER XX.

Thus dwelt poor ———, of few goods poffeft,
A bed, board, tankard, and fix cups at beft ;
Item, Wefley's head, old books, and rotten cheft :
His bed was fcant, for his fhort wife too fhort !
His cups were earthen, all of fmaller fort.

Owen's Juvenal.

Fixt in an elbow chair at eafe,
I choofe companions as I pleafe.   Swift.

Hail, precious pages ! that amufe and teach,
Exalt the genius, and improve the breaft,
A feaft for ages.—O thou banquet nice !
Where the foul riots with fecure excefs.
What heart-felt blifs ! What pleafure-wing'd hours !

Dr. S. Davis.

DEAR FRIEND,

WITH the remainder of the money we purchafed houfhold goods, but as we then had not fufficient to furnifh a room, we worked hard, and lived ftill harder, fo that in a fhort time we had a room furnifhed with our own goods; and I believe that it is not poffible for you to imagine with what pleafure and fatisfaction we looked round the room and furveyed our property : I believe that Alexander the Great never reflected on his immenfe acquifitions with half the heart-felt enjoyment which we experienced on this capital attainment.

" How happy is the man whofe early lot,
" Hath made him mafter of a furnifh'd cot."

After our room was furnifhed, as we ftill enjoyed a better ftate of health than we did at Briftol and Taunton, and had alfo more work and higher wages, we often added fomething to our ftock of wearing apparel.

Induftrious habits in each bofom reigns,
And induftry begets a love of gain ;
Hence all the good from opulence that fpring.

Goldsmith.

G

Nor did I forget the old book-shops: but frequently added an old book to my small collection; and I really have often purchased books with the money that should have been expended in purchasing something to eat; a striking instance of which follows:

At the time we were purchasing houshold goods, we kept ourselves very short of money, and on Christmas-eve we had but half-a-crown left to buy a Christmas dinner. My wife defired that I would go to market, and purchase this festival dinner, and off I set for that purpose; but in the way I saw an old book-shop, and I could not refist the temptation of going in; intending only to expend sixpence or nine-pence out of my half-crown. But I stumbled upon Young's Night Thoughts—forgot my dinner—down went the half-crown—and I hastened home, vastly delighted with the acquisition. When my wife asked me where was our Christmas dinner? I told her it was in my pocket.—"In your pocket! (said she), that is a strange place. How could you think of stuffing a joint of meat into your pocket?" I assured her that it would take no harm. But as I was in no haste to take it out, she began to be more particular, and enquired what I had got, &c. On which I began to harangue on the superiority of intellectual pleasures over sensual gratifications, and observed that the brute creation enjoyed the latter in a much higher degree than man. And that a man, that was not possessed of intellectual enjoyments, was but a two-legged brute.

I was proceeding in this strain: "And so (said she,) instead of buying a dinner, I suppose you have, as you have done before, been buying books with the money?"

"Pray, what is the value of Newton or Locke?
"Do they lessen the price of potatoes or corn?
"When poverty comes, can they soften the shock,
"Or teach us how hunger is patiently borne?
"You spend half your life-time in poring on books;
"What a mountain of wit must be cramm'd in that skull!
"And yet, if a man were to judge by your looks,
"Perhaps he would think you confoundedly dull."

I confessed I had bought Young's Night Thoughts: "And I think (said I) that I have acted wisely for had I bought *a dinner*, we ſhould have eaten it to-morrow, and the pleaſure would have been ſoon over ;

> " But in the volumes of the mighty dead,
> " We feaſt on joys to vulgar minds unknown."

Should we live fifty years longer, we ſhall have the *Night Thoughts* to feaſt upon." This was too powerful an argument to admit of any farther debate; in ſhort, my wife was convinced. Down I ſat, and began to read with as much enthuſiaſm as the good doctor poſſeſſed when he wrote it ; and ſo much did it excite my attention as well as approbation, that I retained the greateſt part of it in my memory. A couplet of Perſius, as Engliſhed, might have been applied to me :

> " —— For this you gain your meagre looks,
> " And ſacrifice your dinner to your books."

Sometime in June 1774, as we ſat at work in our room, Mr. Boyd, one of Mr. Weſley's people, called and informed me that a little ſhop and parlour were to be let in Featherſtone-ſtreet ; adding, that if I was to take it, I might there get ſome work as a maſter. I without heſitation told him that I liked the idea, and hinted that I would ſell books alſo. Mr. Boyd then aſked me how I came to think of ſelling books ? I informed him that until that moment it had never once entered into my thoughts ; but that when he propoſed my taking the ſhop, it inſtantaneouſly occured to my mind, that for ſeveral months paſt I had obſerved a great increaſe in a certain old book ſhop ; and that I was perſuaded I knew as much of old books as the perſon who kept it. I farther obſerved, that I loved books, and that if I could but be a book-ſeller, I ſhould then have plenty of books to read, which was the greateſt motive I could conceive to induce me to make the attempt. My friend on this aſſured me, that he would get the ſhop for me, and with a laugh added, " When you are Lord Mayor, you ſhall uſe all your intereſt to get me made an Alderman." Which I engaged not to forget to perform.

G 2

" In all my wand'rings round this world of care,
" In all my griefs, and God has giv'n my fhare;
" I ftill had hopes to fee fome better days."

My *private library* at this time confifted of Fletcher's Checks to Antinomianifm, &c. 5 volumes; Watts's Improvement of the Mind; Young's Night Thoughts; Wake's Tranflation of the Apoftolical Epiftles; Fleetwood's Life of Chrift; the firft twenty numbers of Hinton's Dictionary of the Arts and Sciences; fome of Mr. Wefley's Journals, and fome of the pious lives publifhed by him; and about a dozen other volumes of the latter fort, befides odd magazines, &c. To fet me up in ftyle, Mr. Boyd recommended me to the friends of an holy brother lately gone to heaven, and of whom I purchafed a bagful of old books, chiefly divinity, for a guinea.

> How muft he ftruggle in the fhades of night,
> To break thro' poverty's dark mifts to light!
> Oh, what a tafk before he gains his end!
> A tafk indeed!—exclaims *my dear old* friend.   SWAIN.

With this flock, and fome odd fcraps of leather, which together with all my books were worth about five pounds, I opened fhop on Midfummer-day 1774, in Featherftone-ftreet, in the parifh of St. Luke; and I was as well pleafed in furveying my little fhop with my name over it, as was Nebuchadnezzar, when he faid, " Is not this great Babylon that I have built?" And my good wife often perceiving the pleafure that I took in my fhop, pioufly cautioned me againft fetting my mind on the riches of this world, and affured me that it was all but vanity. "You are very right, my dear (I fometimes replied,) and to keep our minds as fpiritual as we can, we will always attend our clafs and band-meetings, hear as many fermons, &c. at the Foundery on week days as poffible, and on fabbath days we will mind nothing but the good of our fouls; our fmall beer fhall be fetched in on Saturday nights, nor will we drefs even a potatoe on the fabbath. We will ftill attend the preaching at five o'clock in the morning; at eight, go to the prayer meeting; at ten, to the public worfhip at the

Foundery; hear Mr. Perry at Cripplegate, at two;
be at the preaching at the Foundery, at five; meet
with the general society, at six; meet in the united
bands at seven, and again be at the prayer meeting at
eight; and then come home, and read and pray by
ourselves."

I am,

Dear Friend,

You--

_____

LETTER XXI.

— Strange vicissitudes of human fate!
Still alt'ring, never in a steady state;
Good after ill, and after pain delight;
Alternate, like the scenes of day and night.
Since every one who lives is born to die,
And none can boast intire felicity:
With equal mind what happens let us bear,
Nor joy, nor grieve too much for things beyond our care.
Like pilgrims, to the appointed place we tend:
The world's an Inn, and death's the journey's end.
                    DRYDEN's Palemon and Arcite.

DEAR FRIEND,

NOtwithstanding the obscurity of
the street, and the mean appearance of my shop, yet
I soon found customers for what few books I had;
and I as soon laid out the money in other old trash
which was daily brought for sale.

At that time Mr. Wesley's people had a sum of
money, which was kept on purpose to lend out, for
three months, without interest, to such of their society whose characters were good, and who wanted a
temporary relief. To increase my little stock, I bor-

G. 3

rowed five pounds out of this fund, which was of great service to me.

In our new situation we lived in a very frugal manner, often dining on potatoes, and quenching our thirst with water, being absolutely determined, if possible, to make some provision for such dismal times as sickness, shortness of work, &c. which we had been so frequently involved in before, and could scarce help expecting to be our fate again. My wife foreboded it much more than I did, being of a more melancholy turn of mind.

> ———— Women ever love
> To brood o'er sorrows, and indulge their woe.
> FRANCKLIN's Sophocles.

And yet when we really were involved in sickness and poverty, she bore all with patience and fortitude.

> Imagin'd ills in frightful shapes appear,
> While present evils we with patience bear ;
> Phantoms, and empty forms are fear'd the most,
> As those who scorn'd the man, yet dread the ghost.
> DRAPER.

I lived in this street six months, and in that time increased my stock from five pounds, to twenty-five pounds.

> London——the public there are candid and generous, and before my merit can have time to create me enemies, I'll save money, and a fig for the Sultan and Sophy.   ROVER.

This immense stock I deemed too valuable to be buried in Featherstone-street ; and a shop and parlour being to let in Chiswell-street, No. 46, I took them. This was at that time, and for fourteen years afterwards, a very dull and obscure situation : as few ever passed through it, besides Spitalfield weavers on *hanging days*, and methodists on *preaching nights* ; but still it was much better adapted for business than Featherstone-street.

A short time after I came into Chiswell-street to live, an odd circumstance occurred which caused a great deal of talk ; Mrs. Chapman, who many years

kept a livery stable in Coleman-street, had a cat big
with kitten ; this cat was one day seen to fly at a
fowl, that was roasting by the fire, which she repeated
several times, so that she was at last put out of the
room ; when this fowl was dressed and eat, they gave
poor puss the bones, but this was not enough, for
when she lay in, they found that she had marked her
kitten, as instead of two feet before, she had two
wings, with some short feathers on them ; the singu-
larity of this kitten drew great numbers to visit her,
which occasioned so much trouble to Mrs. Chapman,
that she signed the death-warrant, and poor puss was
drowned, and afterwards buried in the dung heap.

I thought this story would read as well in my Life,
as in the Philosophical Transactions, which prevented me from troubling those learned authors with
it.

A few weeks after I was settled in my new shop, I
bade a final adieu to the *gentle craft*, and converted my
little stock of leather, &c. into old books ; and a
great sale I had, considering my stock; which was
not only extremely small, but contained very little
variety, as it principally consisted of divinity ; for as
I had not much knowledge. so I seldom ventured out
of my depth. Indeed, there was one class of books,
which for the first year or two that I called myself a
bookseller, I would not sell, for such was my ignorance, bigotry, superstition (or what you please) that
I conscientiously destroyed such books as fell into my
hands, which were written by free-thinkers ; for
really supposing them to be dictated by his sable high-
ness, I would neither read them myself, nor sell them
to others.

You will perhaps be surprised when I inform you,
that there are in London (and I suppose in other populous places) persons who purchase every article
which they have occasion for (and also many articles
which they have no occasion for, nor ever will) at
stalls, beggarly shops, pawnbrokers, &c. under the
idea of purchasing *cheaper* than they could at respectable shops, and of men of property. A considerable
number of this species of customers I had in the be-

ginning, who forfook my fhop as foon as I began to
appear more refpectable, by introducing better order,
poffeffing more valuable books, and having acquired
a better judgment, &c. Notwithftanding which, I
declare to you, upon my honour, that thefe very
bargain-hunters have given me double the price that
I now charge for thoufands and tens of thoufands of
volumes. For as a tradefman increafes in refpectabi-
lity and opulence, his opportunities of purchafing increafe proportionably, and the more he buys and
fells, the more he becomes a judge of the real value
of his goods. It was for want of this experience and
judgment, ftock, &c. that for feveral years I was in
the habit of charging more than double the price I
now do for many thoufand articles. But profeffed
bargain-hunters often purchafe old *locks* at the ftalls
in Moorfields, when half the wards are rufted off or
taken out, and give more for them than they would
have paid for new ones to any reputable ironmonger.
And what numerous inftances of this infatuation do
we meet with daily at fales by auction, not of books
only, but of many other articles? Of which I could
here adduce a variety of glaring inftances: but (not
to tire you) a few of recent date fhall fuffice.—At
the fale of Mr. Rigby's books at Mr. Chriftie's, Mar-
tyn's Dictionary of Natural Hiftory fold for *fifteen
guineas*, which then ftood in my catalogue at *four
pounds fifteen fhillings*; Pilkington's Dictionary of
Painters, at *feven guineas*, ufually fold at three;
Francis's Horace, *two pounds eleven fhillings*, and many
others in the fame manner. At Sir George Cole-
brook's fale, the octavo edition of the Tatler fold for
two guineas and a half. At a fale a few weeks fince,
Rapin's Hiftory, in folio, the two firft volumes only
(inftead of five) fold for upwards of *five pounds!* I
charge for the fame from *ten fhillings and fixpence to one
pound ten fhillings*. I fell great numbers of books to
pawnbrokers, who fell them out of their windows at
much higher prices, the purchafers believing that
they are buying bargains, and that fuch articles have
been pawned; nor is this commerce confined to books

only, but extends to various other articles, of which they always buy the worſt of every kind of article they ſell. I will even add, that many ſhops which are called pawnbrokers, never take in any pawns, yet can live by ſelling things which are ſuppoſed to be kept over time.

I went on proſperouſly until ſome time in September 1775, when I was ſuddenly taken ill of a dreadful fever; and eight or ten days after, my wife was ſeized with the ſame diſorder.

> Human hopes, now mounting high,
> On the ſwelling ſurge of joy ;
> Now with unexpected woe,
> Sinking to the depths below. WEST's Pindar.

At that time I only kept a boy to help in my ſhop, ſo that I fear, while I lay ill, my wife had too much care and anxiety on her mind. I have been told that, before ſhe was confined to her bed, ſhe walked about in a delirious ſtate; in which ſhe did not long continue, but contrary to all expectation died, in a fit of enthuſiaſtic rant, on the ninth of November, ſurrounded with ſeveral methodiſtical preachers.

> Invidious death ! how doſt thou rend in ſunder,
> Whom love has knit and ſympathy made one ?
> A tie ſo ſtubborn——— BLAIR's Grave.

She was in reality one of the beſt of women; and although for about four years ſhe was ill the greateſt part of the time, which involved me in the very depth of poverty and diſtreſs, yet I never once repented having married her.

> ——— Still buſy meddling memory,
> In barbarous ſucceſſion, muſters up
> The paſt endearments of our ſofter hours,
> Tenacious of his theme. BLAIR's Grave.

'Tis true, ſhe was enthuſiaſtical to an extreme, and of courſe very ſuperſtitious and viſionary, but as I was very far gone myſelf, I did not think that a fault in her.

> Go, take thy ſeat, the heav'nly choirs among,
> But leave thy virtues to the world below.
> ORLANDO FURIOSO.

Indeed she much exceeded me, and most others that ever fell under my observation.

> She ne'er indulg'd a recreation,
> That could endanger her salvation;
> But chose the most austere restraints,
> And spoke the language of the saints.   HUMPHREYS.

She in reality *totally* neglected and disregarded *every kind of pleasure whatever*, but those of a spiritual (or visionary) nature. Methinks I here see you smile; but I assure you she made *no* exception; but was a complete devotee, and what is more remarkable without pride or ill-nature.

> Intentions so pure, and such meekness of spirit,
> Must of course, and of right, Heaven's kingdom inherit.
>   SIMKIN.

I am,

Dear Friend,

Yours.

LETTER XXII.

> " I've strange news to give you! but when you receive it,
> " 'Tis impossible, Sir, that you should believe it!
> " But as I've been told this agreeable story,
> " I'll digress for a moment to lay it before ye."

DEAR SIR,

A Friend of mine, of whose veracity I entertain the highest opinion, has favoured me with an account of a lady, who has to the full as much, indeed more of the spirit, but without the good-nature of Nancy Lackington. The fact is as follows:

> " 'Tis true 'tis a pity: and pity 'tis 'tis true."

Mr. R—t, a genteel tradesman with whom I am acquainted, having lost his second wife early in 1790, courted and married one of the holy sisters a few months afterwards. They had lived together about six months, when Mr. R—t, one Sunday, being a sober religious man, took down Doddridge's Lectures, and began to read them to his wife and family. But this holy sister found fault with her husband for reading such learned rational discourses, which savoured too much of human reason and vain philosophy, and wished he would read something more spiritual and edifying. He attempted to convince her that Dr. Doddridge was not only a good rational divine, but to the full as spiritual as any divine ought to be; and that to be more spiritual he must be less rational, and of course become fanatical and visionary. But these observations of the husband so displeased his spiritual wife, that she retired to bed, and left her husband to read Doddridge's Lectures as long as he chose to his children by a former wife.

The next morning, while Mr. R—t was out on business, this holy sister, without saying one syllable to any person, packed up all her clothes, crammed them into a hackney-coach, and away she went. Mr. R—t, poor soul! on coming home, discovered his immense loss, and, in an almost frantic state, spent the first fortnight in fruitless attempts to discover her retreat.

" Three weeks after her elopement, I was (says
" Mr. R—t) going down Cheapside one day, and
" saw a lady something like my wife; but as she was
" somewhat disguised, and I could not see her face,
" I was not sure. At last I ventured to look under
" her bonnet, and found, that, sure enough, it was
" she. I then walked three times backwards and
" forwards in Cheapside, endeavouring to persuade
" her to return with me, or to discover where she
" lived; but she obstinately refused to return, or to let
" me see her retreat; and here (says Mr. R—t) I
" begged that she would grant me a kiss; but she
" would not willingly. However, after some bustle
" in the street, I took a farewel kiss. Poor dear

G 6

" foul! (figh'd he) fhe is rather *too fpiritual* ; for not-
" withftanding I laid by her fide near fix months, fhe
" never would be prevailed upon to do any thing
" carnal; and although I did all in my power to get
" the better of her fpiritual fcruples, yet fhe was al-
" ways fo in love with Chrift her heavenly fpoufe,
" that when fhe eloped from me, fhe was, I affure
" you, as good a virgin as when I married her."

I muft give you a ftory or two of the fame nature
with the preceding :

A gentleman of London happening to be on a vifit at Briftol about three years fince, fell in love with
a handfome young lady who was one of the holy
fifterhood; after a few weeks acquaintance he made
her an offer of his perfon and fortune, and the young
lady, after proper inquiry had been made into the
gentleman's family, fortune, &c. confented to make
our lover happy. They were foon after married,
and the fame day fet off in a poft-chaife towards London, in order to fleep the firft night at an inn, and fo
fave the lady the blufhes occafioned by the jokes common on fuch occafions; this happy couple had been
in bed about an hour when the cry of murder alarmed
the houfe; this alarm, proceeding from the room that
was occupied by the bride and bridegroom, drew the
company that way ; the inn-keeper knocked at the
door, and demanded admittance; our Benedict appeared at the door, and informed the hoft that his
lady had been taken fuddenly ill in a kind of fit, he
believed, but that fhe was better; and after the innkeeper's wife had been fent into the room to fee the
young lady, and had found her well, all retired to
bed.

They had, however, not lain more than two hours,
when the cry of murder, fire, &c. again alarmed the
houfe, and drew many out of their beds once more.

Our young gentleman then dreffed himfelf, and,
opening the door, informed the company that he had
that morning been married to the young lady in bed,
and that being married, he had infifted on being admitted to the privilege of an hufband, but that the
young lady had talked much about the good of her

poor foul, her fpiritual hufband, &c; and that inftead of granting what he conceived to be the right of every hufband, fhe had thought proper to difturb all in the houfe. He added, that having been thus made very ridiculous, he would take effectual care to prevent a repetition of the fame abfurd conduct.

He then ordered a poft-chaife, and fet off for London, leaving our faint in bed to enjoy her fpiritual contemplations in their full extent; nor has he ever fince paid her any attention.

> " The poor man having wander'd round 'em,
> " Left all her beauties as he found 'em. '

Some time fince, being in a large town in the Weft, fhe was pointed out to me by a friend, as fhe was walking in the ftreet.

I am alfo imformed, from undoubted authority, that in the fame town there now refides a couple who have been married upwards of three years, and as yet the hufband is not certain as to the fex of his wife: and on every attempt of the hufband for that purpofe, the fervants are alarmed with the fcreams of the pious lady, who would not permit fuch carnal communication for the world.

The preceding ftories put me in mind of what Ovid fays was practifed by young maids on the feftival of the celebrated nymph *Anna Porenna*, thus tranflated by I—I know not who:

> " With promifes the amorous god fhe led,
> " And with fond hopes his eager paffion fed;
> " At length 'tis done, the goddefs yields, fhe cry'd
> " My pray'rs have gain'd the victory o'er pride.
> " With joy the god prepares the golden bed;
> " Thither, her face conceal'd, is Anna led;
> " Juft on the brink of blifs, fhe ftands confefs'd;—
> " The difappointed lover is her jeft,
> " While rage and fhame alternate fwell his breaft.

I know that there are now in Wefley's fociety, in London, fome women who, ever fince they were converted, have refufed to fleep with their hufbands, and that fome of thofe will not pay the leaft attention to any temporal concern whatever, being, as

they term it, wholly wrapped up in divine contemplation, having their souls abforbed in divine love,
fo as not to be interrupted by the trifling concerns of
a hufband, family, &c.

> Reflection loves to wake and fhed a tear
> O'er human weaknefs— many a noble mind,
> By fuperftition cramp'd, has here refign'd
> The rights of reafon God and nature gave,
> Man's higheft privilege :—Here many a heart,
> Of that fweet focial intercourfe debarr'd
> Which gives to polifh'd life its higheft tafte,
> Harden'd; to joy's, to pity's melting touch
> Infenfible and cold—prayer here has taught
> Her lovely voterefs the art to check
> Each rifing wifh, each tumult of the foul ;
> Refign'd — —— — — —
> To live to heav'n alone, and pafs away,
> Like fome fair flow'r that on the wild heath blows,
> And ftrews its with'ring leaves upon the blaft.
>   Rev. J. WHITEHOUSE.

Mrs. G——, left her hufband and children, one
of whom was fucking at her breaft, and came from
Ireland to London; and when fhe was upbraided
with her unnatural behaviour, fhe replied, " It was
the will of the Lord ; fhe had left all for Chrift's
fake, and followed the guidings of his fpirit. To fit
under the preaching of Mr. Wefley, was of more
importance to her than hufband and children." For
a long time fhe lived on what fhe had brought away
from her hufband ; after that was gone, fhe lived a
half-ftarved life, by taking in plain work. What
became of her at laft I could never learn.

> Each warm affection and paternal care,
> Left unrequited for the pomp of pray'r ;
> Each focial duty, each endearing tie,
> The foul's beft bond, its native fympathy.
> And thofe few virtues which our natures own,
> Alike forgotten, or alike unknown.   BIRCH.

I am,

Dear Friend,

Yours.

LETTER XXIII.

Women that leave no stone unturn'd,
In which the cause might be concern'd.   HUDIBRAS.

The *man without sin,* the *methodist* Rabbi,
Has perfectly cur'd the chlorosis of Tabby:
And, if right, I can judge from her shape and her face,
She soon may produce an infant of grace.
Now they say that all people in her situation
Are very fine subjects for regeneration.
New BATH Guide.

DEAR FRIEND,

BECAUSE some of the holy
sisters are in their amours altogether spiritual, you
are by no means to understand that they are all totally
divested of the carnal propensity.

Some of these good creatures are so far from thinking that their husbands are too carnal in their affections, that they really think that they are not enough
so; and instances are not wanting, in which, owing
to their having husbands too spiritual, they have
been willing to receive assistance from the husbands of
other women.

It is but about a year since a certain celebrated
preacher used to administer carnal consolation to the
wife of his clerk. This holy communication was repeated so often, and so open, that at last it came to
the clerk's ears, who watching an opportunity, one
day surprised the pious pair at their *devotion,* and so
belaboured the preacher with his walking staff, that
the public were for near a month deprived of the
benefits resulting from his remarkable gift of eloquence.

" The pious methodist, may chance to fail,
" Like Æsop's fox, entangl'd by the tail."

As I am got into the story-telling way, I cannot
resist the temptation of telling another; for, as Mat
Bramble says,

" —— Here my subject is not barren;
" But in rare anecdotic matter rich."

A certain holy sister who lately kept a house in a
country village, within ten miles of London, and
took in (as they called it) Mr. Wesley's preachers; by
taking *in* is only meant, that when they came in turn
to preach in the village, she used to supply each with
victuals and a bed (*no doubt* but they slept *alone*).
This lady was so very remarkable for her *spiritul experience* and divine gifts;

Heaven has its chosen favourites, and on those·
With partial hand, its double gift bestows;
While common souls, like coarser stuffs laid by,
Are not prepar'd to take the brighter dye.

                              J. H. BROWNE, Esq.

These gracious gifts attracted many to her house,
besides such as came in the regular course of their
duty, and among the former a preacher from London,
from whom I learnt the affair.

If any of her sisters said,
Calista, you're a lovely maid;
For shame! cry'd our religious lass,
Sure you forget all flesh is grass;
The beauty of each blooming finner,
Will soon give churchyard worms a dinner;
The fairest features of the face
Are vanity compar'd to grace.

                              FONTAINE by HUMPHREYS.

This preacher happening to want a wife, and being very spiritually-minded, actually married her in
December 1790, merely for her geat gifts and graces,
as her fortune was not above the fiftieth part as much
as his own. They had not been married a week,
when this simple preacher discovered that his gifted
gracious saint was an incarnate devil, who had married him only to rob, plunder, and —— him.

Whate'er it be, 'to wisest men and best
Seeming at first all heav'nly under virgin veil,
Soft, modest, meek, demure;
Once join'd, the contrary she proves, a thorn,
Intestine, for within defensive arms
A cleaving mischief; in his way to virtue

Adverfe and turbulent, or by her charms
Draws him away enflav'd
With dotage, and his fenfe deprav'd,
To folly and fhameful deeds which ruin ends.

MILTON's Samfon Agoniftes.

And in a few months, between her and her gal-
lants, they bullied him out of a fettlement to the
amount of four times the fum fhe brought him, and
the poor pious preacher thinks that he has cheaply
got rid of her.

Ah, foolifh woman ! may fhe one day fee
How deep fhe's plung'd herfelf in infamy,
And with true penitence wafh out the ftain ;—
But—mifchief on't—why fhould,I pray in vain ;
For fhe's but harden'd at the name of grace,
No blufh was ever feen t'adorn her face.   GOULD.

The reafon why I intereft myfelf in his behalf is,
becaufe I am confident that he really is an honeft
well-meaning man at the bottom ; but withal one
that does not poffefs the greateft fhare of underftanding, and who being formerly but a mean mechanic,
never had any education ; but although he is a great
enthufiaft, yet he is one of the good-natured inoffen-
five fort, who will do no harm to any. perfon, but,
on the contrary, all the good in his power. I am
only forry, as he lately was an honeft ufeful tradefman, that he fhould have fo much fpiritual quixotifm
in him, as at thirty years of age to fhut up his fhop
and turn preacher, without being able to read his
primer ; which I can affure you is the cafe.

What though his wits could ne'er difpenfe
One page of grammar, or of fenfe ;
What though his learning be fo flight,
He fcarcely knows to fpell or write ;
What though his fkull be cudgel-proof,
He's orthodox, and that's enough.   TOM BRAINLESS.

But thefe heavenly teachers only fpeak as the
Spirit giveth utterance, of courfe all human learning
is entirely fuperfluous :

—— As he does not chufe to cull,
His faith by any fcripture rule,

But by the vapours that torment
His brains, from hypocondria fent,
Which into dreams and vifions turn,
And make the zeal fo fircely burn,
That reafon lofes the afcendant,
And all within grows independant.
He proves all fuch as do accord
With him the chofen of the Lord;
But that all others are accurft,
'Tis plain in Canticles the firft.

BUTLER's Pofth. Works.

The following very extraordinary fact took place about the time that I firft came to live in Chifwell-ftreet: Mr. R— a furgeon, who lived many years near Moorfields, happened to have a methodiftical lady (fome relation to him) that boarded in the houfe, and ferved as a companion to Mrs. R—; the furgeon fome how or other got to bed to this holy woman, and after fome time Mrs. R— beame acquainted with their illicit amours; fhe took not the leaft notice of the difcovery, but kept in good humour with both until fhe had an opportunity of being revenged of her rival. One afternoon, her hufband being from home, fhe took care to fend the fervants out of the way, and then went up ftairs to this boarder's bed-room, and found her taking her afternoon nap on the bed; upon which fhe fecured her hands, by tying them, one to each of the pofts at the head of the bed; in doing which the lady awaked and began to laugh, as thinking it was fome bit of humour; Mrs. R— laughed alfo, and proceeded to tye her legs, one to each of the pofts at the foot of the bed, which the other permitted, ftill thinking it was fome harmlefs whim; but alas! fhe was foon convinced to the con-trary, for as foon as Mrs. R— had made her fecure, fhe (horrid to relate) took a pen-knife, and cut off one half of the externals of the offending part. Now, faid fhe, in *favage triumph*, let Mr. R—— take half, or a whole one, which he likes beft. She then fent for her hufband, and told him that Mrs. —— wanted his immediate affiftance, which he found to be too true, as fhe was nearly dead with the lofs of blood; however, he with much care and attention, for many weeks, at laſt healed the wound. She then was deſired by Mrs. R— to get herſelf another place to board at, leſt ſhe ſhould loſe the other half—the poor lady took her advice, and after this dreadful misfortune gave herſelf up entirely to devotion, and was ſoon after admitted into the ſelect bands, among the entirely holy ſiſters, who *having ſuffered much in the fleſh*, are made perfect in grace, and free from the very remains of ſin.

A few years ſince the methodiſt-preachers got footing in Wellington (the famous birth-place of your humble ſervant) and eſtabliſhed a ſociety, ſoon after which, one of their preachers (at Collompton, a neighbouring town) happened to like a young ſervant girl, who was one of the holy ſiſters, (ſhe having gone through the new birth) better than his wife, becauſe ſhe was an unenlightened, unconverted woman. And this ſervant girl proving with child, the news ſoon reached Wellington ; and a very wealthy gentleman, who entertained the preachers there, followed the preacher of Collompton's example, and got his own pious maid with child.

> " Bleſſed ſhe tho' once rejected,
> " Like a little wandering ſheep ;
> " Poor maid, one morning was elected
> " By a viſion in her ſleep."

After this ſome of the ſociety in Wellington began to have all things in common, and ſeveral more of the holy ſiſters proved prolific ; which ſo alarmed the pariſh, that ſome of the heads of it inſiſted that the preachers ſhould not be permitted to exhibit there any longer. " For, if (ſaid they) the methodiſt-ſociety continues, we ſhall have the pariſh full of baſtards."

A ſimilar affair happened at a country town, ten or twelve miles from Oxford, about two years ſince, where a very handſome powerful preacher made converts of a great number of women, both married and ſingle, who were wonderfully affected, and great numbers flocked to his ſtandard.

> He had a roguiſh twinkling in his eye,
> And ſhone all glittering with ungodly dew;

If a tight damfel chanc'd to be tripping by,
    Which when obferv'd, he fhrunk into his mew,
    And ftrait would recollect his piety anew.

Caftle of Indolence.

But he had not laboured there more than a year, before the churchwardens were made acquainted with his powerful operations on five young female faints, who all fwore baftards to this holy, fpiritual labourer in the vineyard; upon which the gentlemen of the town exerted themfelves, and prevented the farther propagation of methodifm; as

" The ladies by fympathy feem to difcover
" The advantage of having a fpiritual lover.
" They were fadly afraid that wives, widows, and miffes,
" Would confine to the—all their favours and kiffes."

There was in Salifbury, fome few years ago, a congregation of methodifts in connection with the late Mr. Wefley; and amongft the poorer members, a young man, who with honourable profeffions, paid his addreffes to a young woman. They generally met in the dufk of the evening, after their daily labour was ended. One evening in particular he preffed her to marry him; it was mutually agreed on, and the day fixt for the celebration of their nuptials; and by way of binding the bargain (as odd as it may feem) he prefented the young woman with half-a-guinea. A few evenings after, being in company with her as ufual, he began to offer rudenefs to her; alledging in excufe, that as they were to be married in a few days, the congrefs would be perfectly innocent. But the girl refented the ufage highly; and foon after, complained to the other methodifts in that city, of the infult fhe had received from him. The young man was accordingly challenged with it; but he ftiffly denied the whole; alledging that he had not been in her company for fome time paft; that he had made no matrimonial contract with her; and confequently did not give her the half-guinea afferted; and the man who ufually worked with him in the fame fhop, averred pofitively that he was prefent with them on the evening in queftion, at his ufual employment. Upon this, the methodifts *wifely* concluded, that it must have been the devil who had carried on this affair with the young woman; that when he gave her the half guinea, she had sold herself to him, and that on the day fixt for the marriage, he would come and fetch her away; or at least that some great evil would befal her.

Peter Pindar, in his ode to the devil, says,

"What thousands hourly bent on sin,
"With supplications call thee in,
  "To aid them to pursue it;
"Yet when detected, with a lie
"Ripe at their finger's ends, they cry,
  "The devil bid me do it."

As Mr. Wesley was to be at Newbury soon, they prudently determined upon sending a deputation of certain of their members to him, for his advice in so critical an affair; which was accordingly done.—After having stated the case to him; instead of opening their eyes, as so learned a man ought to have done; he treated the whole as truth; and directed them to fast and pray on that day when they expected satan to make his appearance; and after the deputies had left Newbury, he said to the good people of the house where he then was, *I thought a little fasting and prayer would not do them any harm.*

The author of a letter to Dr. Coke and Mr. More, published since the first edition of my Memoirs, informs us, that a gentleman of Chesham had a daughter about seventeen years of age, whom he put into the hands of a methodist parson, to have her converted, and was exceedingly kind and liberal to him; and we are informed that this rascal converted her first, and debauched her afterwards.

So you see, my dear friend, by the above examples (were it necessary, I could give you many more) that not *all* the converted and sanctified females are become so absorbed in the spiritual delights of the mystical union, as to be totally insensible to carnal connections; as we find that many among them are blessed with a mind so capacious, as to be able to participate in the pleasures of both worlds.

——————— In this naughty world
The garb of virtue is assum'd by vice,
And hard it is for an experienc'd eye
To say who merits.   HUDDIS.

I am,

Dear Friend,

Yours.

————————————————————

LETTER XXIV.

Domestic happiness, thou only bliss
Of paradise that has surviv'd the fall!
Thou art the nurse of virtue, in thine arms
She smiles appearing, as in truth she is,
Heav'n born, and destin'd for the skies again.   COWPER.

Woman, man's chiefest good, by heav'n design'd
To glad the heart, and humanize the mind;
To sooth each angry care, abate the strife,
And lull the passions as we walk through life.
                            Art of living in LONDON.

DEAR FRIEND,

A FTER a long digression, I must
now return to my own affairs.

I continued in the above-mentioned dreadful fever
many weeks, and my life was despaired of by all who
came near me. During which time, my wife, whom
I affectionately loved, died and was buried, without
my once having a sight of her.

She was—I cannot say how good—God knows.
                                        ADRIAN.

What added much to my misfortunes, several
nurses that were hired to take care of me and my
wife, proved so abandoned and depraved as to have
lost all sense of moral obligation, and every tender

feeling for one who to all appearance was just on the point of death: several of these monsters in female shape robbed my drawers of linen, &c. and kept themselves drunk with gin, while I lay unable to move in my bed, and was ready to perish, partly owing to want of cleanliness and proper care.   Thus situated, I must inevitably have fallen a victim, had it not been for my sister Dorothy, wife of Mr. Northam of Lambeth, and my sister Elizabeth, wife of Mr. Bell in Soho.

————— dreadful are the ills
Which cruel fortune brings on human kind.
                                        FRANCKLIN's Sophocles

These kind sisters, as soon as they were informed of the deplorable state in which I lay, notwithstanding some misunderstanding which subsisted between us, and prevented me from sending for them, hastened to me, and each sat up with me alternately, so that I had one or the other with me every night; and, contrary to all expectation, I recovered.   But this recovery was in a very slow manner.

Health, loviest handmaid of the immortal train,
   With thee may all my future moments flow,
Of this short life what fleeting hours remain ;
   Come thou and tinge them with thy chearful glow.
                                        BELOE.

As soon as I was able to enquire into the state of my affairs, I found that Mr. Wheeler, sack and rope-maker in Old-street, Messrs. Bottomley and Shaw, carpenters and sash-makers in Bunhill-row, had saved me from ruin, by locking up my shop, which contained my little *all*.   Had not this been done, the nurses would no doubt have contrived means to have emptied my shop, as effectually as they had done my drawers.

The above gentlemen not only took care of my shop, but also advanced money to pay such expences as occurred; and as my wife was dead, they assisted in making my will in favour of my mother.

These worthy gentlemen belong to Mr. Wesley's society (notwithstanding they have imbibed many

enthusiastic whims) they would be an honour to any
society, and are a credit to human nature. I hope
that I never shall recollect their kindness without being filled with the warmest sentiments of gratitude
towards them.

I never had any opportunity of returning Mr.
Wheeler's kindness. But Messrs. Bottomley and
Shaw have received many hundred pounds of me for
work, and are still my carpenters, and ever shall be
as long as I shall live near them, and have a house
to repair.

> " He that hath Nature in him must be grateful :
> " 'Tis the Creator's primary great law,
> " That links the chain of being to each other,
> " Joining the greater to the lesser nature,
> " Tying the weak and strong, the poor and powerful,
> " Subduing men to brutes, and even brutes to men."

There is a fine passage in Ajax, a tragedy by So-
phocles, as translated by Dr. Francklin, and as it is a
wife speaking to her husband, is the more remarkable.
Tecmessa says to Ajax,

> " ———— Thou art my all,
> " My only safeguard : do not, do not leave me !
> " Nought so becomes a man as gratitude
> " For good received, and noble deeds are still
> " The offspring of benevolence, whilst he
> " With whom remembrance dies of blessings past,
> " Is vile and worthless."

There are also two fine lines on this subject in W.
Whitehead's Epistle to Dr. Lowth, which I must quote.

> " ——— The next virtue to bestowing good,
> " Thou know'st, is gratitude for good bestow'd."

On my recovery I also learnt that Miss Dorcas
Turton (the young woman that kept the house, and
of whom I then rented the shop, parlour, kitchen and
garret) having out of kindness to my wife, occasionally assisted her during her illness, had caught the
same dreadful disorder ; she was then very dangerously
ill, and people shunned the house as much as if the
plague had been in it. So that when I opened my
shop again, I was stared at as though I had actually

returned from the other world; and it was a considerable time before many of my former customers could credit that I really was in existence, it having been repeatedly reported that I was also dead.

Montaigne says " That sorrow is a passion which the world has endeavoured to honour, by cloathing it with the godly titles of wisdom, virtue, &c. which is a foolish and vile disguise; the Italians call it by its proper name, *ill-nature*; for, in truth (says he) it is always a mean base passion; and for that reason the stoicks forbid their wise men to be any way affected with it."

Whether Montaigne is right or not, I will not determine; but I got rid of my sorrow as fast as I could, thinking that I could not give a better proof of my having loved my late wife, than by getting another as soon as I could.

> Man may be happy if he will,
> I've said so often, and I think so still;
> Doctrine to make the millions stare!
> Know then, each mortal is an actual Jove;
> Can brew what weather he shall most approve,
> Or wind, or calm, or foul, or fair.
>
> But here's the mischief—man's an ass, I say;
> Too fond of thunder, light'ning, storm, and rain;
> He hides the charming, chearing ray,
> That spreads a smile, o'er hill and plain!
> Dark he must court the scull, and spade, and shroud,
> The mistress of his soul must be a cloud!

> PETER PINDAR.

Miss Dorcas Turton was a charming young woman, and you must now be made farther acquainted with her. She is the daughter of Mr. Samuel Turton of Staffordshire; her mother, by marriage, still retained her maiden name, which was Miss Jemima Turton, of Oxfordshire, grand-daughter of the honourable Sir John Turton, Knight, one of the Judges of the Court of King's Bench. Mr. Samuel Turton had a large fortune of his own, and about twenty thousand pounds with his wife Miss Jemima, but by law-suits, and an unhappy turn for gaming, he dissipated nearly the

H

whole of it, and was obliged to have recourse to trade to help to support his family.

> " 'Tis loft at dice, what ancient honour won,
> " Hard, when the father plays away the fon."

He opened a fhop as a fadler's ironmonger; but being but little acquainted with trade, and as his old propenfity to gaming never quitted him, it is no wonder that he did not fucceed in his bufinefs; and to crown all his other follies, he was bound for a falfe friend in a large fum; this completed his ruin.

His wife died in Jan. 1773, and his final ruin enfued a few months after; fo that from that time to his death he was partly fupported by his daughter Mifs Dorcas Turton, who cheerfully fubmitted to keep a fchool, and worked very hard at plain work, by which means fhe kept her father from want.

> The worft of ills to poverty ally'd,
> Is the proud fcuff, it hurts man's honeft pride.
>
> OWEN's Juvenal.

The old gentleman died a few months after I came into the fhop. Being partly acquainted with this young lady's goodnefs to her father, I concluded that fo amiable a daughter was very likely to make a good wife; I alfo knew that fhe was immoderately fond of books, and would frequently devote half of the night to reading; this turn of mind in her was the greateft of all recommendations to me, who having acquired a few ideas, was at that time reftlefs to increafe them: fo that I was in raptures with the bare thoughts of having a woman to read with, and alfo to read to me.

> Of all the pleafures, noble and refin'd,
> Which form the tafte and cultivate the mind,
> In ev'ry realm where fcience darts its beams,
> From Thule's ice to Afric's golden ftreams,
> From climes where Phœbus pours his orient ray,
> To the fair regions of declining day,
> The " Feaft of Reafon," which from READING fprings,
> To reas'ning man the higheft folace brings.
> 'Tis BOOKS a lafting pleafure can fupply,
> Charm while we live, and teach us how to die.
>
> LACKINGTON's Shop Bill.

I embraced the first opportunity after her recovery to make her acquainted with my mind; and as we were no strangers to each other's characters and circumstances, there was no need of a long formal courtship; so I prevailed on her not to defer our union longer than the 30th of January, 1776, when, for the second time. I entered into the holy state of matrimony.

> ——— Wedded Love is founded on esteem,
> Which the fair merits of the mind engage :
> For those are charms that never can decay,
> But Time, which gives new whiteness to the swan,
> Improves their lustre.   FENTON.

I am,

Dear Friend,

Yours.

LETTER XXV.

> Reason re-baptized me when adult :
> Weigh'd true from false, in her impartial scale.
> Truth, radiant goddess ! sallies on my soul !
> And puts delusion's dusky train to flight.   YOUNG.
>
> All the mystic lights were quench'd.   LEE.
>
> To thee, Philosophy ! to thee the light,
> The guide of mortals through their mental night,
> By whom the world in all its views is shewn,
> Our guide through nature's works, and in our own,
> Who place in order being's wond'rous chain,
> Save where those puzzling, stubborn links remain,
> By art divine involv'd, which man can ne'er explain.
>   CRABBE.

DEAR FRIEND,

I Am now in February 1776, arrived at an important period of my life. Being lately recovered from a very painful, dangerous, and hope-

H 2

less illness, I found myself once more in a confirmed state of health, surrounded by my little stock in trade, which was but just saved from thieves, and which to me was an immense treasure.

> Pass some fleeting moments by,
> All at once the tempests fly;
> Instant shifts the clouded scene;
> Heav'n renews its smiles serene.   West's PINDAR.

The following lines by Isaac Hawkins Browne, Esq. on Pleasure and Pain are also worth quoting:

> " Cease then, ah! cease, fond mortal to repine
>   " At laws, which Nature wisely did ordain;
> " Pleasure, what is it? rightly to define,
>   " 'Tis but a short-lived interval from Pain;
> " Or, rather each alternately renew'd,
> " Gives to our lives a sweet vicissitude."

Add to the above, my having won a second time in a game where the odds were so much against me; or to use another simile, my having drawn another prize in the lottery of wedlock, and thus like John Buncle, repaired the loss of one very valuable woman by the acquisition of another still more valuable.

> O woman! let the libertine decry,
> Rail at the virtuous love he never felt,
> Nor wish'd to feel.—Among the sex there are
> Numbers as greatly good as they are fair;
> Where rival virtues strive which brightens most,
> Beauty the smallest excellence they boast;
> Where all unite substantial bliss to prove,
> And give mankind in them a taste of joys above.
>   HAYWARD.

Dr. Watts, in his poem entitled Few Happy Matches, supposes that souls come forth in pairs, male and female, and that the reason why there are so many unhappy matches, is occasioned by many souls losing their partners in the way to this lower world. That the happy matches takes place when souls arrive safe, and meeting again instinctively, impel the bodies they animate towards each other, so as to produce an hymeneal union. Thus, according to the good doctor's hypothesis, it must be very dangerous indeed for a person to be married more than once;

but perhaps such cases as mine, might be exceptions to the general rule, and three souls might come out together; but how very fortunate was I to meet with both my partners.

> Marriage is itself, I take it,
> Just as the parties please to make it.   HUMPHREYS.

Reflecting on the above united circumstances, I found in my heart an unusual sensation, such as until then I had been a stranger to, and something within me adopted the sentiments of Anacreon, when he said,

> " Hence, sorrows, hence, nor rudely dare
> " Disturb my transient span;
> " Be mine to live (adieu to care)
> " As cheerful as I can."

My mind began to expand, intellectual light and pleasure broke in and dispelled the gloom of fanatical melancholy; the sourness of my natural temper, which had been much increased by superstition, (called by Swift, " the spleen of the soul,") in part gave way, and was succeeded by cheerfulness, and some degree of good-nature.

> As when a wretch from thick polluted air,
> And dungeon-horrors by kind fate discharg'd,
> Climbs some fair eminence, where æther pure,
> Surrounds him, and Elysian prospects rise,
> His heart exults, his spirits cast their load;
> As if new born he triumphs in the change.   YOUNG.

It was in one of these cheerful moods that I one day took up the Life of John Buncle; and it is impossible for my friend to imagine with what eagerness and pleasure I read through the whole four volumes of this whimsical, sensible, pleasing work; it was written by Thomas Amory, Esq. (who was living in the year 1788, at the great age of 97). I know not of any work more proper to be put into the hands of a poor ignorant, bigotted, superstitious methodist; but the misfortune is, that scarce one of them will read any thing but what suits with their own narrow notions, so that they shut themselves up in darkness, and exclude every ray of intellectual light; which puts me in mind of the enthusiasts on the banks of the Ganges, who will not look at any thing beyond the tips of their noses. By the time I had gone through the last volume,

> My soul had took its freedom up.   GREEN.

John Buncle's merry life puts me in mind of Peter Pindar's sensible, whimsical lines:

> " Who told man that he must be curs'd on earth ?
> " The GOD of NATURE ? no such thing !
> " Heav'n whisper'd him, the moment of his birth,
> " Don't cry, my lad, but dance and sing ;
> " Don't be too wise, and be an ape,
> " In colours let the soul be dress'd, not crape.

> " Roses shall smooth LIFE's journey, and adorn ;
> " Yet mind me if, through want of grace,
> " Thou mean'st to fling the blessing in my face,
> " Thou hast full leave to tread upon a thorn."

> Yet some there are, of men I think the worst,
> Poor imps ! unhappy if they can't be curs'd ;
>   For ever brooding over mis'ry's eggs,
> As though life's pleasure were a deadly sin ;
> Musing for ever for a gin
>   To catch their happiness by the legs.

I also received great benefits from reading Coventry's Philemon to Hydaspes; it consists of dialogues on false religion, extravagant devotion, &c. in which are many very curious remarks on visionaries of various ages and sects. This work is complete in five parts octavo. There has also been a decent Scotch edition, published in twelves ; both editions are rather scarce.

I now began to enjoy many innocent pleasures and recreations in life, without the fear of being eternally damn'd for a laugh, a joke, or for spending a sociable evening with a few friends, going to the play-house, &c. &c.

> ——— The hours so spent shall live,
> Not unapplauded in the book of heav'n ;
> For dear and precious as the moments are
> Permitted man, they are not all for deeds
> Of active virtue, give me none to vice,
> And heav'n will not separation ask,

> For many a summer's day and winter's eve,
> So spent as best amuses us,
> We trifle all, and he that best deserves,
> Is but a trifler—'tis a trifling world.   Village Curate.

In short, I saw that true religion was no way incompatible with, or an enemy to rational pleasures of any kind. As life (says one) is the gift of heaven, it is religion to enjoy it.

> Fools by excess make varied pleasure pall,
> The wife man's moderate, and enjoys them all.
>   VOLTAIRE, by Franklin.

I now also began to read with great pleasure the rational and moderate divines of all denominations: and a year or two after I began with metaphysics, in the intricate, though pleasing, labyrinths of which I have occasionally since wandered, nor am I ever likely to find my way out.

> " Like a guide in a mist have I rambled about,
> " And now come at last where at first I set out;
> " And unless for new lights we have reason to hope,
> " In darkness it must be my fortune to grope."

I am not in the least uneasy on that head, as I have no doubt of being in my last moments able to adopt the language of one of the greatest men that ever existed.

> " Great God, whose being by thy works is known,
> " Hear my last words from thy eternal throne:
> " If I mistook, 'twas while thy law I sought,
> " I may have err'd, but thou wert in each thought;
> " Fearless I look beyond the opening grave,
> " And cannot think the God who being gave,
> " The God whose favours made my bliss o'erflow,
> " Has doom'd me, after death, to endless woe."

In the mean time I can sincerely pronounce the following lines of Mr. Pope:

> " If I am right, thy grace impart,
>   " Still in the right to stay;
> " If I am wrong, O teach my heart,
>   " To find the better way."

Having begun to think rationally, and reason freely on religious matters, you may be sure I did not long remain in Mr. Wesley's society. No:

> A ray of welcome light disclosed my path!
> Joyful I left the shadowy realms of death,
> And hail'd the op'ning glories of the sky.
>
> BOYD's Dante's Inferno.

What is remarkable, I well remember that some years before, Mr. Wesley told his society in Broadmead, Bristol, in my hearing, that he could never keep a bookseller six months in his flock (all fanatics are enemies to reason). He was then pointing out the danger that attended close reasoning in matters of religion and spiritual concerns, in reading controversies, &c. At that time I had not the least idea of my ever becoming a bookseller; but I no sooner began to give scope to my reasoning faculties, than the above remarkable assertion occured to my mind.

But that which rather hastened my departure from methodism was this:—The methodist preachers were continually reprobating the practice of masters and mistresses keeping servants at home on Sundays, to dress dinners, which prevented them from hearing the word of God (by the word of God they mean their own jargon of nonsense); assuring them if the souls of such servants were damned, they might in a great measure lay their damnation at the doors of such masters and mistresses, who rather than eat a cold dinner, would be guilty of breaking the sabbath, and risking the souls of their servants. How great was my surprize, when I discovered that these very men who were continually preaching up fasting, abstinence, &c. to their congregation, and who wanted others to dine off cold dinners, or eat bread and cheese, &c. would themselves not even *sup*, without roasted fowls, &c.

This I found to be fact, as I several times had occasion, after attending the preaching, to go into the kitchen behind the *old Foundery* (which at that time was Mr. Wesley's preaching-house); there I saw women who had been kept from hearing the sermon, &c. they being employed in roasting fowls, and otherwise providing good suppers for the preachers.

" A cart-load, lo! their stomachs steal;
" Yet swear they cannot make a meal !"

" So," said I, " you lay burthens on other men's shoulders, but will not so much as touch them yourselves with one of your fingers."

A ridiculous instance of the same nature happened also some years since at Taunton. One of Mr. Wesley's preachers, whose name was Cotterrell, assured his congregation, from time to time, that every baker that baked meat on Sundays would be damned, and every person that partook of such meat would also be damned ; on which a poor baker shut up his oven on Sundays; the consequence was, that he lost his customers, as such bakers as baked their victuals on Sunday, had their custom on other days, of course the poor baker's family was nearly reduced to the workhouse : when one Sunday passing by the house, where he knew the preacher was to dine, he was very much surprized to see a baked leg of pork carried into the house, and after a few minutes reflection, he rushed in, and found the pious preacher eating part of the baked leg of pork ; on which he bid farewel to the methodists, and again took care for his family.

It is perhaps worth remarking, that many poor hair-dressers in Mr. Wesley's society are reduced to extreme poverty; they cannot get employment, as they will not dress hair on Sundays; and I find that a poor milkwoman, who until the beginning of the year 1792, maintained her family in a decent manner, was lately frightened out of her understanding by a methodist preacher; her crime was selling milk on Sundays. The poor wretch is now confined in Bedlam, and her five children are in a workhouse. But driving people mad they treat as a trifling affair. A few weeks since, a methodist preacher in Grub-street, in one of his discourses, made use of the following language to his auditory.—" You spread a report I am informed, that my doctrine has such effect upon some, that they run mad; but I should much rather send five thousand to Bedlam, than that one soul should be sent to hell."

I at this time know a bookseller, who being a methodist, is so conscientious as to have his hair dressed on the evening of every Saturday, and to prevent its being discomposed in the night, he on those nights always sleeps in his elbow chair. Indeed some tell the story different, and say, that his hair is dressed Saturday morning, and by sleeping in his chair he saves the expence of dressing on Sundays; others say, that the first is the fact, and that he hinted at it in his shop-bills, in order that the public might know where to find a tradesman that had a very tender conscience.

I was one day called aside, and a hand-bill was given me: thinking it to be a quack doctor's bill for a certain disease, I expressed my surprise at its being given to me in such a particular manner; but on reading it, I found it contained a particular account of the wonderful conversion of a John Biggs, when he was twenty-one years of age. Mr. Biggs says, that ever since that time he has had *communion with God his Father every hour.* He publishes this bill (he says) for the glory of God; but that the public might have an opportunity of dealing with this wonderful saint and perfectly holy man, he put his address in capitals, John Biggs, No. 98, Strand. I keep this bill as a curiosity.

The following note was some years since given to the clerk, for the clergyman at St. Michael's church, Bristol:—" I, Mary Lockhart, return Almighty God my most hearty thanks, for the benefits received in my soul, through the burning and shining lights, Mr. Cennick and Mr. Hall. I have not only received remission for my sins past, present, and to come, but am now entered into the rest (or made perfect) of the children of God. Mary Lockhart."

I will conclude this letter in the words of Col. Lambert, in the comedy of the Hypocrite.—" I cannot see with temper, sir, so many religious mountebanks impose on the unwary multitude; wretches, who make a trade of religion, and shew no uncom-

mon concern for the next world, only to raise their
fortunes with greater security in this. I always respect piety and virtue, but there are pretenders to religion, as well as to courage; and as the truly brave
are not such as make much noise about their valour,
so, I apprehend, the truly good seldom or never deal
in much grimace. I can never pay the same regard
to the mask that I do to the face."

Where is the man, who, prodigal of mind,
In one wide wish embraces human kind?
All pride of sects, all party zeal above,
Whose *guide* is reason, and whose god is love,
Fair nature's friend, a foe to fraud and art—
Where is the man, so welcome to my heart!

J. LANGHORNE.

I am,

Dear Friend,

Yours.

LETTER XXVI.

Good morrow to thee: How dost do?
I only just call'd in, to shew
My love, upon this blessed day,
As I by chance came by this way.

BUTLER's Posth. Works.

" Let not your weak unknowing hand
" Presume God's bolts to throw,
" And deal damnation round the land,
" On each you judge his foe."

DEAR FRIEND,

I Had no sooner left Mr. Wesley's
society, and begun to talk a little more like a rational
being, but I found that I had incurred the hatred of
some, the pity of others, the envy of many, and the
displeasure of *all* Mr. Wesley's—*old women!*

H 6

No feared confcience is fo fell,
As that which has been burnt with zeal;
For chriftian charity's as well
A great impediment to zeal,
As zeal a peftilent difeafe,
To charity and peace.   BUTLER's Remains.

So that for a long time I was conftantly teafed with
their impertinent nonfenfe. I believe that never was
a poor devil fo plagued.

Superftition is dreadful in her wrath,
Her dire Anathemas againft you dart.   HENRIADE.

Some as they paffed by my door in their way to
the Foundery, would only make a ftop and lift up
their hands, turn up the whites of their eyes, fhake
their heads, groan and pafs on. Many would call in
and take me afide, and after making rueful faces,
addrefs me with, " Oh, Brother Lackington! I am
very forry to find that you who began in the Spirit
are now like to end in the flefh. Pray, Brother, do
remember Lot's wife." Another would interrupt me
in my bufinefs, to tell me, that " He that putteth
his hand to the plough, and looketh back, is unfit
for the kingdom." Another had juft called as he was
paffing by, to caution me againft the bewitching
fnares of profperity. Others again called to know
if I was as happy then as I was when I conftantly
fought the Lord with my brethren, in prayer meeting, in clafs, in band, &c. When I affured them
that I was more happy, they in a very folemn manner affured me, that I was under a very great delufion
of the devil; and when I by chance happened to
laugh at their enthufiaftic rant, fome have run out of
my fhop, declaring that they were afraid to ftay
under the fame roof with me, left the houfe fhould
fall on their heads.

Each zealot thus elate with ghoftly pride,
Adores his God, and hates the world befide.
                                   J. LANGHORNE.

Sometimes I have been accofted in fuch an alarming manner as though the houfe was on fire, with
" Oh! brother! brother! you are faft afleep! and

the flames of hell are taking hold of you;" which reminds me of the following lines :

> —— Were hell demolish'd now,
> Another must be had for you ;
> That providence were falsely nam'd,
> If such a monster is not dam'd.
>
> Lord Gardenston.

A certain preacher assured me, in the presence of several gentlemen, that the devil would soon toss me about in the flames of hell with a pitchfork. This same eloquent mild preacher used occasionally to strip to his shirt to *dodge* the devil.

Mr. E. a gentleman of my acquaintance, going through some alley, one Sunday, hearing a very uncommon noise, was led by curiosity to the house from whence it proceeded, and there he saw elevated above an assembly of old women, &c. this taylor, stript in his shirt, with his wig off, and the collar of his shirt unbuttoned, sweating, foaming at the mouth, and bellowing like a baited bull. In the above manner it seems he would often amuse himself and his congregation for near two hours ;

> Cursing from his sweating tub,
> The cavaliers of Belzebub.   Butler's Posth. Works.

Some of the *Tabernacle* saints assured me, that I never had one grain of saving grace, and that when I thought myself a child of God, I was only deluded by the devil, who being now quite sure of me, did not think it worth his while to deceive me any longer. Others advised me to take care of sinning against light and knowledge, and piously hoped that it was not quite too late ; that I had not (they hoped) committed the *unpardonable* sin against the Holy Ghost. Others again, who happened to be in a better humour, often told me that they should see me brought back to the true sheepfold, as they really hoped I had once been in a state of grace, and if so, that I always was in grace, in spite of all I could do : the Lord would never quit his hold of me; that I might fall *foully*, but that it was impossible for me to fall *finally*, as in the end I should be brought back or the shoulders of the everlasting gospel; for when God came to number his jewels, not one would be missing.

One of these righteous men, after passing some encomiums on me for my moral character, assured me that I had by no means fallen so low as many of God's dear children had fallen; but fall as low as they possibly can, said he, they are still God's children, for although they may "be black with sin, they are fair within." He then read to me the following passage out of a pamplet written against Mr. Fletcher by R. Hill: "David stood as completely "justified in the everlasting righteousness of Christ, "at the time when he caused Uriah to be murdered, "and was committing adultery with his wife, as he "was in any part of his life. For all the sins of the "elect, be they more or be they less, be they past, pre- "sent, or to come, were for ever done away. So that "every one of those elect stand spotless in the sight "of God." Is not this a very comfortable kind of doctrine? The pernicious consequences of such tenets, impressed on the minds of the ignorant followers of these quacks in religion, must be obvious to every person capable of reflection. They have nothing to do but enlist themselves in the band of the elect, and no matter then how criminal their life!

Thus, my dear friend, I was for a long time coaxed by some, threatened with all the tortures of the damned by others, and constantly teased by all the methodists who came near me.

"Surrounded by foes, as I sat in my chair,
"Who attacked like dogs that are baiting a bear."

I at last determined to laugh at all their ridiculous perversions of the scripture, and their spiritual cant. As Peter Pindar says;

"My honest anger boil'd to view
"The snuffling, long-fac'd, canting crew."

For as Dr. Dalton justly remarks,

"A conscience void of blame her front erect,
"Her God she fears, all other fear rejects."

The confequence (as might be expected) was, they
pioufly and charitably configned me over to be tor-
mented by the devil, and every where declared that
I was turned a downright Atheift. But the afperfions
of fuch fanatics gave me no concern ; for

> —— If there's a power above us,
> (And that there is, all nature cries aloud
> Thro' all her works) he muft delight in Virtue ;
> And that which he delights in muft be happy."
>
> ADDISON'S Cato.

And no matter " when or where." After relating
fuch ridiculous ftuff as the above, I think that I cannot conclude this better than with Swift's humorous
and fatirical account of the Day of Judgment ; fo
humorous that I would not have quoted it, had it
not been written by a divine of the Church of England.

> " With a whirl of thought oppreſs'd,
> " I funk from reverie to reft,
> " An horrid vifion feiz'd my head,
> " I faw the graves give up their dead :
> " Jove arm'd with terrors burfts the fkies !
> " And thunder roars, and light'ning flies !
> " Amaz'd, confus'd, its fate unknown,
> " The world ftands trembling at his throne !
> " While each pale finner hung his head,
> " Jove nodding, fhook the heavens and faid,
> " Offending race of human kind,
> " By nature, reafon, learning blind ;
> " You who thro' frailty ftept afide,
> " And you who never fell thro' pride,
> " You who in different fects were ftrain'd,
> " And come to fee each other damn'd !
> " (So fome folks told you, but they knew
> " No more of Jove's defigns than you)
> " The world's mad bufinefs now is o'er,
> " And I refent thefe pranks no more.
> " —— I to fuch blockheads fet my wit !
> " I damn fuch fools ! go, go, you're bit."

I am,

Dear Friend,

Yours,

LETTER XXVII.

—— Say, what founds my ear invade,
From Delphi's venerable shade ?
The temple rocks, the laurel waves !
  The god ! the god ! the sybil cries.
Her figure swells ; she foames, she raves !
  Her figure swells to more than mortal size.
Streams of rapture roll along,
  Silver notes ascend the skies :
Wake, Echo, wake, and catch the song,
  Oh, catch it ere it dies.
The sybil speaks, the dream is o'er,
The holy harpings charm no more,
In vain she checks the god's controul,
  His madding spirit fills the frame,
And moulds the features of her soul,
  Breathing a prophetic flame.
The cavern frowns ! its hundred mouths unclose !
And, in the thunder's voice the fate of empire flows !

Superstition, a Poem.

DEAR FRIEND,

THERE is a very extraordinary passage in Rousseau on Fanaticism. It is printed in his Thoughts, published by Debrett, vol. I. page 11.

"Bayle (says he) has acutely proved that Fanati-
"cism is more pernicious than Atheism. This is in-
"contestable. What he has been very careful, how-
"ever, not to mention, and, what is not less true is,
"that Fanaticism, although sanguinary and cruel, is
"still an exalted passion, which elevates the heart of
"man, raises him above the fear of death, multi-
"plies his resources exceedingly, and which only
"wants to be better directed, to be productive of the
"most sublime virtues. (He adds) the argumenta-
"tive spirit of controversy and philosophy, on the
"contrary, attaches us to life, enervates and debases
"the soul, concentrates all passions in the baseness
"of self-interest, and thus gradually saps the real
"foundation of all society."

I have somewhere read of a man, who having
been cured of madness, he, instead of thanking his
friends and the physician, was displeased with them,
for having deprived him of the happiness he possessed
in a state of insanity. And methinks Rousseau seems
to be much of the same mind. But how was it possible that he should so glaringly contradict himself in
so few lines? Plutarch was the first that asserted, that
superstition was worse than Atheism. Lord Bacon, in
his Essays, says the same; and Bayle has incontestably
proved it, as Rousseau acknowledges. We know
from a great authority that "Fanaticism is to superstition what a delirium is to a fever, and fury to anger.
He who has extasies and visions, who takes dreams
for realities, and his imagination for prophesies, is an
enthusiast; and he who sticks not at supporting his
folly by murder, is a fanatic;" and yet Rousseau,
when he acknowledges that fanaticism is sanguinary
and cruel, calls it "an exalted passion, which elevates the heart of man, and raises him above the
fear of death, multiplies his recourses exceedingly."
Of all the absurdities wrote by great men, this seems
to me the greatest. If we except that which he asserts
in the following lines: "Philosophy attaches to life,
enervates and debases the soul, concentrates all the
passions in the business of self-interest, and thus gradually, says he, saps the real foundation of all society?" That the very reverse of what Rousseau here
asserts is the truth, must be obvious to every rational
being: no one can help thinking he must have
wrote these lines in a fit of insanity, in a fanatical
conventicle. "The superstitious (says Plutarch) are
in continual fear of the divine powers, whom they
suppose to be cruel, and hurtful beings; and he that
fears the divine powers fears every thing. The land,
the sea, air, sky, darkness, light, silence and dreams.
Even slaves forget their cruel masters, and prisoners
their fetters; but superstition fills the soul even in
sleep, with prodigious forms and ghostly spectres."

But still some frightful tales, some furious threats,
By——— form'd those grave and holy cheats,

Invent new fears, whose horrid looks should fright,
And damp thy thoughts.   CREECH's Lucretius.

A much greater man than Rousseau says, " The only remedy for the infectious disease of Fanaticism, is a *philosophical* temper, which spreading through society, at length softens manners, and obviates the excesses of the distemper; for whenever it gets ground, the best way is to fly from it and stay till the air is purified. The laws and religion are no preservative against this mental pestilence; religion so far from being a salutary aliment in these cases, in infected brains, becomes poison."

" The laws likewise have proved very ineffectual against this spiritual rage; it is indeed like reading an order of council to a lunatic. The creatures are firmly persuaded, that the spirit by which they are actuated is above all laws, and that their enthusiasm is the only law they are to regard."

" What can be answered to a person who tells you, that he had rather obey God than man; and who, in consequence of that choice, is certain to gain heaven by cutting your throat ?"

" Hence, to the realms of night, dire demon,
" Thy chain of adamant can bind
" That little world, the human mind,
" And sink its noblest powers to impotence.
" Wake the lion's loudest roar,
" Clot his shaggy mane with gore,
" With flashing fury bid his eye-balls shine,
" Meek is his savage sullen soul to thine!
" Thy touch Superstition! has steel'd the breast,
" Where thro' her rainbow-shower, soft pity smil'd;
" Has clos'd the heart each god like virtue blest,
" To all the silent pleadings of his child.
" At thy command he plants the dagger deep,
" At thy command exults, tho' nature bid him weep."

Was it possible to keep the enthusiast at all times free from fanaticism, I believe the mischief to society would not be so great, as in that case, enthusiasm would be a more harmless madness; but it seems impossible to keep the two characters separate, which is the reason that the terms are often used by writers indiscriminately.

Enthusiasts and fanatics are in general conscious of their own inability to reason, hence they all exclaim against it, and "immediate revelation being a much easier way to establish their opinions," they have recourse to it in all difficulties, and nothing is more common among the methodists, than to hear them assert that they become acquainted with the truth of all the mysteries of Christianity, by their being revealed to them by "the Spirit of the Lord." Mr. Locke says, (speaking of enthusiasts) "They understand that God has promised to enlighten the mind, by a ray darted into the mind immediately from the fountain of light; and who then has so good a title to expect it, as those who are his peculiar people."

"Their minds being thus prepared, whatever groundless opinion comes to settle itself strongly upon their fancies, is an illumination from God. And whatever odd action, they find in themselves a strong inclination to do, that impulse is concluded to be a call from heaven, and must be obeyed; it is a commission from above, and they cannot err in executing it.

"This I take to be properly enthusiasm, which, though founded neither on reason nor divine revelation, but rising from the conceits of a warmed, or over-weening brain, works yet where it once gets footing, more powerfully on the persuasions and actions of men, than either of those two, or both together; men being most forwardly obedient to the impulses they receive from themselves, and the whole man is sure to act more vigorously where the whole is carried by a natural motion. For strong conceit, like a new principle, carries all easily with it, when got above common sense; and freed from all restraint, of reason, and check of reflection, it is heightened into a divine authority, in concurrence with our own temper and inclination."

—————— I feel him now
Like a strong spirit, charm'd into a tree,
That leaps and moves the wood without a wind:
The roused god, as all the while he lay
Entomb'd alive, starts, and dilates himself;

He struggles, and he tears my aged trunk
With holy fury: my old arteries burst;
My shrivell'd skin, like parchment, crackles at the holy fire
DRYDEN's Œdipus.

These impulses and revelations have been made the
pretext not only for thousands of absurdities and ridiculous whims, but also for every kind of wickedness. It is but a few years since, there were in Po-
land a sect of these fanatics, who all at once were seized
with an impulse to kill their own children, which
they did most devoutly, in order to secure the salvation of those innocent victims. Lucretius says,

" Such impious use was of religion made,
" Such dev'lish acts religion could persuade."

What, my dear friend, can preserve mankind from
this pestilence so effectually as philosophy, which
Rousseau attempts to degrade. " Painful and corporal punishment (says Beccaria) should never be applied to fanaticism, for being founded on pride, it
glories in persecution. Infamy and ridicule only
should be employed against fanatics; in the first,
their pride will be overbalanced by the pride of the
people; and we judge of the power of the second, if
we consider that even truth is obliged to summon all
her force, attacked with error armed with ridicule.
Thus by opposing one passion to another, and opinion
to opinion, a wise legislator puts an end to the admiration of the populace occasioned by a false principle,
the original absurdity of which is veiled by some
well deduced consequences."

It is for the above reasons that I have held up to
public ridicule that sect of fanatics, among whom I
lost so much of my time in the early part of my life;
and for the same reasons I hope you will read with
patience a few more of my letters, in which I purpose to excite you to join with me in laughing a little
more at the absurdities of the methodists.

I am, dear friend, yours,

LETTER XXVIII.

In London streets is often seen
A hum-drum saint with holy mien,
His looks most primitively wear
An ancient Abrahamick air,
And like bad copies of a face,
The good original disgrace.

BUTLER's Posth. Works.

" Some there are who seek for private holes,
" Securely in the dark to damn their souls,
" Wear vizards of hypocrisy to steal,
" And slink away in masquerade, to hell."

DEAR FRIEND,

IT being generally known that I
had for many years been a strict methodist, since I
have freed myself from their shackles, I have been
often asked if I did not believe or rather know, that
the methodists were a vile sect of hypocrites altogether? My reply has been uniformly in the negative.
I am certain that they are not in general so. The
major part of them indeed are very ignorant (as is the
case with enthusiasts of every religion); but I believe
that a great number of the methodists are sincere, honest, friendly people; in justice to those of that description it may not be amiss to observe, that many artful,
sly, designing persons, having noticed their character,
connection, &c. and knowing that a religious person
is in general supposed to be honest and conscientious,
have been induced to join their societies, and by assuming an appearance of extraordinary sanctity, have
the better been enabled to cheat and defraud such as
were not guarded against their hypocritical wiles.
Rochefoucault says, that " truth does not so much
good in the world, as its appearance does mischief."

Making religion a disguise,
Or cloak to all their villanies.

BUTLER's Posth. Works.

I have also reason to believe that there are not a few, who think they can as it were afford to cheat and defraud, on the score of having right notions of religion in their head, hearing what they deem orthodox teachers, going to prayer-meetings, &c.

There are again others who think, that grace is so free and so easy to be had, or in other words, that as they can have pardon for all kinds of sins, and that at any time whenever they please, they under this idea make very little conscience of running up large scores, to which practice I fear such doctrines as I noticed in my last, from the pen of Mr. Hill, have not a little contributed.

> The wrath of gods, tho' dreadful, is but slow,
> With tardy footsteps comes th' avenging blow,
> If all the bad are punish'd, 'twill be long
> Ere my turn comes to suffer in the throng.
> I may find mercy from the power divine,
> They oft o'erlook such moderate guilt as mine,
> Crimes, quite the same, oft meet a different end.
>
> OWEN's Juvenal.

I have often thought that great hurt has been done to society by the methodist preachers, both in town and country, attending condemned malefactors, as by their fanatical conversation, visionary hymns, bold and impious applications of the scriptures, &c. many dreadful offenders against law and justice, have had their passions and imaginations so worked upon, that they have been sent to the other world in such raptures, as would better become martyrs innocently suffering in a glorious cause, than criminals of the first magnitude.

A great number of narratives of these sudden conversions and triumphant exits have been compiled, many of them published, and circulated with the greatest avidity, to the private emolument of the editors, and doubtless to the great edification of all sinners, long habituated to a course of villainous depredations on the lives and properties of the honest part of the community; and many such accounts as have not appeared in print, have been assiduously pro-

claimed in all methodist chapels and barns, throughout the three kingdoms; by which the good and pious
of every denomination have been scandalized, and
notorious offenders encouraged to persevere, trusting
sooner or later, to be honoured with a similar degree
of notice; and thus by a kind of hocus pocus, be suddenly transformed into saints.

The following remarks made by the compilers of
the Monthly Review for 1788, p. 286. and are so applicable to the present subject, that I hope my introducing
the passage will not be deemed improper. After mentioning a couplet in one of the methodistical hymns;
where it said,

> *Believe*, and all your sin's forgiven.
> " Only *believe*, and your's is heaven."

they proceed thus:

" Such doctrine no doubt must be comfortable to
poor wretches so circumstanced as those were to whom
this pious preacher had the goodness to address his
discourse; but some (and those not men of shallow
reflection) have questioned whether it is altogether
right, thus to free the most flagitious outcasts of society from the terrors of an *after-reckoning*; since it is
too well known, that most of them make little account
of their punishment in *this* world. Instead of the
" fearful *looking for of* (future) *judgment*," they are
enraptured with the prospect of a joyful flight " to
the expanded arms of a loving Saviour—longing to
embrace his long lost children." Surely this is not
the way (humanely speaking) to check the alarming
progress of moral depravity; to which, one would
think, *no* kind of *encouragement* ought to be given."

I must observe farther, that the unguarded manner
in which the methodist preachers make tenders of
pardon and salvation, has induced many to join their
fraternity, whose consciences wanted very large plais-
ters indeed! many of those had need to be put under a
course of mortification and penance, but they generally adopt another method; a few quack nostrums,
which they call faith and assurance, dries up the
wound, and they then make themselves as hateful by

affecting to have squeamish consciences, as they really have been obnoxious, for having consciences of very wide latitude indeed. And notwithstanding the affected change, they often are as bad, or worse than ever. Butler says,

> " ——That which owns the fairest pretext,
> " Is often found the indirect'st.
> " Hence 'tis, that hypocrites still paint
> " Much fairer than the real saint;
> " And knaves appear more just and true
> " Than honest men, who make less shew."

As a friend, permit me to advise you never to purchase any thing at a shop where the master of it crams any of his pious nonsense into his shopbill, &c. as you may be assured you will, nine times out of ten, find them, in the end, arrant hypocrites, and as such, make no scruple of cheating in the way of trade, if possible.

This puts me in mind of one of these pious brethren in Petticoat-lane, who wrote in his shop-window, " Rumps and Burs sold here, and Baked Sheep's heads will be continued every night, *if the Lord permit.*" The Lord had no objection: so Rumps, Burs, and Baked *Sheep's heads* were sold there for a long time. And I remember to have seen on a board, near Bedminster-down, " Tripe and cow-heels sold here as usual, except on the Lord's-day, which *the Lord help me to keep holy.*" And on my enquiring about the person who exhibited this remarkable shew-board, at the inn just by, I was informed that the pious tripe-seller generally got drunk on Sundays, after he returned from the barn-preaching; which accounts for his not selling tripe on that day, having full employment (though possibly not so inoffensive) elsewhere.

I also saw in a village near Plymouth, in Devonshire, " Roger Tuttel, *by God's grace and mercy,* kills rats, moles, and all sorts of vermin and venomous creatures." But I need not have gone so far for pious cant, as, no doubt you must remember that a few years since, a certain pious common-councilman of the metropolis, advertised in the public papers for a porter that could carry *three hundred* weight, take care of horses, and *serve the Lord*. Of the same worthy personage I have heard it asserted, that so very conscientious is he, that he once staved a barrel of beer in his cellar, because he detected it *working* on the sabbath-day, which brought to my recollection four lines in drunken Barnaby's Journey:

> " To Banbury came I ; O prophane one !
> " Where I saw a puritane one,
> " Hanging of his cat on Monday,
> " For killing of a mouse on Sunday."

Mr. L—e, a gentleman of my acquaintance informed me, that a methodist neighbour of his, in St. Martin's-lane, who keeps a parcel of fowls, every Saturday night makes a point of conscience of tying together the legs of every cock he has, in order to prevent them from breaking the sabbath, by gallanting the hens on Sundays; as Col. Lambert says Dr. Cantwell used to do by the turkey-cocks.

I have a few more observations to make on this remarkable sect, but fearing I have already tired you, shall reserve them for my next.

> Seeming devotion doth but gild the knave,
> That's neither faithful, honest, just, or brave,
> But where religion does with virtue join,
> It makes a hero like an angel shine. WALLER.

I am,

Dear Friend,

Yours.

I

LETTER XXIX.

Under this ftone refts Hudbras,
A knight as errant as e'er was:
The controverfy only lies,
Whether he was more fool than wife;
Full oft he fuffer'd bangs and drubs,
And full as oft took pains in tubs:
And for the good old caufe ftood buff,
'Gainft many a bitter kick and cuff,
Of which the moft that can be faid,
He pray'd and preach'd, and preach'd and pray'd.
                              BUTLER'S Pofth. Works.

DEAR FRIEND,

IT is very remarkable that while I
was writing the laft five lines of my former letter to
you, on Wednefday the 2d of March, 1791, I received the news of the death of Mr. John Wefley,
who I am informed died that morning at his own
houfe, in the City-road, Moorfields, in the eighty-
eighth year of his age. He had no illnefs, but the
wheels of the machine being worn out, it ftopt of
courfe. As I am on the fubject of methodifm, I
hope you will not deem it impertinent, if I devote a
few lines to this great parent of a numerous fect,
whom I well knew, and feel a pleafure in fpeaking of
with fome refpect.

Several days preceding his interment, being laid in
his coffin, in his gown and band, he was expofed to
the view of all his friends who came, and the public;
and I fuppofe that forty or fifty thoufand perfons had
a fight of him. But the concourfe of people was fo
great, that many were glad to get out of the crowd
without feeing him at all; and although a number of
conftables were prefent, yet the pick-pockets contrived to eafe many of their purfes, watches, &c.

To prevent as much as poffible the dreadful effects
of a mob, he was interred on Wednefday, March the
9th, between five and fix o'clock in the morning, in the
burial ground behind his own chapel in the City-road.

After which, Dr. Whitehead (the physician) preached his funeral sermon; but notwithstanding the early hour, many thousands attended more than the chapel would hold, although it is very large.

As soon as it was known that Mr. Wesley was deceased, a number of needy brethren deemed it a fair opportunity of profiting by it, and each immediately set his ingenuity to work, to compose what he chose to call a *life* of him; and for some weeks since the funeral the chapel-yard and its vicinity have exhibited a truly ludicrous scene, on every night of preaching, owing to the different writers and venders of these hasty performances exerting themselves to secure a good sale; one bawling out that *his* is the *right* life; a second, with a pious shake of the head, declares *his* the real life; a third protests *he* has got the *only genuine* account; and a fourth calls them all vile cheats and impostors, &c. so that between all these competitors, the saints are so divided and perplexed in their opinions, that some decline purchasing either; others willing " to try all, and keep that which is good," buy of each of these respectable venders of the life and last account of that celebrated character; while the uninterested passenger is apt to form a conclusion that the house of prayer is again become a den of thieves. Thus we see those holy candidates for heaven are so influenced by self-interest, that it

> Turns meek and secret sneaking ones,
> To raw-heads fierce and bloody bones.   HUDIBRAS.

I cannot help thinking that Mr. John Wesley, the father of the methodists, was one of the most respectable enthusiasts that ever lived; as it is generally thought that he believed all that he taught others, and lived the same pious exemplary life, that he would have his followers practice. The sale of his numerous writings produced nett profits to the amount of near TWO THOUSAND POUNDS per annum; and the weekly collection of the classes in London and Westminster amounted to a very large sum; besides this, great sums were collected at the sacraments and love-feasts, for quarterly tickets, private and public subscriptions, &c. &c. In a pamphlet which was published in the beginning of the year 1792, by an old member of their society, it is asserted that for the last ten years, the sums collected in Great Britain and Ireland, have amounted to no less than FOUR HUNDRED THOUSAND POUNDS per annum, which reminds me of Peter Pindar's humorous lines:

> " I've often read these pious whims,
> " Methodist's sweet damnation hymns,
> " That chant of heav'nly riches,
> " What have they done? Those heav'nly strains,
> " Devou'ly squeez'd from canting brains,
> " But fill'd their earthly breeches."

Besides the above, many private collections are made in all his societies throughout the three kingdoms, so that Mr. Wesley might have amassed an immense fortune, had riches been his object. But instead of accumulating wealth, he expended all his own private property: and I have been often informed, from good authority, that he never denied relief to a poor person that asked him. To needy tradesmen I have known him to give ten or twenty pounds at once. In going a few yards from his study to the pulpit, he generally gave away an handful of half-crowns to poor old people of his society. He was indeed charitable to an extreme, as he often gave to unworthy objects, nor would he keep money sufficient to hold out on his journies, One of his friends informs me that he left but 4l. 10s. behind him: and I have heard him declare that he would not die worth twenty pounds, except his books for sale, which he has left to the " general methodist fund, for carrying on the work of God, by itinerant preachers," charged only with a rent of eighty-five pounds a year, which he has left to the wife and children of his brother Charles.

His learning and great abilities are well known. But I cannot help noticing that in one of his publications (stepping out of his line) he betrayed extreme weakness and credulity, though no doubt his intentions were good. What I allude to is his *Primitive Physic*, a work certainly of a dangerous tendency, as

the majority of remedies therein prescribed are most
assuredly inefficacious, and many of them very dangerous, if administered. The consequence of the
first is, that while poor ignorant people are trying
these remedies (besides the very great probability of
their mistaking the case) the diseases perhaps become
so inveterate as to resist the power of more efficacious
remedies properly applied ; and with regard to those
of a highly dangerous nature, how rash to trust them
in the hands of such uninformed people as this book
was almost solely intended for, especially when sanc-
tioned by the name of an author whose influence impressed the minds of the unfortunate patients with the
most powerful conviction. Many fatal effects, I fear,
have been produced by a blind adherence to this
compilation ; which carries with it more the appearance of being the production of an ignorant opi-
nionated old woman, than of the man of science and
education. One melancholy instance is fresh in my
memory ; a much esteemed friend having fallen an
immediate sacrifice to an imprudent application of
one of these remedies.

Permit me just to give you one specimen of the
author's wonderful abilities, by quoting a receipt,
which if not an *infallible remedy*, must at least be acknowledged to be a singular one.

" To cure a windy Cholic."

" Suck a healthy woman daily; this (says Mr.
Wesley) was tried by my father."

Should you, my dear friend, be desirous of per-
using a variety of remedies, equally *judicious* as well
as *efficacious* with those of Mr. Wesley, you will meet
with ample satisfaction by turning to " *Dom Pernety's
Voyage to the Falkland Islands*," page 153 to 162.
quarto edition.

Many of the receipts there inserted are so truly
curious, I can scarce refrain from treating you with
a few specimens, but some of them being *very* indelicate, I must be cautious in selecting; for, like Simpkin,

" I pity the ladies so modest and nice."

I 3

Take the two following, one being no doubt an effectual remedy for a grievous complaint of that useful quadruped the horse; the other at least equally certain for the cure of one of the most dangerous disorders human nature is subject to.

" To Cure a Foundered Horse."

" Let him take one or two spoonfuls of *common salt* in half a pint of water!"

" For a malignant Fever."

" A live tench applied to the feet for *twelve hours,* then buried *quietly,* or thrown down *the house of office,* and the patient will soon recover."

It was a circumstance peculiarly happy for the practitioners of physic, though no doubt a terrible misfortune to the public, that the difference in religious principles of these two reverend gentlemen proved an effectual bar to the union of their medical abilities, which appear so exactly correspondent; had such an event taken place, that horrid monster *disease* might by this time have been banished from the earth, and the sons of Æsculapius would be doomed to feed on their own compositions or starve! The Rev. Dr. Fordyce, in a late publication, has also given the world a remedy for the cramp, as *delicate* as efficacious.

But here, I think I see you smile at my censuring Mr. Wesley for *stepping out of his line,* when at the. very moment I am committing the same error by obtruding my judgment upon the science of physic.— I shall only reply, many thought I did the same when I commenced bookseller: and a friend once taught me the adage, (be not offended, 'tis the only scrap of Latin I shall give you) " *Ne sutor ultra crepidam.*" But the event has proved it otherwise, and I flatter myself every candid and judicious person capable of judging will think with me on the above subject. I also must inform you, that in one disorder I have been successful even in physic. The fact is this: Mrs. Lackington havingseveral times been cured of the dropsy in the chest, by broom tea; I prescribed it to others, nor has it once failed. The last instance was in 1792, a young lady, an only daughter, being nearly loft to her family, fhe having had the dropfy two years, by my defire took broom tea, a little at a time, once or twice a day, weak or ftrong as fhe could bear. She continued this for feveral months, by which fhe perfectly recovered her health, and I hope fhe will foon have a good hufband, and get another kind of dropfy. But to refume my narrative.

What a pity that fuch a character as Mr. Wefley was, upon the whole, fhould have been a dupe and a rank enthufiaft! A believer in dreams, vifions, immediate revelations, miraculous cures, witchcraft, and many other ridiculous abfurdities, as appears from many paffages of his Journals, to the great difgrace of his abilities and learning; which puts one in mind of Cæfar, who in his Commentaries turns bridge builder, and a maker of engines; of Periander, who although he was an excellent phyfician, quitted phyfic to write bad verfes; Sir Ifaac Newton's Expofition of the Revelations, Milton's Paradife Regained, Dr. Johnfon's unmanly and childifh Devotions, &c. &c. and (to compare fmall things with greater) J. L's turning author.

> This Verro's fault, by frequent praifes fir'd,
> He feveral parts at try'd, in each admir'd;
> That Verro was not ev'ry way complete,
> 'Twas long unknown, and might have been fo yet;
> But—mad, th' unhappy man purfu'd
> That only thing heav'n meant he never fhould;
> And thus his proper road to fame neglected,
> He's ridicul'd for that he but effected. DALACOURT.

However, I think we may fafely affirm that Mr. Wefley was a good fincere and honeft enthufiaft, who denied himfelf many things; and really thought that he difregarded the praife and blame of the world, when he was more courted, refpected, and followed than any man living, ruling over a hundred and twenty thoufand people with an abfolute fway; the love of power feems to have been the main fpring of all his actions. I am inclined to believe that his death will be attended with confequences fomewhat fimilar to thofe which followed the death of Alexander the Great. His fpiritual generals will be putting

in their pretenfions, and foon divide their mafter's
conquefts. His death happened at a time rather
critical to the methodifts, as the *Swedenborgians,* or
New Jerufa'emifts, are gaining ground very faft. Many
of the methodifts, both preachers and hearers, are
already gone over to their party; many more will
now, undoubtedly, follow: and the death of that
great female champion of methodifm, the Countefs
of Huntingdon, which has fince happened, will in
all probability occafion another confiderable defection
from *that* branch of methodifts, and an additional re-
inforcement to the Swedenborgians; a proof of the
fondnefs of mankind for novelty, and the marvellous,
even in religious matters.

Great difcoveries and improvements have of late
years been made in various branches of the arts and
fciences; but valuable and important as thefe difcoveries are, how trifling do they appear when compared with the aftonifhing and wonderful difcoveries
which have been made by the Swedenborgians, who
are, it feems, *beyond a doubt,* " *the only true church of*
God," by them the " *true fcience of the language of*
correfpondence" is difcovered, fo that mankind are no
longer left in the dark; the divine arcana is now laid
open, and myfteries are no longer myfteries. " God
in me fpeaks to God in you;" fo that I can talk to
you of feafting on chariots and horfes, and be perfectly underftood. Although they read any chapter
in the Bible, without exception, publicly in the congregations, yet this excites no blufh in *the moft prudifh*
lady, or the moft delicate virgin, they being quite
fpiritual, and acquainted with the " *true language of*
correfpondence." They never notice indelicate expreffions, being wholly occupied in applying the fpiritual correfponding words. Thefe, my friend, are
glorious difcoveries indeed. And what a pity it is
that fo many thoufand pious learned men fhould
have wafted fo much time in endeavouring to explain
the myfterious parts of the Prophets and the Revelations to no purpofe, but to increafe the trade of bookfellers. It was very providential for them that the
Swedenborgians did not appear in the more early

ages of the church; but a very great loss to mankind
in general; the more so, as it seems the great man,
after whom the sect are named, composed the whole
of his numerous works under the immediate guidance
of the Holy Ghost, which are more valuable than the
Bible. I must just take notice of another wonderful
community.

In the beginning of the year 1786, a strange sect
of religious fanatics sprung up near Dumfries in
Scotland; the first of whom seems to have been a
Lady Buchan, as from her they were called Buchan-
ites. They were but few in number, and all lived in
one house together, both men and women, and had
all things in common. In 1791 an Englishman of
some property joined their society, and gave all that
he had to the common stock. The next day Lady
Buchan proclaimed a fast, which was to be strictly
kept for six weeks; this was no ways pleasing to the
Englishman, so that after he had fasted two days, he
applied to the sheriff, in order to recover his property
from out of the stock of the holy community; but the
sheriff informed him, that as it was a free gift, it was
not in his power to recover it.

Lady Buchan at times called herself the Holy
Spirit, and in that character applied to many people
in order to make them converts to this new sect.

The chief article of their faith was, that they
should never taste of death, but should be translated,
and when any one of them happened to die, the rest
said that it was for want of faith; and when Lady Buchan died, they insisted on keeping her unburied,
declaring that she could not be dead: under this af-
surance she was kept a long time; the magistrates
however at last had her buried by force, to prevent
any bad consequence that might arise from the horrid
stench, which began to make the neighbourhood in-
supportable.

A little before she expired, she called her followers
near her, and informed them, that she had a secret
to communicate to them, which was, that she was
the Virgin Mary, the real mother of Jesus; the same
woman mentioned in the Revelations as being clothed

I 5

with the fun, &c. who was driven into the wilderneſs;
that ſhe had been wandering in the world ever ſince
our Saviour's days; that though ſhe here appeared
to die, they need not be diſcouraged, for ſhe would
only ſleep a little, and in a ſhort time viſit them
again, and conduct them to the New Jeruſalem. I
had this curious account from ſome gentlemen in
Scotland, except that part where ſhe calls herſelf the
Virgin, which I added from the Bee for July 1791.

A ſhort time after Mr. Weſley's chapel was finiſhed
in the City-road, an old gentleman was buried in the
burial ground behind it, who on his death-bed informed his wife, that he ſhould ſoon come to life
again; on which account the door of the vault was
not faſtened, and the old lady paid him a viſit every
day, expecting the performance of his promiſe, this
practice did ſhe continue two years, when the poor
old lady paid him her laſt viſit, and was laid by his
ſide.

I will make ſome further remarks on the methodiſts
in my next.

I am,

Dear Friend,

Yours.

LETTER XXX.

More haughty than the reft, the ——
Appear with belly gaunt, and famifh'd face:
Never was fo deform'd a babe of grace.   DRYDEN.

—————— Ollos made of conflagration,
Of gulphs, of brimftone, and damnation,
Eternal torments, furnace, worm,
Hell-fire, a whirlwind, and a ftorm;
With Mammon, Satan, and perdition,
And *Beelzebub* to help the dish on; .
Belial, and *Lucifer*, and all
The nicknames which *Old Nick* we call.   E. LLOYD.

DEAR FRIEND,

ALTHOUGH Mr. Wefley was
poffeffed of a very great fhare both of natural and acquired abilities, yet I fuppofe it fcarcely neceffary to
inform you, that this is by no means the cafe with his
preachers in general; for although there are amongft
them fome truly fenfible, intelligent men, yet the
major part are very ignorant and extremely illiterate:
many of thefe excellent fpiritual guides, cannot read
a chapter in the Bible, though containing the deep
myfteries, which they have the rafhnefs and pre-
fumption to pretend to explain. Many others cannot
write their own names.

A motly crew, from various callings fprung;
    Some of you have been gipfies, others failors;
Some drays have whiftling driven, or carts of dung,
    And others mighty barbers been and taylors.
                              MAT. BRAMBLE.

But fo great is the ignorance of Mr. Wefley's people
in general, that they often neglect the more rational
and fenfible of their preachers, and are better pleafed
with fuch as are even deftitute of common fenfe;
really believing that the incoherent nonfenfe which
they from time to time pour forth, is dictated by the
Holy Spirit.

I 6.

Thus folly attends to the vapid oration,
And madness mistakes for an apt inspiration.

ANTHONY PASQUIN.

As these noisy declaimers never scruple to call themselves the " servants of the most high God," Ambassadors from heaven, &c. Peter Pindar, speaking of
one of that stamp, seems to think that if he was sent
from God, heaven had made a bad choice : take his
own words :

> " Where'er I hear that stupid parson H—,
> " God's house with ev'ry nonsense fill,
> " And when with blasphemy each sentence cramm'd,
> " And when I hear the impostor cry,
> " I've news, you raggamuffins, from the sky ;
> " I'm come to tell ye, that you'll all be damn'd :
> " I'm come from God, ye strumpets—come from God—
> " I'm God Almighty's servant, hear my voice.
> " Which if it were so, would be vastly odd,
> " Since Heav'n would show bad judgment in the choice."

It is always observable, that the more ignorant
people are, the more confidence they possess. This
confidence, or *impudence*, passes with the vulgar, as a
mark of their being in the right ; and the more the
ignorance of the preachers is discovered, the more
are they brought down to their own standard. Again,
the more ignorant preachers having very contracted
ideas of real religion and manly virtue, of course supply the want of it with a ridiculous fuss about trifles,
which passes with the ignorant for a more sanctified
deportment, and hence arises much of the mischief
which has been so justly charged on the methodists.
For by making the path to heaven so very narrow,
and beset with ten thousand bugbears, many despair-
ing to be ever able to walk in it, have thrown off all
religion and morality, and sunk into the abyss of
vice and wickedness. Others have their tempers so
soured, as to become lost to all the tender connexions
of husband, wife, father, child, &c. really believing
that they are *literally* to *hate* father, mother, &c for
Christ's sake. Thus is sweet domestic peace and happiness for ever blasted :

Enlivening hope, and fond defire,
  Refign the heart to fpleen and care ;
Scarce frighted love maintains her fire,
  And rapture faddens to defpair.   DR. JOHNSON.

Many have in a fit of defpondency put a period to
their exiftence, it having become a burthen too intolerable to be borne. Some have been fo infatuated
with the idea of fafting to mortify the flefh, that their
ftrict perfeverance in it has been productive of the
moft ferious confequences : Two inftances of which
lately occurred in one family, in the City-road—
The miftrefs was deprived of her fenfes, and the maid
literally fafted herfelf to death. Bedlam and private
mad-houfes now contain many very melancholy inftances of the dreadful effects of religious defpondency; not to mention the hundreds that have died
from time to time in fuch places, and the numerous
fuicides which have been traced to the fame fource.

———— Gloomy fcene,
Eftrang'd from all the chearful ways of men,
There fuperftition works her baneful pow'r,
And darkens all the melancholy hour.
Unnumber'd fears corrode and haunt his breaft,
With all that whim or ignorance can fuggeft.
In vain for him kind nature pours her fweets ;
The vifionary faint no joy admits,
But fick with pious fpleen fantaftic woes,
And for heav'n's fake, heav'n's offer'd good foregoes.
                              W. MELMOTH.

I knew one man who for many years believed himfelf to be the Holy Ghoft, and endeavoured to make
his acquaintance believe the fame : in other refpects
he appeared to be in his right fenfes.

Mr. Bentley fays, in his letter to the members of
the houfe of commons, dated May 12th, 1791, that,
although he had a fortune of one thoufand pounds,
and naturally liked good living, yet that he lived on
horfe and afs flefh, barley bread, ftinking butter, &c.
and when he found that his eating fuch things gave
offence to his neighbours, he left off eating afs flefh,
and only lived on vegetables, as the common fort of
food by their dearnefs hurt his *confcience*.

A few years fince I faw in a field not feven miles
from China-hall, Mr. Taylor, a fhip-carpenter, of

Deptford, tossing up his bible in the air. This he often repeated, and raved at a strange rate. Amongst other things, (pointing to a building at some distance,) " *That* (said he) is the *devil's* house, and it shall not stand three days longer!" On the third day after this, I saw with surprize an account in one of the public papers of that very building having been set on fire, and burnt to the ground; and thus the poor itinerant disciples of Thespis who exhibited there, lost the whole of their wardrobe and scenery.

This religious maniac afterwards preached very often in Smithfield and Moorfields; but he did not wholly depend on the operations of the Holy Spirit, as at last he seldom began to preach until he was nearly drunk, or filled with another kind of spirit, and then he was " a very powerful preacher indeed."

> Great were his looks, his eyes with hollow stare.
> Deep, deep within the burning sockets roll'd, .
> Like Gorgon's crest, or stern Alecto's hair,
> His tempest beaten locks erect and bold,
> With horrid shade his temples seem'd to fold,
> His beard, the rest conceal'd, a black disguise.
> ORLANDO FURIOSO.

But the good man happening several times to exert himself rather too much, had nearly tumbled head-long out of his portable pulpit; these accidents the mob *uncharitably* ascribed to the liquor that he had drank, and with mud, stones, dead cats, &c. drove him off every time he came, until at last our preacher took his leave of them with saying, " That he perceived it was in vain to attempt their conversion, as he saw that God had given them over to the hardness of their hearts."

I must inform you that this devout zealous preacher lived many years before this, and some years after, with a very holy sister, and begot sons and daughters, without being brought into bondage, by submitting to the carnal ordinance of marriage.

> If he errs now and then, and his faults meet detection,
> It but proves that the best are not heirs of perfection.
> ANTHONY PASQUIN..

I have been lately informed, that his enthusiasm and superstition, at last, entirely deprived him of the small remains of reason, and that he died in a private mad-house.

But although this holy man deserted them, yet other spiritual knights-errant were not wanting, so that a little time before the heaps of stone; which lay for years in Moorfields were removed, for the purpose of building on the spot, I have seen five or six in a day preaching their initiation sermons from those elevated situations, until they could collect a sufficient sum of money to purchase pulpits. Some of these excellent preachers received the whole of their divine education, and took up their degrees in Moorfields; and in due time, after having given ample and satisfactory proofs of being properly qualified, have been admitted to professorships in the noble College, situated on the south side of those fields, generally known by the name of *Bedlam*. You must know, Sir, that many of the lazy part of the community set up stalls in Moorfields, to buy and sell apples, old iron, &c. several of these having heard such edifying discourses frequently repeated as they sat at their stalls, and observing the success which those kind of preachers met with, boldly resolved to make trial of their spiritual gifts on the heaps of stones, and have now totally abandoned their stalls, and are gone forth as ambassadors of heaven.

> —— Thus poor Crispin, crazy for the praise,
> Of pulpit eloquence, to preach essays,
> His 'prentice clerk ; his cobbling stool his stage ;
> Flies to the fields with tabernacle rage!
> With Rowland's skill erects his orbs of sight,
> Or turns them ravish'd! on the inward light !
> New faith, all-saving faith, proclaims aloud !
> Now deals damnation to the trembling crowd,
> Ask'd why for preaching he deserts his stall,
> (Bred at Moorfields, or Tot'nham) hear him bawl,
> Because as how I feels I has a call.
>
>   BUSBY's Age of Genius.

One of these who cannot read, lately informed me, that he had quitted all temporal concerns for the good of poor ignorant sinners.

They added that by which themfelves were winners,
It ferv'd no purpofes but faving finners.

R. Bentley, Esq.

John Turpin, a waiter at an Inn in Dartmouth, fome time late in 1791, made free with fome of his mafter's plate, and was whipped at the tail of a cart round the town, after which he went to Totnefs, about 12 miles from Dartmouth, and commenced methodift preacher; and a few months after he had the affurance to return to Dartmouth to proclaim his converfion, and to preach what he was pleafed to call the gofpel, and in that capacity he foon collected together as great a number of people round his pulpit, as before he had done round his cart; and among others he made a convert of the clerk of the parifh, who entertained him in his houfe at free coft. Some time in the fpring 1792, as he was one Sunday morning going towards the church with the clerk, he pretended to be feized on a fudden with griping pains, and told the clerk that he muft go back, on which the old fool of a clerk gave him the key of his houfe, and alfo a key of a clofet where he kept fome brandy, and advifed him to go and take a glafs. On the old man's return from church, he miffed a watch, and on farther fearch he miffed another watch, and upwards of twenty guineas in gold. And as the preacher was not to be found, he hired horfes, and with a conftable fet off in purfuit of this heavenly-minded rafcal, and about fifteen miles from Dartmouth they took him, with the whole of the property on him.

At Exeter Affizes in March he was tried, found guilty and condemned to be hanged; but was reprieved, and is fince fent to Botany-Bay, where perhaps he may have addrefs enough to get himfelf made chaplain to Barrington, as on his trial he told the judge, that if he would fend him to Botany-Bay, he would do much towards the glory of God, in fending one among the abandoned tranfports, who call them to repentance, and bring them to Chrift the friend of finners.

But before I take my leave of the fubject, I will in few words inform you how the preachers were go-

verned and fupported. Mr. Wefley every year ordered the major part of his travelling preachers in
Great Britain and Ireland, which were upwards of
two hundred in number, to meet together, one year
at London, the next at Briftol, and the following at
Manchefter; this meeting he called a conference. At
thofe conferences, the bufinefs of the whole fociety
was tranfacted, new 'preachers admitted, and fome
turned off, or filenced; complaints heard, differences
adjufted, &c. Mr. Wefley having divided Great
Britain into circuits, at thofe conferences, he appointed the preachers to every circuit for the following
year ; and as he woll knew the general want of abilities among his preachers, he limited their time of
preaching in one circuit to a year, and fo in fome
meafure, made up the want of abilities by variety ;
moft of thofe circuits had three or four preachers
every year, and in many country places, they had
but one fermon a week from the travelling preachers,
fo that each preacher preached about twelve fermons
(fometimes it may be twenty) at each place. In
every circuit one of the preachers was called the affift-
ant ; to him the various contributions were paid, and
of him might be had any of Mr. Wefley's publications. He alfo admitted new members, or turned
out any who were judged unworthy of bearing the
high appellation of a methodift.

Each itinerant preacher had a horfe found him,
which, with himfelf, are maintained by fome brother
or fifter wherever they go, as the preachers do not
put up at any inn, and yet they have as regular ftages
to call at as the coaches have, they having made converts at convenient diftances in moft parts of Great
Britain and Ireland.

Each travelling preacher was then allowed twelve
pounds a year, to find himfelf cloaths, pay turn-
pikes, &c. exclufive of what he could get privately out
of the old women's pockets. But befides thofe circuit-preachers, there were in the year 1790, in Europe and America, thirteen or fourteen hundred," of
local holdersforth, who do not preach out of their

own neighbourhood, and those in general are most ignorant of all.

Many of the circuit-preachers only travel until they can marry a rich widow, or some ignorant young convert with money, which has often been the cause of great unhappiness in many respectable families. The following poetical description of the methodist preachers, is so much to my purpose, that I must insert it:

" Every *mechanic* will commence
" *Orator*, without *mood* or *tense*;
" *Pudding* is *pudding* still they know,
" Whether it has a plum or no.
" So, tho' the preacher have no skill,
" A *sermon* is a *sermon* still.

" The Bricklay'r throws his trowel by
" And now *builds mansions in the sky*;
" The *Cobler*, touch'd with *holy pride*,
" Flings his *old shoes* and *last* aside,
" And now devoutly sets about
" Cobbling of *souls* that ne'er *wear out*;
" The *Baker* now *a preacher* grown,
" Finds *man lives not by bread alone*,
" And now his customers he feeds
" With *pray'rs*, with *sermons*, *groans*, and *creeds*;
" The *Tinman*, mov'd by warmth within,
" Hammers the gospel just like *tin*;
" *Weavers* inspir'd, their *shuttles* leave,
" *Sermons* and *flimsy hymns* to weave;
" *Barbers* unreap'd will leave the chin,
" To trim, and shave the *man within*;
" The *Waterman* forgets his *wherry*,
" And opens a *celestial ferry*;
" The *Brewer*, bit by frenzy's grub,
" The *mashing* for the *preaching* tub
" Resigns, *those waters* to explore,
" Which if you drink, you thirst no more;
" The *Gard'ner*, weary of his trade,
" Tir'd of the mattock and the spade,
" Chang'd to *Appollos* in a trice,
" *Waters the plants of paradise*;
" The *Fisherman* no longer set
" For *fish* the meshes of their net,
" But catch, like *Peter*, *men of sin*,
" For *catching* is to *take them in*."

I now take a final leave of methodism, with assuring you, that in giving a general idea of the tenets

and practices of a numerous sect who have excited
much public attention, I have invariably had in
view to " speak of them as they are, nothing to ex-
tenuate, nor set down aught in malice." Should you
wish to see the errors of the methodists particularly
exposed, you may read Bishop Lavington's " Enthusiasm of the methodists and papists compared." It is
esteemed a very good work, and will amuse as well as
instruct you. In my next, I intended to have re-
sumed the account of my own affairs; but an extraordinary publication will tempt me to add one letter
more on the methodists.

I am,

Dear Friend,

Yours.

LETTER XXXI.

Religion, fairest maid on earth,
As meek as good, who drew her breath
From the blest union when in heaven,
Pleasure was bride to virtue given;
Religion ever pleas'd to pray,
Possess'd the precious gift one day;
Hypocrisy, of Cunning born,
Crept in and stole it ere the morn.   CHURCHILL.

DEAR FRIEND,

ALTHOUGH I was many years
in connexion with Mr. Wesley's people, it seems,
according to a pamphlet published a few months
after the two first editions of my Memoirs, that I was
but superficially acquainted with Mr. Wesley and his
preachers. The pamphlet is entitled, " A Letter to
the Rev. T. Coke, LL. D. and Mr. H. Moore."

To which is added, "An Appeal and Remonftrance to the People called Methodifts, by an old Member of the Society." This old member informs us, that he has been acquainted with the methodifts twenty-eight years, and if their preachers are but half as bad as he has drawn them, they are a detestable fet of fly deceiving villains. The letter was occafioned by Dr. Coke and Mr. Moore's propofols for publifhing Mr. Wefley's Life, in oppofition to that advertifed (under the fanction of the executors) to be written by Dr. Whitehead.

This writer informs us, that after Mr. Wefley's manufcripts and private papers had been given up to Dr. Whitehead, the Doctor appointed to write his Life, and this Life announced to the public by the executors as the only authentic work ; on a mifunder-ftanding taking place between Dr. Whitehead and the preachers, becaufe the Doctor would not fubmit his work to be infpected, altered, &c. and alfo becaufe the Doctor would not confent to give the preachers at the conference, nearly the whole of the profits de-rived from his labours, they then fent a circular letter figned by nine of their head preachers, to all their focieties, advifing them *to return the fubfcriptions that they had taken for Dr. Whitehead's Life of Mr. Wefley, and to procure all the fubfcriptions in their power for another Life of Mr. Wefley*, to be written by Dr. Coke and Mr. Moore.

The following quotations I think will pleafe you, page 8, &c. " That Mr. Wefley was a great man is an undeniable truth ; *that* is comparatively—Great amongft little people."

" Nothing can exhibit his character as an ambi-tious man, more than the following anecdote, which I can give from the moft authentic authority. When a boy, he was in the Charter-Houfe School ; the Rev. *A. Tooke*, the author of the *Pantheon*, was then mafter, and obferving that his pupil, who was remarkably forward in his ftudies, yet he conftantly affociated with the inferior claffes, and it was his cuftom to be furrounded by a number of the little boys, haranguing them. Mr. Tooke once accidentally broke in upon.

him when in the middle of an oration, and interrupted him, by desiring him to follow him into the parlour. Mr. Wesley, offended by being thus abruptly deprived of an opportunity of displaying his superior abilities, obeyed his master very reluctantly. When they had got into the parlour Mr. Tooke said to him : " John, I wonder that you, who are so much above the lower forms, should constantly associate with them ; for you should now consider yourself as a man, and affect the company of the bigger boys, who are your equals." Our hero, who could hardly stifle his resentment while his master spoke, boldly replied :—
" *Better to rule in hell, than serve in heaven.*"

" Mr. Tooke dismissed his pupil with this remarkable observation to the assistant master.—That boy, though designed for the Church, will never get a living in it : for his ambitious soul will never acknowledge a superior, or be confined to a parish.

" That he was superior to the prejudices he inculcated to his followers, and with what contempt he sometimes treated the lay-preachers, the following will shew :—Being at supper one Sunday night, (a short time before his death) with several of the preachers, one of them observed that whenever Mr. Wesley travelled, he was always invited to the houses of the neighbouring nobility and gentry ; but when the preachers travelled, no notice was taken of them, which he could not account for. Mr. Wesley replied, " It was the way of the world to court the great, but I say, love me love my dog !" enjoying his triumph with a hearty laugh at their expence.

After this old member's Letter comes his Appeal and Remonstrance to the Methodists, which, as coming from an old methodist, contains some very extraordinary assertions and facts, and letters more extraordinary. I shall give you some extracts from it in page 28. " Faith is the ground-work of (methodist) evidence—it precludes the necessity of every virtue—it is to be feared it has sent more of its votaries to Bedlam than to heaven—is to wise men a stumbling-block an unintelligible jargon of mystical

nonsenfe, which common fenfe and common honefty
reject."

Page 30, &c. "It has been computed that the
contributions raifed among the members of the different focieties in Great Britain and Ireland, for the
laft ten years, has amounted to no lefs than FOUR
HUNDRED THOUSAND POUNDS per annum.
It has been further proved that about one eighth part
of this fum is appropriated to the purpofes for which
it was raifed, and the remainder is difpofed of at the
difcretion of the conference, the preachers, and the
ftewards.   This calculation does not include the
enormous fums known to be raifed privately by the
influence of the preachers in their refpective circuits,
under the various pretenfions of diftrefs, &c.

"However, I do not pretend to vouch for the ac-
curacy of this calculation, yet I think it by no means
exaggerated. What has come within my own knowledge I can affert with confidence, and I challenge
any one to refute it.

"Of *Kingfwood School*, I can fpeak with certainty:
for this foundation, many thoufands have been raifed
which never will, and I believe never were intended
to be applied to that charity. During eight years
that I was at Kingfwood, it not only fupported itfelf,
but produced a confiderable annual furplus.

"One of the mafters of King's School, being deficient in his accounts, he was judged an improper
perfon to enjoy any place of truft, and was accordingly
difmiffed, and appointed to a circuit as a *travelling
preacher*—but any will do for that, who has but *impudence* and *hypocrify*—no matter whether he poffeffes a
grain of *honefty*. Now if this was the cafe with refpect to Kingfwood, may we not conclude that the
fame iniquitous principle pervaded the adminiftration
of the finances in all the different departments?"

Page 33, &c. "O how long, ye *fheep*, will ye be
the prey of *wolves*, who fleece and devour you at
pleafure! and, ye *fools*, be the dupes of *knavery* and
hypocrify?

"Open your eyes, and behold the *villain* and *hypo*-

vice unmasked, in instances of the most flagitious crimes, and deeds of the blackest dye! perpetrated by wretches, whom you tamely suffer to devour your substance, and whom you cheerfully contribute to support in idleness and luxury, which brings into contempt the gospel, and whose example has done more harm to religion, than that of the most abandoned and profligate open sinner: admitting at the same time that there may be, and I hope there are, some honest and sincere men amongst them.

"To begin then with the late Rev. J. Wesley. As the founder and head, he must be considered as the *primum mobile*, or first mover of this mighty machine of *hypocrisy, fraud*, and *villainy!* Yet were his motives originally laudable in their intention, virtuous in their object, but unhappy in their consequences. This I will endeavour to make appear, by an impartial review of his life, character, and conduct. I flatter myself that I am in some measure qualified, being totally divested of prejudice, and having no interest either in representing him as a *saint* or a *devil*.

"From what I have observed during near twenty-eight years that I have known him, I have uniformly found him ambitious, imperious, and positive even to obstinacy. His learning and knowledge various and general, but superficial; his judgment too hasty and decisive to be always just – his penetration acute: yet was he constantly the dupe to his credulity and his unaccountable and universal good opinion of mankind. Humane, generous, and just. In his private opinions liberal to a degree inconsistent with strict Christianity; in his public declarations rigid almost to intolerance. From this observation of the inconsistency of his private opinions and public declarations, I have often been inclined to doubt his sincerity, even in the profession of the Christian faith. In his temper impetuous, and impatient of contradiction; but in his heart, a stranger to malice or resentment; incapable of particular attachment to any individual: he knew no ties of blood or claims of kindred; never violently or durably affected by grief, sorrow, or any of the passions to which humanity is subject; susceptible of the grossest flattery, and the most fulsome panegyric was constantly accepted and rewarded. In his views and expectations, sanguine and unbounded, but though often disappointed, never dejected: of his benevolence and charity much has been said; but it is to be observed, benevolence is but a passive virtue, and his charity was no more than bribery; he knew no other use of money but to give it away, and he found out that an hundred pounds would go farther in half-crowns than in pounds; so that his charity was little more than parade, as he hardly ever essentially relieved an object of distress: in fact his charity was no more than putting money to interest, as the example excited his followers to the practice of the same virtue, and doubled their subscriptions and contributions. In his constitution warm, and consequently amorous; in his manner of living luxurious and strictly epicurean, and fond of dishes highly relished, and fond of drinking the richest wines, in which he indulged often, but never to excess. He was indebted more to his commanding, positive, and authoritative manner, than to any intrinsically superior abilities.

"Having thus given the outlines of his character, I shall only observe, that he appears to have been more a philosopher than a Christian: and shall then proceed to some anecdotes and circumstances which will corroborate my assertions, and justify my conclusion.

"As the *work of God*, as it is called, was the sphere of action in which he was more particularly and conspicuously engaged, and as I have ventured to question the sincerity of his professions, it is proper that I should state my reasons for so doing. First, then, of conversion: in the *methodistical* sense of the word, for in the true sense, I apprehend to be neither more nor less, than forsaking vice and practising virtue; but however, the methodistical sense imports quite a different thing, and it is in that sense we shall view it. I have made it an invariable observation, that Mr. Wesley, although he was often in company of sensitle men, who were capable of forming an opinion, and presumed to judge for themselves by the light of nature, the evidence of the senses, and the aid of reason and philosophy; but of such, he never attempted the conversion. In his own family, and amongst his relations, he never attempted, or if he did attempt, he never succeeded: except now and then with a female, in whom he found a heart susceptible of any impression he pleased to give. It is remarkable, that even the children of Mr. C. W. were never converted—because they, and most of his relations, possessed sense enough to discover hypocrisy, and honesty enough to reject the advantage they might have derived from assuming it. But what is still more extraordinary, is, that out of so many hundreds, who have been educated at *Kingswood*, in the most rigid discipline of methodism, hardly any have embraced their tenets, or become members of the society. The reason is pretty obvious, they were taught too much to imbibe the ridiculous prejudices the founder wished to be instilled into their minds: philosophy and methodism are utterly incompatible. When the human mind is formed by the study of philosophy, it expands itself to the contemplation of things.

" It is true indeed, the *work* was sometimes attended with power among the children at *Kingswood*. *Conversions* were frequent; but never durable. I myself was converted some ten or a dozen times; but unluckily, my *class leader* was detected in having stolen a pair of silver buckles. This was a dreadful stroke to the *work*, and a glorious triumph to the *wicked one*. The whole fabric of *faith*, *grace*, and all its concomitant vices, as *hypocrisy*, &c. &c. experienced a total overthrow! The serious boys, as they are called by way of eminence, fell into the utmost contempt, and ever after, the *leader* of a *class* was stiled *Captain* of the *Gang*: a *convert* and a *thief*, were synonimous terms.

" A general conversion among the boys was once effected, by the late excellent Mr. *Fletcher*: one poor boy only excepted, who unfortunately resisted the

K

influence of the Holy Spirit; for which he was feverely flogged, which did not fail of the defired effect, and impreffed proper notions of religion on his mind. Unhappily thefe operations of the fpirit, though violent, were but of fhort duration.

" As the converfion of men and women is a more ferious concern than that of children, I will defcribe one, to which I was an eye-witnefs among the poor colliers at *Kingfwood*. One of thofe prefumptuous and impious fanatical wretches, who affume the character of minifters of God, and take upon them in his moft holy name, to denounce his curfes and vengeance againft thofe who are far lefs guilty than themfelves: a fellow of this defcription, of the name of *Sanderfon*, preaching to a congregation of ignorant, but harmlefs people; this fellow took upon himfelf, in the name of God, to condemn them all to eternal damnation, painting their deplorable ftate in the moft dreadful colours: fome of his hearers were foon evidently affected by this difcourfe, which he took care to improve, and taking the advantage of the kindling fpark, addreffed himfelf more particularly to them, whom he foon " made roar for the difquietude of their fouls." The whole congregation were quickly affected in the like manner; one and all exclaimed, " What fhall I do to be faved? Oh! I'm damned! I'm damned! I'm damned to all eternity! What fhall I do? Oh! Oh! Oh!" Our performer obferving to what a ftate he had reduced his audience, redoubled his threats of divine wrath and vengeance, and with a voice terrible as thunder, demanded, " Is there any backfliders in the prefence of God?" A dead and folemn paufe enfued—till he exclaimed, " Here is an old grey headed finner:" at the fame time ftriking with his hand violently on the bald pate of an honeft old man who fat under the defk; the poor man gave a deep groan; whether from conviction, or from the pain of the blow, I know not, for it was far from being gentle. The farce was not yet concluded, when they were ftrongly *convulfed* with thefe *convictions*, he fell down upon his knees, and with the greateft fervency, accompanied with abundance of tears, he

entreated the Lord in mighty prayer, to have com-
passion on the poor desponding sinners whom he had
brought to a proper sense of their danger: the prayer
continued about ten minutes, accompanied by the
sighs and groans of the converted and alarmed sinners,
in concert making a most divine harmony: when suddenly starting up, he pretended to have received a
gracious answer to his prayer, and with a joyful and
smiling countenance, pointing towards the window,
exclaimed: Behold the Lamb! Where! Where!
Where! was the cry of every contrite and returning
sinner, (and they were all of that description.) There!
(continued the preacher, extending his arms towards
the window where he pretended first to have espied
the Lamb). In Heaven! In *Colo!* making interces-
sion for your sins! And I have his authority to proclaim unto you—" your sins are forgiven—depart in
peace."—O, my dearest brethren, how sweet is the
sound of those extatic words! " Behold the Lamb
of God, who taketh away the sins of the world!"
But could you but feel the peculiar energy, the divine force, the rapturous and cheering import of the
original, your mouths would be filled with praise, and
your hearts with divine joy, holy exultation, and un-
speakable gratitude.—Only mark the sound of the
words, even that will convey an inexpressible pleasure
to your souls, " *Hecca hangus Dei ! Ki dollit pekkaltus
Monday!*" The school-boys (who were seated in a
pew detached from the congregation on account of
their prophane and contemptuous behaviour during
service) immediately burst into a loud laugh, on one
of the congregation saying, " O the blessed man!
We shall see him again on MONDAY."

In some pages following we have an account of the
methodist preacher's first converting his benefactor's
daughter, and then debauching her; also of a preacher
at Beverly, in Yorkshire, that collected fifteen pounds
for a poor man in great distress, and gave him only
fifteen shillings, reserving to himself fourteen pounds
five shillings for the trouble of collecting it, with
which, and twenty pounds more he was entrusted

with, he decamped the next day, to the aſtoniſhment of the ſimple on whom he had impoſed.

I wiſh the author, as he propoſes, may ſoon give us a more particular account of the methodiſts, preachers, and people, and alſo of ſome of Mr. Weſley's private opinions, &c.

This pamphlet concludes with very curious letters written by Mr. J. Weſley; and he informs us, in a note, that the publiſher has his addreſs, in order to direct any perſon to the author, where they may ſee the original letters. I here give you the whole of theſe extraordinary letters in order to help you to

Break thoſe fetters bigots would impoſe,
To aggravate the ſenſe of human woes!

W. T. FITZGERALD.

Page 50, &c.

"DEAR SIR,

FOR your obliging letter which I received this morning, I return you thanks.

"Our opinions for the moſt part perfectly coincide reſpecting the ſtability of the connexion, after my head is laid in the duſt. This, however, is a ſubject, about which I am not ſo anxious as you ſeem to imagine; on the contrary, it is a matter of the utmoſt indifference to me; as I have long foreſeen that a diviſion muſt neceſſarily enſue, from cauſes ſo various, unavoidable, and certain, that I have long ſince given over all thoughts and hopes of ſettling it on a permanent foundation. You do not ſeem to be aware of the moſt effective cauſe that will bring about a diviſion. You apprehend the moſt ſerious conſequences from a ſtruggle between the preachers for power and pre-eminence, and there being none among them of ſufficient authority or abilities to ſupport the dignity, or command the reſpect and exact the implicit obedience, which is ſo neceſſary to uphold our conſtitution on its preſent principles. This is one thing that will operate very powerfully againſt unity in the connexion, and is, perhaps, what I might poſſibly have prevented, had not a ſtill greater

difficulty arisen in my mind : I have often wished for
some person of abilities to succeed me as the head of
the church I have with such indefatigable pains, and
astonishing success, established; but convinced that
none but very superior abilities would be equal to the
undertaking, was I to adopt a successor of this description, I fear he might gain so much influence among
the people, as to usurp a share, if not the whole of
that absolute and uncontroulable power, which I have
hitherto, and am determined I will maintain so long
as I live: never will I bear a rival near my throne.——
You, no doubt, see the policy of continually changing the preachers from one circuit to another at short
periods: for should any of them become popular with
their different congregations, and insinuate themselves
into the favour of their hearers, they might possibly
obtain such influence, as to establish themselves inde-
pendently of me, and the general connexion. Besides,
the novelty of the continual change excites curiosity,
and is the more necessary, as few of our preachers
have abilities to render themselves in any degree tolerable, any longer than they are new.

The principal cause which will inevitably effect a
diminution and division in the connexion after my
death, will be the failure of subscriptions and contributions towards the support of the cause, for money is
as much the finews of religious, as of military power.
If it is with the greatest difficulty that even I can
keep them together, for want of this very necessary
article, I think no one else can. Another cause,
which, with others, will effect the division, is the
disputes and contentions that will arise between the
preachers and the parties that will espouse the several
causes, by which means much truth will be brought to
light, which will reflect so much to their disadvantage,
that the eyes of the people will be opened to f e their
motives and principles, nor will they any longer contribute to their support, when they find all their pretensions to sanctity and love are founded on motives
of interest and ambition. The consequence of which
will be, a few of the most popular will establish them-

felves in the refpective places where they have gained fufficient influence over the minds of the people; the reft muft revert to their original humble callings. But this no way concerns me: I have obtained the object of my views, by eftablifhing a name that will not foon perifh from the face of the earth; I have founded a fect which will boaft my name, long after my difcipline and doctrines are forgotten.

"My character and reputation for fanctity is now beyond the reach of calumny; nor will any thing that may hereafter come to light, or be faid concerning me, to my prejudice, however true, gain credit.

"My unfoil'd name, th' aufterenefs of my life,
Will vouch againft it.
And fo the accufation overweigh
That it will ftifle in its own report,
And fmell of calumny."

"Another caufe that will operate more powerfully and effectually than any of the peceding, is the rays of philofophy which begin now to pervade all ranks, rapidly difpelling the mifts of ignorance, which has been long in a great degree the mother of devotion, of flavifh prejudice, and the enthufiaftic bigotry of religious opinions: the decline of the papal power is owing to the fame irrefiftible caufe, nor can it be fuppofed that methodifm can ftand its ground, when brought to the teft of truth, reafon, and philofophy.

I am, &c.

J. W."

City Road, Thurfday Morn.

Our author informs us, that the following was written to a very amiable and accomplifhed lady, fome years ago. The lady was about three and twenty years of age.

" MADAM,

"IT is with the utmoft diffidence I prefume to addrefs fuperior excellence: emboldened by a violent yet virtuous paffion, kindled by the irrefiftible rays, and encouraged by the fweetly attractive force of tranfcendant beauty, the elegant fimplicity of your manners, the facinating melody of your voice, and above all, the inexpressible fire of an eye, that the extravagance of the muses has given to the goddess of love: but which nature has bestowed on you alone.

> They sparkle with the right *Promethean* fire!"

"Believe me, my dear Madam, this is not the language of romance; but the genuine exuberant effusions of an enraptured soul. The impression of your charms was no less instantaneous than irresistible: when first I saw you, so forcibly was I struck with admiration and love of your divine perfections, that my soul was filled with sensations so wild and extravagant, yet delightful and pure! But I will not indulge in declaring what are my real sentiments, lest I should incur a suspicion of flattery. Your mind, superior to fulsome panegyric, unsusceptible of the incense of affected adulation, would, with just indignation, spurn at those impertinent compliments, which are commonly offered with a view to impose upon the vanity and credulity of the weaker part of your sex: I will not attempt it; but confine myself to the dictates of sincerity and truth, nor shall a compliment escape my pen, that is not the sentiment of a devoted heart.

"As beauty has no positive criterion, and fancy alone directs the judgment and influences the choice, we find different people see it in various lights, forms, and colours; I may therefore, without a suspicion of flattery, declare, that in my eye you are the most agreeable object, and most perfect work of created nature: nor does your mind seem to partake less of the divinity than your person.

> "I view thee over with a lover's eye;
> No fault hast thou, or I no fault can spy."

"The reason I did not before declare myself, was the profound and respectful distance I thought it became me to observe, from a conscious sense of my own comparative unworthiness to approach, much less to hope for favour from, the quintessence of all female perfection.—Forgive me, my dear Eliza, and compassionate a heart too deeply impressed with your divine image, ever to be erased by time, nor can any power, but the cold hand of death, ever obliterate from my mind the fond imagination and sweet remembrance of Eliza's charms! Nor can even death itself divide the union that subsists between kindred souls.

"Yesterday, my dear Eliza, the charms of your conversation detained me too late to meet the *penitents*, as I had promised to do; but

"With thee conversing, I forget
"All times, all seasons, and their change."

"I hope, however, the disappointment of my company did not deprive them of a blessing.

"This being my birth-day, reflections on the revolution of years and the shortness of life, naturally intrude on my mind. I am now *eighty-one* years of age, and I thank God I enjoy the same vigour of constitution I possessed at *twenty-one*! None of the infirmities that usually accompany years, either corporal or mental; and I think it not impossible that I may fulfil my hundred years, the residue of which shall be devoted to love and Eliza.

J. W."

I sent a person to the author of the above pamphlet, to desire him to give me a sight of the original of the preceding letters; but he returned for answer, that he had sent them back to the persons to whom they were written; so that I cannot be certain as to their authenticity.

Voltaire, in that letter in which he writes in the character of Father Charles Goujer to his brethren the Jesuits, says, "A man may believe in God, and yet kill his father; but is it possible he should believe in God, and pass his whole life amidst deliberate crimes, and an uninterrupted series of fraud and imposture? The man that killed his father must repent in his last moments; but I defy you to find in history one single divine who ever acknowledged his crimes on his death-bed."

In this letter Voltaire is not writing as a Deist, but as a real Christian, and is proving that such priests as lived such diabolical lives could never believe in the religion which they taught to others. "Think you (says he) that such as are polluted with incest,

aſſaſſinations, ſo many ſovereign pontiffs ſurrounded
by miſtreſſes and baſtards, laughing at the credulity
of mankind, in the boſom of riot and debauchery;
think you, that theſe ever-lifted up to God hands filled
with gold, or ſtained with blood? Did one of them
ever repent in their retirement? No. I will forfeit
ten thouſand crowns, if you can produce me one penitent divine."

Methinks Voltaire might have added, or one penitent
hypocrite among the laity. For of all vice hypocriſy
moſt degrades and hardens the mind; and I declare
that I never ſaw, or heard of a repenting hypocrite in
religion. And although it is acknowledged that the
methodiſts are enthuſiaſtical, ſuperſtitious, and fanatical, yet that by no means excuſes ſuch as connect
themſelves with them, merely from mercenary motives; for, notwithſtanding they may have much better
informed heads, yet are ſunk by hypocriſy beneath
the dregs of mankind; and the moſt ignorant, uninformed, ſelf-conceited fanatic among them, if he is
really ſincere in what he profeſſes, is a reſpectable,
dignified character, when compared with the ſneak-
ing, cunning, religious, hypocritical raſcal, who
has been claiming an acquaintance with God and divine things, the better to cheat and defraud mankind.

Hypocrites!

"———————— Theſe herd together,
" The *common* damn'd ſhun their ſociety,
" And look upon themſelves as fiends leſs foul."

I am,

Dear Friend,

Yours,

LETTER XXXII.

Whoe'er fo lives that proving we may find,
A faithful, honeft, equal, open mind ;
To no foul luft, or impious wifh a flave,
Mild to a brother, bold againft a knave ;
Whom innocence with fortitude fupplies,
Who follows nature clofe, this man is wife.

Poem on Friendfhip.

Paffions 'tis true, may hurry us along ;
Sometimes the juft may deviate into wrong.

VOLTAIRE, by Francklin.

DEAR FRIEND,

MY new wife's attachment to books was a very fortunate circumftance for us both, not only as it was a perpetual fource of rational amufement, but alfo as it tended to promote my trade : her extreme love for books made her delight to be in the fhop, fo that fhe foon became perfectly acquainted with every part of it, and (as my ftock increafed) with other rooms where I kept books, and could readily get any article that was afked for. Accordingly, when I was out on bufinefs my fhop was well attended. This conftant attention, and good ufage, procured me many cuftomers, and I foon perceived that I could fell double and treble the quantity of books if I had a larger ftock. But how to enlarge it, I knew not, except by flow degrees, as my profits fhould enable me ; for as I was almoft a ftranger in London, I had but few acquaintances, and thefe few were not of the opulent fort. I alfo faw that the town abounded with cheats, fwindlers, &c. who obtained money and other property, under falfe pretences, of which the credulous were defrauded, which often prevented me from endeavouring to borrow, left I fhould be fufpected of having the fame bad defigns.

I was feveral times fo hard put to it, for cafh to purchafe parcels of books which were offered to me, that I more than once pawned my watch, and a suit of cloaths, and twice I pawned some books for money to purchase others.

Soon after I commenced bookseller, I became acquainted with what Pope calls " the noblest work of God," an HONEST man. This was Mr. JOHN DENIS, an oil-man in Cannon-street (father of the present Mr. John Denis, bookseller). This gentleman had often visited me during my long illness, and having seen me tranquil and serene when on the very point of death, he formed a favourable conclusion that I too must be an honest man, as I had so quiet a conscience at such an awful period. Having retained these ideas of me after my recovery, and being perfectly well acquainted with my circumstances, he one day offered to become a partner in my business, and to advance money in proportion to my stock. This confidential offer I soon accepted; early in 1778 he became partner; and we very soon laid out his money in secondhand books, which increased the stock at once to double.

I soon after this proposed printing a sale catalogue, to which, after making a few objections, Mr. Denis consented. This catalogue of twelve thousand volumes (such as they were) was published in 1779. My partner's name was not in the title-page, the address was only " J. LACKINGTON & Co. No. 46, Chiswell-street." This our first publication produced very opposite effects on those who perused it: in some it excited much mirth, in others an equal proportion of anger. The major part of it was written by me, but Mr. Denis wrote many pages of it; and as his own private library consisted of scarce old mystical and alchymical books, printed above a century ago, many of them were in bad condition; this led him to insert *neat* in the catalogue to many articles, which were only neat when compared with such as were in very bad condition; so that when we produced such books as were called *neat* in our catalogue, we often got ourselves laughed at, and sometimes our *neat* articles were heartily *damned*. We had also a deal of trouble on another score; Mr. Denis inferted a number of articles without the authors names, and affured me that the books were well known, and to mention the authors was often ufelefs. The fact was, Mr. Denis knew who wrote thofe articles; but was foon convinced that many others did not, as we were often obliged to produce them merely to let our cuftomers fee who were the authors; we however took twenty pounds the firft week the books were on fale, which we thought a large fum: The increafe of our ftock augmented our cuftomers in proportion; fo that Mr. Denis, finding that his money turned to a better account in bookfelling than in the funds, very foon lent the ftock neat two hundred pounds, which I ftill turned to a good account. We went on very friendly and profperoufly for a little more than two years; when one night Mr. Denis hinted, that he thought I was making purchafes too faft, on which I grew warm, and reminded him of an article in our partnerfhip agreement, by which I was to be fole purchafer, and was at liberty to make what purchafes I fhould judge proper. I alfo reminded him of the profits which my purchafes produced, and he reminded me of his having more money in the trade than I had. We were indeed both very warm; and on my faying, that if he was difpleafed with any part of my conduct, he was at liberty to quit the partnerfhip; he in great warmth replied that he would. The above paffed at Mr. Denis's houfe in Hoxton-fquare; I then bade him good night. When Mr. Denis called at the fhop the next day, he afked me if I continued in the fame mind I was in the preceding night? I affured him that I did. He then demanded of me whether I infifted on his keeping his word to quit the partnerfhip? I replied, I did not infift on it, as I had taken him a partner for three years, nearly one third part of which time was unexpired; but, I added, that, as I had always found him ftrictly a man of his word, I fuppofed he would prove himfelf fo in the prefent inftance, and nor affert one thing at night and another in the morning. On which he obferved, that as he was not provided with a fhop, he muft take fome time to look for one.

I told him that he might take as long a time as he thought neceſſary. This was in March 1780. He appointed the twentieth of May following. On that day we accordingly diſſolved the partnerſhip; and, as he had more money in the trade than myſelf, he took my notes for what I was deficient, which was a great favour done to me. We parted in great friendſhip, which continued to the day of his death; he generally called every morning to ſee us, and learn our concerns, and we conſtantly informed him of all that had paſſed the preceding day; as how much caſh we had taken, what were the profits, what purchaſes we had made, what bills we had to pay, &c. and he ſometimes lent me money to help to pay them.

At his death he left behind him in his private library the beſt collection of ſcarce valuable myſtical and alchymical books, that ever was collected by one perſon. In his lifetime he prized theſe kinds of books above every thing; in collecting them he never cared what price he paid for them. This led him to think, after he became a bookſeller, that other book-collectors ſhould pay their money as freely as he had done his, which was often a ſubject of debate between him and me, as I was for ſelling every thing cheap, in order to ſecure thoſe cuſtomers already obtained, as well as increaſe their numbers.

In Selden's Table Talk is the following odd paſſage: " The giving a bookſeller his price for his " books has this advantage; he that will do ſo, ſhall " have the refuſal of whatſoever comes to his hand, " and ſo by that means get many things which other- " wiſe he never ſhould have ſeen." - He adds, " So " it is in giving a bawd her own price." But I hope he did not mean to compare the bookſellers to old bawds. Different profeſſions are oddly jumbled together in the following lines:

" No ſurgeon will extract a tooth,
" No ſtrumpet exerciſe her trade,
No parſon preach eternal truth
" Where not a ſixpence can be made."

Mr. Denis was, at the time of his death, about fifty years of age. He informed me that in his childhood and youth he was weakly to an extreme; so that no one who knew him ever thought he could live to be twenty years of age; however, he enjoyed an uninterrupted state of health for nearly the last forty years of his life; this he ascribed to his strictly adhering to the rules laid down by *Cornaro* and *Tryon* in their books on Health, Long Life and Happiness. His unexpected death was in consequence of a fever, caught by sitting in a cold damp room.

> " O'er the sad reliques of each friend sincere,
> " The happiest mortal, sure, may spare a tear."

I am,

Dear Friend,

Yours.

LETTER XXXIII.

> There is a tide in the affairs of men,
> Which taken at the flood leads on to fortune,
> Omitted, all the voyage of their life
> Is bound in shallows and in miseries:
> On such a sea are we now afloat,
> And we must take the current when it serves,
> Or lose our ventures.   SHAKESPEARE'S *Julius Cæsar*.

DEAR FRIEND,

IT was some time in the year 1780, when I resolved from that period to give no person whatever any credit. I was induced to make this resolution from various motives: I had observed, that where credit was given, most bills were not paid within six months, many not within a twelvemonth, and some not within two years. Indeed, many tradesmen have accounts of seven years standing; and some bills are never paid. The losses sustained by the interest of money in long credits, and by those bills that were not paid at all; the inconveniences attending not having the ready-money to lay out in trade to the best advantage, together with the great loss of time in keeping accounts, and collecting debts, convinced me, that if I could but establish a ready-money business *without any exceptions*, I should be enabled to sell every article very cheap.

> " Let all the learn'd say all they can,
> " 'Tis ready-money makes the man."

When I communicated my ideas on this subject to some of my acquaintances, I was much laughed at and ridiculed; and it was thought, that I might as well attempt to rebuild the tower of Babel, as to establish a large business without giving credit. But notwithstanding this discouragement, and even *You*, my dear friend, expressing your doubts of the practicability of my scheme, I determined to make the experiment; and began by plainly marking in every book facing the title the lowest price that I would take for it; which being much lower than the common market prices, I not only retained my former customers, but soon increased their numbers. But, my dear Sir, you can scarce imagine what difficulties I encountered for several years together. I even sometimes thought of relinquishing this my favourite scheme altogether, as by it I was obliged to deny credit to my very acquaintance; I was also under a necessity of refusing it to the most respectable characters, as *no exception* was, or now is made, not even in favour of nobility; my porters being strictly enjoined, by one general order, to bring back all books not previously paid for, except they receive the amount on delivery. Again, many in the country found it difficult to remit small sums that were under bankers notes, (which difficulty is now done away, as all post-masters receive small sums of money, and give drafts for the same on the post office in London) and others to whom I was a stranger, did not like to send the money first, as not knowing how I should treat them,

and fuspecting by the price of the articles, there muft
certainly be fome deception. Many unacquainted
with my plan of bufinefs, were much offended, until
the advantages accruing to them from it were duly
explained, when they very readily acceded to it. As
to the anger of fuch, who, though they were acquainted with it, were ftill determined to deal on
credit only, I confidered that as of little confequence,
from an opinion that fome of them would have been
as much enraged when their bills were fent in, had
credit been given them.

I had alfo difficulties of another nature to encounter; when firft I began to fell very cheap, many
came to my fhop prepoffeffed againft my goods, and
of courfe often faw faults where none exifted ; fo that
the beft editions were merely from prejudice deemed
very bad editions, and the beft bindings faid to be inferior workmanfhip, for no other reafon, but becaufe
I fold them fo cheap; and I often received letters
from the country, to know if fuch and fuch articles
were REALLY as I ftated them in my catalogues, and
if they REALLY *were the beft editions, if* REALLY *in
calf*; and REALLY *elegantly bound*; with many other
reallys. Oh, my friend! I *really* was afraid for fome
years that I fhould be *really* mad with vexation. But
thefe letters of *reallys* have for years happily ceafed,
and the public are now *really* and thoroughly convinced that I will not affert in my catalogues what is
not *really* true. But imagine, if you can, what I
muft have felt, on hearing the very beft of goods de-
preciated, on no other account whatever, but becaufe
they were not charged at a higher price.

It is alfo worth obferving, that there were not
wanting among the bookfellers, fome who were mean
enough to affert that all my books were bound in
fheep, and many other unmanly artifices were practifed, all of which fo far from injuring me, as bafely
intended, turned to my account; for when gentlemen were brought to my fhop by their friends, to
purchafe fome trifling article, or were led into it by
curiofity, they were often very much furprized to fee
many thoufands of volumes in elegant and fuperb

bindings. The natural conclusion was, that if I had not held forth to the public better terms than others, I should not have been so much envied and misrepresented.

> " —— To malice sure I'm much oblig'd,
> " On every side by calumny besieg'd;
> " Yet Envy I could almost call thee Friend."

So that whether I am righteous or not, all these afflictions have worked together for my good. But I assure you, that my temporal salvation was not effected without " *conditions*." As every envious transaction was to me an additional spur to exertion, I am therefore not a little indebted to Messrs. ENVY, DETRACTION, & Co. for my present prosperity; though I assure you, this is the only debt I am determined not to pay. Green says,

> Happy the man who innocent,
> Grieves not at ills he can't prevent:
> And when he can't prevent foul play,
> Enjoys the follies of the fray.   SPLEEN.

I am,

Dear Friend,

Yours.

LETTER XXXIV.

" Conſtant at ſhop and Change, his gains were ſure:
" His givings rare; ſave halfpence to the poor."

When Fortune, various goddeſs, low'rs,
Collect your ſtrength, exert your pow'rs,
But when ſhe breathes a kinder gale,
Be wiſe and furl your ſwelling ſail.

FRANCIS'S HORACE.

DEAR FRIEND,

IN the firſt three years after I re-
fuſed to give credit to any perſon, my buſineſs increaſed much, and as the whole of my profit (after
paying all expences) was laid out in books, my ſtock
was continually enlarged, ſo that my Catalogues in
the year ſeventeen hundred and eighty-four, were very
much augmented in ſize. The firſt contained Twelve
thouſand; and the ſecond Thirty thouſand volumes:
this increaſe was not merely in numbers, but alſo in
value, as a very great part of theſe volumes were
better, that is, books of an higher price. But notwithſtanding the great increaſe of my buſineſs, I ſtill
met with many difficulties on account of my ſelling
books cheap; one of theſe I confeſs I did not foreſee:
as the more convinced the public were of my acting
ſtrictly conformable to the plan I had adopted, the
more this objection gained ground, and even to the
preſent day is not *entirely* done away. This difficulty
was, in making private purchaſes of libraries and parcels of books, many of my cuſtomers for ſeveral years
had no objection to *buying* of me becauſe I ſold cheap,
but were not equally inclined to *ſell* me ſuch books as
they had no uſe for, or libraries that were left them
at the death of relations, &c. They reaſoned (very
plauſibly, it muſt be confeſſed) thus: " Lackington
ſells very cheap; he therefore will not give much for
what is offered him for ſale. I will go to thoſe who
ſell very dear; as the more they ſell their books for,
the more they can afford to give for them."

This mode of reasoning, however specious it seems at first, will on due reflection appear nugatory and erroneous, for the following reasons:

I believe no one ever knew or heard of a covetous man that would sell his goods *cheap*: But every one has heard of such characters selling *very dear*; and when a covetous person makes a purchase, is it likely that he should offer a generous price? Is he not when buying influenced by the same avaricious disposition as when selling? And on the other hand, I cannot help thinking (I am aware of the inference) that one who has been constantly selling cheap for a series of years must possess some degree of generosity; that this disposition has prevailed in me when I have been called to purchase, and when libraries or parcels of books have been sent to me, thousands in the three kingdoms can witness. And however paradoxical it may appear, I will add, that I can afford to give more for books now, than I could if I sold them much dearer. For, were I to sell them dear, I should be ten times longer in selling them; and the expences for warehouse-room, insurance from fire, together with the interest of the money lying long in a dead stock, would prevent my giving a large price when books were offered for sale.

But it did not appear in this point of view to the public in the more early stages of my business, until being often sent for after other booksellers had made offers for libraries, and finding that I would give more than they had offered, it was communicated from one to another until it became publicly known; and the following method which I adopted some years since has put the matter beyond the shadow of a doubt.

When I am called upon to purchase any library or parcel of books, either myself or my assistants carefully examine them, and if desired to fix a price, I mention at a word the utmost that I will give for them, which I always take care shall be as much as any bookseller can afford to give; but if the seller entertains any doubts respecting the price offered, and chooses to try other booksellers, he pays me five per cent. for valuing the books; and as he knows what I have valued them at, he tries among the trade, and when he finds that he cannot get any greater sum offered, on returning to me, he not only receives the price I at first offered, but also a return of the five per cent. which was paid me for the valuation.

But to such as fix a price on their own books I make no charge (if in, or very near town) either taking them at the price at which they are offered to me, or if that appear too much, immediately declining the purchase.

This equitable mode I have the pleasure to find has given the public the utmost satisfaction.

> " ———— Though some little merit I boast,
> " Yet rais'd by indulgence to fame,
> " I sink in confusion, bewilder'd and lost,
> " And wonder I am what I am."

I am,

Dear Friend,

Yours.

LETTER XXXV.

> Behold, Sir Balaam, now a man of spirit,
> Ascribes his gettings to his parts and merit.
>
> POPE.

> Weak truth can't your reputation save,
> The knaves will all agree to call you knave :
> Wrong'd shall he live, insulted, o'er opprest,
> Who dares be less a villain than the rest.
>
> Satyr against Man.

DEAR FRIEND,

WHEN I was first initiated into the various manœuvres practised by booksellers, I found it customary among them, (which practice still continues) that when any books had not gone off so rapidly as expected, or so fast as to pay for keeping them in store, they would put what remained of such articles into private sales, where only booksellers are admitted, and of them only such as were invited by having catalogues sent them. At one of these sales I have frequently seen seventy or eighty thousand volumes sold after dinner, including books of every description, good, bad, and indifferent; by this means they were distributed through the trade.

When first invited to these trade sales, I was very much surprised to learn, that it was common for such as purchased remainders, to *destroy* one half or three fourths of such books, and to charge the full publication price, or nearly that, for such as they kept on hand; and there was a kind of standing order amongst the trade, that in case any one was known to sell articles under the publication price, such a person was to be excluded from trade sales; so blind were copyright-holders to their own interest.

For a short time I cautiously complied with this custom; but I soon began to reflect that many of these books so destroyed, possessed much merit, and only wanted to be better known; and that if others were not worth six shillings, they were worth three, or two, and so in proportion for higher or lower priced books.

From that time I resolved not to destroy any books that were worth saving, but to sell them off at half, or a quarter of the publication prices. By selling them in this cheap manner, I have disposed of many hundred thousand volumes, many thousands of which have been intrinsically worth their original prices. This part of my conduct, however, though evidently highly beneficial to the community, and even to booksellers, created me many enemies among the trade; some of the meaner part of whom, instead of employing their time and abilities in attending to the increase of their own business, aimed at reducing mine; and by a variety of pitiful insinuations and dark inuendoes, strained every nerve to injure the reputation I had already acquired with the public, determined, (as they *wisely* concluded) thus to effect my ruin; which indeed they daily prognosticated, with a dæmon-like spirit, must inevitably very speedily follow. This conduct, however, was far from intimidating me, as the effect proved directly opposite to what they wished for and expected, and I found the respect and confidence of the public continually increasing, which added very considerably to the number of my customers: It being an unquestionable fact, that before I adopted this plan, great numbers of persons were very desirous of possessing some particular books, for which however (from various motives) they were not inclined to pay the original price; as some availed themselves of the opportunity of borrowing from a friend, or from a circulating library, or having once read them, though they held the works in esteem, might deem them too dear to purchase; or they might have a copy by them, which from their own and family's frequent use (or lending to friends) might not be in so good a condition as they could wish, though rather than purchase them again at the full price, they would keep those they had; or again, they might be desirous to purchase them to make presents of; or they might have a commission from a correspondent in the country, or abroad, and wished to gain a small profit on the articles for their trouble, not to mention the great numbers that would have been given to the poor.

Thousands of others have been effectually prevented from purchasing (though anxious so to do) whose circumstances in life would not permit them to pay the full price, and thus were totally excluded from the advantage of improving their understandings, and enjoying a rational entertainment. And you may be assured, that it affords me the most pleasing satisfaction, independent of the emoluments which have accrued to me from this plan, when I reflect what prodigious numbers in inferior or *reduced* situations of life, have been essentially benefited in consequence of being thus enabled to indulge their natural propensity for the acquisition of knowledge, on easy terms: nay, I could almost be vain enough to assert, that I have thereby been highly instrumental in diffusing that general defire for READING, now fo prevalent among the inferior orders of fociety: which moft certainly, though it may not prove equally inftructive to all, keeps them from employing their time and money, if not to *bad*, at leaft to *lefs rational* purpofes.

How happy fhould I have deemed myfelf in the earlier ftage of my life, if I could have met with the opportunity which every one capable of reading may now enjoy, of obtaining books at fo eafy a rate; had that been the cafe, the catalogue of my *juvenile library*, with which I prefented you in a former letter, would have made a more refpectable appearance, and I might poffibly have been enabled, when I purchafed Young's Night Thoughts for a *Chriftmas dinner*, to have at the fame time bought a joint of meat, and thus enjoyed both a mental and corporal feaft, as well as pleafed my wife, (which I need not inform you the ladies fay every good hufband ought to do.) But after all, quere, Whether if I had enjoyed fuch an advantage, fhould I ever have thought of commencing bookfeller? If not, fhould I have been the *great man* I now feel myfelf, and hope you acknowledge me to be?

　For life or wealth let Heav'n my lot affign,
　A firm and even foul fhall ftill be mine.　　　C. PITT.

In my next I will make a few obfervations on purchafing manufcripts, bookfellers liberality, authors turning publifhers, &c. In the mean time,

　　　　I am,

　　　　　　Dear Friend,

　　　　　　　　Yours.

LETTER XXXVI.

High in the world of letters and of wit,
Enthron'd like Jove behold opinion fit!
As symbols of her sway, on either hand
Th' unfailing urns of praise and censure stand;
Their ming'ed streams her motley servants shed
On each bold author's self devoted head.　　HAYLEY.

DEAR FRIEND,

I Promised in my last to give you
a few remarks on purchasing manuscripts; and as I
seldom make such purchases, and but rarely publish
any new books, I think you may fairly credit me for
impartiality. Nothing is more common than to hear
authors complaining against publishers, for want of
liberality in purchasing their manuscripts. But I
cannot help thinking that most of these complaints are
groundless; and that were all things considered, publishers (at least many of them) would be allowed to
possess more liberality than any other set of tradesmen,
I mean so far as relates to the purchasing manuscripts
and copy-right.

Not to trouble you with a long enumeration of
instances in confirmation of this assertion, I shall
barely mention the following:

It is owing to the encouragement of booksellers
that the public is possessed of that valuable work
Johnson's Dictionary; and the same liberality to the
doctor in respect to that publication, his edition of
Shakespeare, and the English Poets, will always reflect honour on the parties. So sensible was the
doctor of this, that he asserted booksellers were the
best Mæcenas's.

Pope, the late Sir John Hawkins, Dr. Cullen,
Hume, Dr. Hill, Dr. Robertson, Mr. Gibbon, &c.
&c. are all striking instances of the truth of my
observation.

As I feel a pleasure in mentioning acts of liberality
wherever they occur, suffer me to quote the follow-

ing paffage from Sir John Hawkins's Life of Dr.
Johnson:

"The bookfellers with whom Mr. Chambers had
contracted for his Dictionary, finding that the work
fucceeded beyond their expectations, made him a vo-
luntary prefent of, I think, 500l. Other inftances
of the like generofity have been known, of a profef-
fion of men, who, in the debates on the queftion of
literary property, have been defcribed as fcandalous
monopolizers, fattening at the expence of other men's
ingenuity, and growing opulent by oppreffion." He
alfo fays, that Dr. Hill earned in one year 1500l. by
his pen. In vol. 4, of Bell's Fugitive Pieces, page
182, we are informed that Dr. Goldfmith cleared in
one year 1800l. by his pen.

The late Mr. Elliot, bookfeller, of Edinburgh,
gave Mr. Smellie a thoufand pounds for his Philofophy of Natural Hiftory, when only the heads of the
chapters were wrote. Hume received only 200l. for
one part of the Hiftory of Britain, but for the remainder of that work he had 500l. Dr. Robertfon
was paid for his Hiftory of Scotland but 600l. but
for his Charles V. he received 4500l. Dr. Blair obtained the higheft price for Sermons that ever was
given: they were purchafed by Mr. Cadell in the
Strand, and Mr. Creech of Edinburgh; and after the
firft two volumes of thefe Sermons were publifhed,
Dr. Blair was farther rewarded from another quarter
with a penfion of 200l. a year; Sherlock's Sermons
had a very great fale, as had Dr. White's and many
others, but none ever fold fo well as Dr. Blair's, and
the fale of them is ftill as geat as ever.

It is confidently afferted, that the late Dr. Hawkef-
worth received 6000l. for his compilation of Voyages:
if fo (and I have never heard it contradicted) I leave
it to any confiderate perfon to judge, whether in
paying fo enormous a price, the publifhers did not
run a great rifk, when it is confidered how great the
expences of bringing forward fuch a work muft have
been. I have alfo been informed, that David Mallet,
Efq. was offered 2000l. for Lord Bolingbroke's Phi-
lofophical Works, which he refufed.

L

A very few years since, Mr. R— was paid 1600l. to do a work, but he died without performing, and the money being spent, it was not recoverable. Before Dr. Rees engaged to revise and improve Chambers's Dictionary of Arts and Sciences, very large sums for that purpose had from time to time been obtained from the proprietors, by persons who never fulfilled their engagements.

It ought also to be considered, that frequently the money which is paid for the copy, is but trifling, compared with the expence of printing, paper, advertising, &c. and hundreds of instances may be adduced of publishers having sustained very great losses, and many have been bankrupts, through their liberality in purchasing manuscripts and publishing them; and on the other hand, it must be acknowledged that some publishers have made great fortunes by their copy-rights, but their number is comparatively small.

I have been told of booksellers who frequently offer as low as half a guinea per volume for novels in manuscript; it is a shocking price to be sure, but it should be remembered that as there are some of the trade who are mean enough to wish to obtain valuable copy-rights for nothing; so, on the other hand, many novels have been offered to booksellers; indeed, many have actually been published, that were not worth the expence of paper and printing, so that the copy-right was dear at any price; and it should be remarked, that authors in general are apt to form too great expectations from their productions, many instances of which I could give you, but I will only produce one.

A gentleman a few years since shewed a manuscript to a publisher, which he refused to purchase, but offered to be the publisher if the gentleman would print it, &c. at his own expence, which he readily agreed to do; the publisher then desired to know how many copies should be printed, on which the gentleman began to compute how many families there were in Great Britain, and assured the publisher that every family would at *least* purchase one copy; but the publisher not being of the same opinion, our author then said that he would print sixty thousand copies *only*, but added, he was afraid that another edition could not be got ready as soon as it would be wanted. However, after a long debate, the publisher prevailed on him to print only *twelve hundred and fifty*, instead of *sixty thousand*, but promised in case another edition should be wanted in haste, to make the printers work night and day, in order not to disappoint the public. This work was soon afterwards published and advertised at a great rate, and for a long time, but to the infinite mortification of our author, not one hundred copies were sold, not even enough indeed to pay for the advertisements. In the preceding instance, I am persuaded the publisher did his best to promote the sale of the work; but in general where authors keep their own copy-right they do not succeed, and many books have been consigned to oblivion, through the inattention and mismanagement of publishers, as most of them are envious of the success of such works as do not turn to their own account; very many just complaints are made on this head, so that I am fully of opinion, that for authors to succeed well, they should sell their copy-right, or be previously well acquainted with the characters of their publishers.

Many works might be mentioned that never sold well, whilst the author retained the copy-right, which had a rapid sale after it was sold to the trade; and no wonder, for if the publisher wishes to purchase the copy-right, he sometimes will take care to prevent the sale of the work, in order to make the author out of conceit with the book, and be willing to part with the copy-right for a mere trifle; but this is only true of some publishers; I am sorry that any such should be found, but I am sure as to the fact.

As I have before observed, there are some authors who become their own publishers, but that mode will seldom or ever answer, as fifty to one might be sold by being exposed to view, and recommended in booksellers shops, where ladies and gentlemen are continually calling to purchase some books, and to turn over others, and often by dipping into publications are led to purchase such as they had no intention to buy. But authors fhould be reminded that there are many who would not go to private houfes to look over books when they are not certain to purchafe, and where if they do purchafe, they are to take them home in their pockets, or be at the trouble of fending for them, which is not the cafe when they purchafe at a bookfeller's fhop. And all authors fhould be fure to give the full allowance to the trade, or their works can never have a great fale, as no bookfeller can reafonably be expected to promote the fale of a work in which he is abridged of his ufual profits, and the more liberality authors exercife towards the trade, the greater will be their profits in the end. For it is inconceivable what mifchief bookfellers *can* and often *will* do to authors, as thoufands of books are yearly written for to London, that are never fent; and in thefe cafes many plaufible reafons are affigned by them for fuch omiffions, as, " The book is too dear, or it is out of print; the author is fcarce ever at home; he gives too much trouble; he does not keep his work bound, or fewed; he is gone from his former lodging, and no one knows where to find him; the work is not worth your purchafing; fuch a one has wrote much better on the fubject," &c. &e. and in fuch cafes, what redrefs can an author have for fo effential an injury?

I am,

Dear Friend,

Yours.

LETTER XXXVII.

Books, of all earthly things my chief delight;
My exercife by day, and dreams by night;
Difpaffion'd mafters, friends without deceit,
Who flatter not; companions ever fweet;
With whom I'm always cheerful, from whom rife
Improv'd and better, if not good and wife;
Grave, faithful counfellors, who all'excite,
Inftruct and ftrengthen to behave aright;
Admonifh us, when fortune makes her court,
And when fhe's abfent, folace and fupport.
Happy the man to whom ye are well known,
'Tis his own fault if ever he's alone.   ANONYMOUS.

DEAR FRIEND,

ALTHOUGH the refult of the plan which I adopted for reducing the price of books, as mentioned in my laft, was a vaft incrsafe of purchafers, yet at the fame time I found a prodigious accumulation of my expences; which will not appear ftrange, when I inform you, that I made proportionably large purchafes, fuch as two hundred copies of one book, three hundred of another, five hundred of a third, a thoufand of a fourth, two thoufand of a fifth, nay, fometimes I have purchaſed fix thoufand copies of one book, and at one time I actually had no lefs than TEN THOUSAND COPIES of Watts's Pfalms, and the fame number of his Hymns, in my poffeffion. In addition to thefe, I purchafed very large numbers of many thoufand different articles, at trade fales of all forts, as bankrupt fales, fales of fuch as had retired from bufinefs, others caufed by the death of bookfellers, fales to reduce large ftocks, annual fales, &c. To enable you to form fome idea on the fubject, I muft inform you that at one of the above fales, I have purchafed books to the amount of 5000l. in one afternoon. Not to mention thofe purchafed of authors, and town and country bookfellers, by private contract, &c. to a very confiderable amount. My expences were alfo exceedingly increafed by the ncceffity I was under of keeping each article in a variety of different kinds of bindings, to suit the various taftes of my cuftomers; befides paying my bills for the above, I was always obliged to find ready money to pay for libraries and parcels of fecond-hand books, which after a while poured in upon me from town and country. So that I often look back with aftonifhment at my courage (or temerity, if you plea e) in purchafing, and my wonderful fuccefs in taking money fufficient to pay the extenfive demands that were perpetually made upon me, as there is not another inftance of fuccefs fo rapid and conftant under fuch circumftances. Some indeed there have been, who for two or three years, purchafed away very faft, but could not perfevere, as they were unable to fell with equal rapidity: for no one that has not a quick fale can poffibly fucceed with large numbers. For fuppofing that a bookfeller expends 1000l. in the purchafe of four articles (I have often done that in only one article) and thefe are bought at a quarter the ufual price, the intereft of the money is 50l. a year; befides which, fome allowance muft be made for warehoufe-room, infurance from fire, &c. now granting he might fell a few of each article every year at four times the price he firft paid for them, yet if he does not fell enough to pay the intereft and other expences of thofe that remain, he is, after all, on the lofing fide; which has been the cafe with the major part of fuch as have purchafed a large number of one book, and I have known many inftances of bookfellers purchafing articles at a quarter the price, and felling them at the full price, and yet have not had two per cent. for their money.

For feveral years together I thought I fhould be obliged to defift from purchafing a large number of any one article; for although by not giving any credit I was enabled to fell very cheap, yet the heavy ftock of books in fheets often fo difheartened me, that I more than once refolved to leave off purchafing all fuch articles where the number was very large. But, fomehow, a torrent of bufinefs fuddenly pouring in upon me on all fides, I very foon forgot my refolution of not making large purchases, and now find my account in firmly adhering to that method; and being universally known for making large purchases, most of the trade in town and country, and also authors of every description, are continually furnishing me with opportunities. In this branch of trade it is next to impossible for me ever to have any formidable rivals, as it requires an uncommon exertion, as well as very uncommon success, and that for many years together, to rise to any great degree of eminence in that particular line. The success must be attained too, without the aid of *novelty*, which I found to be of very great service to me: And should any person begin on my plan and succeed extremely well, he could never supersede me, as I am still enlarging my business every year, and the more it is extended the cheaper I can afford to sell; so that though I may be pursued, I cannot be overtaken, except I should (as some others have done) be so infatuated and blinded by prosperity, as to think that the public would continue their favours, even though the plan of business was reversed.

> " Let Lackington remember how he rose,
> " Nor turn his back on men who made him great."

As the first King of Bohemia kept his country shoes by him, to remind him from whence he was taken, I have put a motto on the doors of my carriage, constantly to remind me to what I am indebted for my prosperity, viz.

" SMALL PROFITS DO GREAT THINGS."

And I assure you, Sir, that reflecting on the means by which I have been enabled to support a carriage, adds not a little to the pleasure of riding in it. I believe I may, without being deemed censorious, assert, that there are some who ride in their carriages, who cannot reflect on the means by which they were acquired with an equal degree of satisfaction.

> If splendor charm not, yet avoid the scorn
> That treads on lowly stations, think of some
> Affiduous booby mounting o'er your head,
> And thence with saucy grandeur looking down:

Think of (reflection's ftab!) the pitying friend,
With fhoulder fhrugg'd, and forry. Think that time
Has golden minutes, if difcreetly feiz'd.
Riches and fame are induftry's reward.
The nimble runner courfes fortune down,
And then he banquets, for fhe feeds the bold.

Dr. Sneyd Davies to F. Cornwallis.

I am,

Dear Friend,

Yours.

LETTER XXXVIII.

Thofe who would learning's glorious kingdom find,
The dear-bought treafure of the trading mind,
From many dangers muft themfelves acquit,
And more than Scylla and Charybdis meet.
Oh ! what an ocean muft be voyag'd o'er,
To gain a profpect of the fhining ftore !
Refifting rocks oppofe th' enquiring foul,
And adverfe waves retard it as they roll.
The little knowledge now which man obtains,
From outward objects and from fenfe he gains ;
He like a wretched flave muft plod and fweat,
By day muft toil, by night that toil repeat ;
And yet, at laft, what little fruit he gains,
A beggar's harveft glean'd with mighty pains !

Pomfret.

DEAR FRIEND,

IT has been afked, times innume-
rable, how I acquired any tolerable degree of knowledge, fo as to enable me to form any ideas of the
merits or demerits of books ; or how I became fufficiently acquainted with the prices that books were
commonly fold for, fo as to be able to buy and fell ;
particularly books in the learned and foreign languages. Many have thought that from the beginning

I always kept shopmen to furnish me with instructions necessary to carry on my business; but you and all my old friends and acquaintances well know that not to have been the case; as for the first thirteen years after I became a bookseller, I never had one shopman who knew any thing of the worth of books, or how to write a single page of catalogue properly, much less to compile the whole. I always wrote them myself, so long as my health would permit; indeed I continued the practice for years after my health was much impaired by too constant an application to that and reading; and when I was at last obliged to give up writing them, I for several catalogues stood by and dictated to others; even to the present time I take some little part in their compilation; and as I ever did, I still continue to fix the price to every book that is sold in my shop, except such articles as are both bought and sold again while I am out of town. I have now many assistants in my shop, who buy, sell, and in short transact the major part of my business.

As to the little knowledge of literature I possess, it was acquired by dint of application. In the beginning I attached myself very closely to the study of divinity and moral philosophy, and thus became tolerably acquainted with all the points controverted between divines: after having read the great champions for Christianity, I next read the works of Toulmin, Lord Herbert, Tindal, Chubb, Morgan, Collins, Hammond, Woolston, Annet, Mandeville, Shaftesbury, D'Argens, Bolingbroke, Williams, Helvetius, Voltaire, and many other free-thinkers.

> If to object, system, scene confin'd,
> The sure effect is narrowness of mind.   J. LANGHORNE.

I have also read most of our English poets, and the best translations of the Greek, Latin, Italian, and French poets.

> What pure delights possess the captive soul
> To hear the Mantuan, or Mæonian roll,
> The stream of song still swelling on its way,
> That keeps by turns each human spring in play!

L 5

What pure delight ! when Pindar sweeps the lyre,
Or the gay Anacreon breathes his fire ;
Or courtly Horace wakes Alcæus' lay,
Who slily lashes while he seems to play.'
When, with high Milton's soul, he takes his flight
To Stygian horrors, or the realms of light,
Riding on fancy's boldest wing t' explore
Regions which mortal eye ne'er pierc'd before
When moral Pope the lovely forms displays
Of truth or beauty in his polish'd lays ;
Or Young, envelop'd with funereal gloom,
Rises to radiant glories from the tomb ;
Or Thomson traverses the changing fields,
To cull each hidden flow'r which nature yields ;
Or while the eventful line his thought engage,
Deduc'd from history's religious page,
What pleasing wonder holds him, while the scene
Assumes, successive, each contrasting mien !
Like the proud vessel which the tempest plies,
Now human glory seems to reach the skies ;
Now plunges in th' abyss of adverse fate,
Or struck by justice, or o'erwhelm'd by hate.
How he contemns, with generous pride, a race
Whose bastard morals mark her with disgrace.
For him to life the mimick pencil calls
A new creation round the glowing walls.

Essay on Sensibility.

I have also read with great pleasure, and I hope
with some benefit, most translations of the Greek and
Roman authors in prose ; History, Voyages, Travels,
Natural History, Biography, &c.

Survey the globe, each ruder realm explore,
From reason's faintest ray to Newton soar ;
What different spheres to human bliss assign'd ?
What slow gradations in the scale of mind.
Yet mark in each these mystic wonders wrought,
Oh mark the sleepless energies of thought.

Pleasures of Memory.

At one time I had a strong inclination to learn
French, but as soon as I was enabled to make out and
abridge title pages, sufficiently to insert them right
in my catalogues, I left off what appeared to me more
pleasing as well as more necessary pursuits, reflecting
that as I began so late in life, and had probably but
a very short period to live, (and I paid some regard
to what Helvetius has asserted, viz. that " No man

acquires any new ideas after he is forty-five years of age.") I had no time to bestow on the attainment of languages.

> " 'Tis weak in any man to lavish pains,
> " And rifle and confound his brains."

I therefore contented myself with reading all the translations of the classics, and inserted the originals in my Catalogues as well as I could; and when sometimes I happened to put the *Genitive* or *Dative* case instead of the *Nominative* or *Accusative*, my customers kindly considered this as a venial fault, which they readily pardoned, and bought the books notwithstanding.

As I have indefatigably used my best endeavours to acquire knowledge, I never thought I had the smallest reason to be ashamed on account of my deficiency, especially as I never made pretensions to erudition, or affected to possess what I knew I was deficient in. " A bookseller (says Mr. Paterson in his Joineriana) is in general, a bad judge of every thing—but his stupidity shines most conspicuously in that particular branch of knowledge by which he is to get his bread " Dr. Young's couplet, you will therefore think equally applicable to many others as well as myself:

> Unlearned men of books assume the care,
> As eunuchs are the guardians of the fair.   Love of Fame.

I had almost forgot to inform you, that I have also read most of our best plays, and am so fond of the Theatre, that in the winter season I have often been at Drury-lane or Covent-garden four or five evenings in a week.

> ——— There cultivate my mind
> With the soft thrillings of the tragic muse,
> Divine Melpomene, sweet pity's nurse,
> Queen of the stately step, and flowing pall.
> Nor let Monimia mourn with streaming eyes,
> Her joys incestuous, and polluted love :
> Now let soft Juliet in the gaping tomb
> Print the last kiss on her true Romeo's lips,
> His lips yet reeking from the deadly draught,
> Or Jaffier kneel for one forgiving look.

Nor seldom let the Moor on Desdemona
Pour the misguided threats of jealous rage.
By soft degrees the manly torrent steals
From my swoll'n eyes, and at a brother's woe
My big heart melts in sympathising tears.
What are the splendors of the gaudy court,
Its tinsel trappings, and its pageant pomps?
To me far happier seems the banish'd Lord,
Amid Siberia's unrejoicing wilds.   WARTON.

Another great source of amusement as well as
knowledge I have met with, in reading almost all the
best novels; by the *best*, I mean those written by
Cervantes, Fielding, Smollett, Richardson, Miss
Burney, Voltaire, Marmontel, Sterne, Le Sage,
Goldsmith, Mackenzie, Dr. Moor, Green, C. Smith,
Gunning, Lee, Reeves, Lennox, Radcliff, and some
others. Indeed I have often thought with Fielding,
that some of those publications have given us a more
genuine history of Man, in what are called Romances,
than is sometimes to be found under the more respectable titles of History, Biography, &c. I have
indeed dipped into every thing as Dr. Armstrong advises.

Toy with your books, and as the various fits
Of humour seize you, from philosopy
To fable shift; from serious Antonine
To Rabelais' ravings, and from prose to song;
While reading pleases, but no longer read;
And read aloud resounding Homer's strains,
And wield the thunder of Demosthenes.
The chest so exercised, improves its thoughts,
And quick vibrations thro' the bowels drive
The restless blood, which in unactive days
Would loiter else, through unelastic tubes.
Deem it not trifling, while I recommend
What posture suits; to stand and sit by turns,
As nature prompts, is best, but o'er your leaves
To lean for ever cramps the vital parts,
And robs the fine machinery of its play.
      Art of Preserving Health.

In order to obtain some ideas in Astronomy, Geo-
graphy, Electricity, Pneumatics, &c. I attended a
few lectures given by the late eminent Mr. Ferguson,
the present very ingenious Mr. Walker, and others;
and for some time several gentlemen spent two or

three evenings in a week at my houſe, for the purpoſe of improvement in ſcience. At theſe meetings we made the beſt uſe of our time with globes, teleſcopes, microſcopes, electrical machines, air pumps, air guns, *a good bottle of wine*, and *other philoſophical* inſtruments——

—— He a choſen few around him ſees
Whoſe worth attaches, and whoſe manners pleaſe,
To whom he gives, from whom receives again,
Augmented pleaſure, and diminiſh'd pain.
                              Eſſay on Senſibility.

The mention of which revives in my memory the loſs I ſuſtained by the premature death of a worthy philoſophical friend, whom you have met, when you occaſionally did us the honour of making one of the evening party, and benefiting us by your inſtructions. I could ſay much in his praiſe, but ſhall forbear, as another friend, who was alſo one of this (I may truly ſay) *rational aſſembly*, has compoſed what I think a juſt character of him, free from that fulſome panegyric which too often degrades thoſe it is meant to celebrate, and conveys to all who knew the parties, the idea of having been deſigned as a burleſque inſtead of an encomium; however, as you may not have ſeen it (though in print) and it will engroſs but a very little of your time to peruſe, I ſhall here beg leave to inſert it:

" With what ſurpriſe poſterity ſhall ſee
" A panegyric penn'd without a fee !"

" On Sunday, May 24, 1789, died at his houſe in
" Worſhip-ſtreet, Moorfields, aged 50, Mr. Ralph
" Tinley; one who had not dignity of birth or ele-
" vated rank in life to boaſt of, but who poſſeſſed
" what is far ſuperior to either, a ſolid underſtand-
" ing, amiable manners, a due ſenſe of religion, and
" an induſtrious diſpoſition. Inſtead of riches, Pro-
" vidence bleſſed him with a good ſhare of health,
" and a mind contented with an humble ſituation.
" Thoſe hours which he could ſpare from a proper
" attention to the duties of a huſband and a father,
" and manual labour as a ſhoemaker, were inceſſant-

" ly employed in the improvement of his mind in va-
" rious branches of science; in many of which he
" attained a proficiency, totally divested of that affecta-
" tion of superiority which little minds assume. These
" qualities rendered him respected by all who knew
" him, as an intelligent man, and a most agreeable
" companion. Among other acquisitions, ENTOMO-
" LOGY was his peculiar delight. Thus far the
" prospect is pleasing. It is a painful task to add,
" that this amiable person fell a victim to an unhappy
" error in taking a medicine. The evening previous
" to his decease he spent in a philosophical society, of
" which he had many years been a member, and where
" his attendance had been constant; but finding him-
" self indisposed, he in the morning early had re-
" course to a phial of antimonial wine, which had
" long been in his possession, and of which only a
" small part remained. This, most unfortunately, he
" swallowed; and it having, by long maceration, ac-
" quired an extraordinary degree of strength, and
" being rendered turbid by mixing with the metallic
" particles, it produced the effect of a violent poison,
" occasioning almost instantaneous death. May his
" fate prove a warning to others, to be careful how
" they venture to confide in their own judgment in
" so intricate a science as medicine!—His valuable
" cabinet of insects, both foreign and domestic, sup-
" posed to be one of the completest (of a private col-
" lection) in the kingdom, all scientifically arranged
" with peculiar neatness, and in the finest preserva-
" tion, will (if it falls into proper hands,) remain a
" monument of his knowledge and application."

Honour and shame from no condition rise;
Act well your part, there all the honor lies.
Fortune in men have some small difference made,
One flaunts in rags, one flutters in brocade;
The cobler apron'd, and the parson gown'd,
The friar hooded, and the monarch crown'd,
What differ more (you cry) than crown and cowl?
I'll tell you friend—a wise man and a fool.
You'll find, if once the monarch acts the monk,
Or, cobler-like, the parson will be drunk;
Worth makes the man, and want of it the fellow,
The rest is all but leather or prunella.   POPE.

My thirſt was, and ſtill is ſo great for literature, that I could almoſt ſubſcribe to the opinions of Herillus the philoſopher, who placed in learning the ſovereign good, and maintained that it was alone ſufficient to make us wiſe and happy; others have ſaid that " Learning is the mother of all virtue, and that vice is produced from ignorance." Although that is not ſtrictly true, yet I cannot help regretting the diſadvantages I labour under by having been deprived of the benefits of an early education, as it is a loſs that can ſcarcely be repaired, in any ſituation. How much more difficult then was it for me to attain any degree of proficiency, when involved in the concerns of a large buſineſs ?

> Without a genius learning ſoars in vain,
> And without learning, genius ſinks again ;
> Their force united, crowns the ſprightly reign.
> ELPHINSTON'S Horace.

The inſtructions that I received from men and books were often like the ſeeds ſown among thorns, the cares of the world choaked them :

> My head was full of houſehold cares,
> And neceſſary dull affairs.   Lord LYTTELTON.

So that although I underſtand a little of many branches of literature, yet my knowledge is, after all, I freely confeſs, but ſuperficial; which indeed I need not have told you.

> For me, on this life's ſea which we explore,
> I ſtrive to furniſh out a ſkiff and oar,
> To regulate deſire, the tempeſt check,
> And, if I can, ſave reaſon from a wreck.
> BOILEAU to J—K—, ESQ.

As Montaigne ſaid two hundred years ago, I may ſay now, " I have a ſmatch of every thing, and no-
" thing thoroughly *a-la-mode de Francoiſe*. As to
" my natural parts, I often find them to bow under
" the burden; my fancy and judgment do but grope
" in the dark, ſtaggering, tripping, and ſtumbling ;
" and when I have gone as far I can, I am by no
" means ſatisfied; I ſee more land ſtill before me,
" but ſo wrapped up in clouds, that my dim ſight

" cannot diftinguifh what it is." However, fuper-
ficial as my knowledge is, it affords me an endlefs
fource of pleafure.

> And books are ftill my higheft joy,
> Thefe earlieft pleafe, and lateft cloy.　SOAME JENYNS.

It has alfo been of very great ufe to me in bufinefs,
enabling me to put a value on thoufands of articles,
before I knew what fuch books were commonly fold
at: 'tis true I was fometimes miftaken, and have fold
a very great number of different articles much lower
than I ought, even on my own plan of felling very
cheap, yet that never gave me the fmalleft concern;
but if I difcovered that I had (as fometimes was the
cafe) fold any articles too dear, it gave me much un-
eafinefs; for whether I had any other motives I will
leave to fuch as are acquainted with me to determine;
but I reafoned thus; if I fell a book too dear, I perhaps lofe that cuftomer and his friends for ever; but
if I fell articles confiderably under their real value, the purchafer will come again and recommend
my fhop to his acquaintances; fo that from the principles of felf-intereft I would fell cheap. I always
was inclined to reafon in this matter, and nine years
fince a very trifling circumftance operated much upon
my mind, and fully convinced me my judgment was
right on that head. Mrs. Lackington had bought a
piece of linen to make me fome fhirts; when the linen-draper's man brought it into my fhop, three
ladies were prefent, and on feeing the cloth opened,
afked Mrs. L. what it coft per yard: on being told
the price, they all faid it was very cheap, and each
lady went and purchafed the fame quantity, to make
fhirts for their hufbands; thofe pieces were again dif-
played to their acquaintances, fo that the linen-draper
got a deal of cuftom from that very circumftance;
and I refolved to do likewife. Trivial as this anecdote may appear, you will pardon me for introducing
it, when you reflect that it was productive of very
beneficial confequences, and that many greater effects
have arifen from as trivial caufes. We are even told
that Sir Ifaac Newton would probably never have

ſtudied the ſyſtem of gravitation had he not been under an apple tree, when ſome of the fruit looſened
from the branches and fell to the earth. It was the
queſtion of a ſimple gardener concerning a pump,
that led Galileo to ſtudy and diſcover the weight of
the air. To the tones of a Welch harp, are we indebted for the Bard of Grey; and Gibbon formed
the deſign of that truly great work, his Hiſtory of
the Decline of the Roman Empire, while viewing
the ruins of the Capitol.

> Lull'd in the countleſs chambers of the brain,
> Our thoughts are link'd by many a hidden chain;
> Awake but one, and lo, what myriads riſe!
> Each ſtamps its image as the other flies.
>
> ROGERS's (Banker) Pleaſures of Memory

I am,

Dear Friend,

Yours.

LETTER XXXIX.

> —— Honeſt Engliſhmen, who never were abroad,
> Like England only, and its taſte applaud.
> Strife ſtill ſubſiſts, which yields the better gout;
> Books or the world, the many or the few:
> True taſte to me is by this touchſtone known,
> That's always beſt that's neareſt to my own,
>
> MAN of Taſte.

DEAR FRIEND,

IT has been long ſince remarked,
that a perſon may be well acquainted with books, or
in other words, may be a very learned man, and yet
remain almoſt totally ignorant of men and manners,
as Mallet remarks of a famous divine:

> While Bentley, long to wrangling fchools confin'd,
> And but by books acquainted with mankind,
> Dares, in the fulnefs of the pedant's pride,
> ——————————— Tho' no judge decide.
>
> Verbal Criticifm.

Hence many fine chimerical fyftems of law, government, &c. have been fpun out of the prolific
brains of the learned, which have only ferved to
amufe others as learned and as unacquainted with
mankind as the authors, and have frequently produced a number of remarks, replies, obfervations,
fevere (not to fay fcurrillous) criticifms, and new
fyftems and hypothefes; thefe again gave birth to
frefh remarks, rejoinders, &c. *ad* —— (*infinitum*).
Thefe learned men, after tiring themfelves and the
public, have generally left them juft as wife on the
fubject as when they began; nay often

> From the fame hand how various is the p ge;
> What civil war their brother pamphlets rage?
> Tracts battle tracts, felf-contradictions glare.   Youno.

The reading and ftudying of Hiftory, Voyages,
Travels, &c. will no doubt contribute much to that
ufeful kind of knowledge, but will not alone be fufficient; in order to become a proficient, " MAN, KNOW
THYSELF!" was a precept of the ancient philofo-
phers. But I can fcarce think it poffible for any man
to be well acquainted with himfelf, without his poffeffing a tolerable degree of knowledge of the reft of
mankind.

> " —— His fav'rite ftudy is *mankind*,
> " And the Creator's brighteft image—mind !"

In the former part of my life I faw much of what
is called *low life*, and became acquainted with the
cuftoms, manners, difpofitions, prejudices, &c. of
the labouring part of the community, in various cities,
towns, and villages.

> ——————————— I love to fee
> How hardly fome of their frugal morfel earn,
> It gives my own a zeft, and ferves to damp
> The longing appetite of difcontent.   Hvosis.

For years past, I have spent some of my leisure hours among that class of people who are called opulet or genteel tradesmen; nor have I been totally excluded from higher circles.

> A flow of good spirits I've seen with a smile
> To worth make a shallow pretence:
> And the chat of good breeding with ease, for a while,
> May pass for good nature and sense.
>
> W. WHITEHEAD.

The middle station of life (says Hume) is the most favourable to the acquiring of wisdom and ability, as well as virtue, and a man so fortunate has a better chance of attaining a knowledge both of men and things, than those of a more elevated station. He enters with more familiarity into human life; every thing appears in its natural colours before him; he has more leisure to form observations, and has besides the motive of ambition to push him on in his attainments, being certain that he can never rise to any distinction, or eminence in the world, without his own industry.

> " He suits to nature's reign th' enquiring eye,
> " Skill'd all her soft gradation to descry,
> " From matter's modes, through instinct's narrow sway,
> " To reason's gradual, but unbounded way,
> " These hold ten thousand wonders to his sight,
> " Which prompt enquiry, and inspire delight:
> " Relations, properties, proportions, ends,
> " Burst into light as the research extends,
> " Until unnumber'd sparks around him fall
> " From the great source of light, and life, and all !"

But among all the schools where the knowledge of mankind is to be acquired, I know of none equal to that of a *bookseller's shop*. A bookseller who has any taste in literature, may in some measure be said to feed his mind as cooks and butchers wives get fat by the smell of meat. If the master is of an inquisitive and communicative turn, and is in a considerable line of business, his shop will then be a place of resort for men, women, and children, of various nations, and of more various capacities, dispositions, &c.

> " Who there but wishes to prolong his stay,
> " And on those cases cast a ling'ring look ;
> " For who to thoughtless ignorance a prey
> " Neglects to hold short dalliance with a book.
> " Reports attract the lawyer's parting eyes,
> " Novels Lord Fopling and Sir Plume require,
> " For songs and plays the voice of beauty cries,
> " And sense and nature Grandison desire."

To adduce a few instances by way of illustration :
—Here you may find an old *bawd* enquiring for,
" The Countess of Huntingdon's Hymn-book ;" an
old worn-out *rake*, for " Harris's List of Covent-
garden Ladies ;" simple *Simon*, for " The Art of
writing Love-letters ;" and Dolly for a Dream-book,
or a Book about Moles ; the lady of true taste and delicacy wants Louisa Matthews ; and my lady's *maid*,
" Ovid's Art of Love ;" a *doubting* Christian, calls
for " The Crumbs of Comfort ;" and a practical
Antinomian, for " Eton's Honey-comb of Free Justification ;" the pious *Churchwoman*, for " The Week's
Preparation ;" and the *Atheist*, for " Hammond's
Letter to Dr. Priestley ; Toulmin's Eternity of the
World, and Hume's Dialogues on Natural Religion ;"
the *Mathematician*, for " Sanderson's Fluxions ;" and
the *Beau*, for " The Toilet of Flora ;" the *Cour-
tier*, for " Machiavel's Prince," or " Burke on the
Revolution in France ;" and a *Republican*, for
" Paine's Rights of Man ;" the tap-room *Politician*,
wants " The History of Wat Tyler," or of " The
Fisherman of Naples ;" and an old Chelsea *Pensioner*,
calls for " The History of the Wars of glorious
Queen Anne ;" the *Critic* calls for " Bayle's Histori-
cal Dictionary—Blair's Lectures—Johnson's Lives of
the Poets, and the last month's Reviews ;" and my
Barber wants " The Sessions Paper," or " The Trial
of John the Painter ;" the *Freethinker* asks for
" Hume's Essays," and the young *Student*, for " Le-
land's View of Deistical Writers ;" the *Fortune-teller*
wants " Sibley's Translation of Placidus de Titus,"
or " Sanderson's Secrets of Palmistry ;" and the
Sceptic wants " Cornelius Agrippa's Vanity of the
Arts and Sciences ;" an *old hardened sinner*, wants
" Bunyan's Good News for the vilest of Men ;" and

a moral *Christian* wants " The Whole Duty of Man;"
the *Roman Catholic* wants " The Lives of the Saints ;"
the *Protestants* wants " Fox's Book of Martyrs;" one
afks for " An Account of Animal Magnetifm;"
another for " The Victorious Philofopher's Stone
difcovered;" one wants " The Death of Abel;"
another defires to have " The Spanifh Rogue;" one
wants an " Ecclefiaftical Hiftory;" another, " The
Tyburn Chronicle;" one wants " Johnfon's Lives
of the Highwaymen;" another wants " Gibbons's
Lives of pious Women ;" Mifs *W——h* calls for
" Euclid in *Greek* ;" and a young *divine* for " Juliet
Grenville, a novel;" and the *philofopher* dips into
books on every fubject.

But it would be an endlefs tafk to fet down the various and oppofite articles that are conftantly called
for in my fhop. To talk to thefe different purfuers
after happinefs, or amufement, has given me much
pleafure, and afforded me fome knowledge of mankind, and alfo of books.

> Go, read mankind; he fairly claims the prize,
> Who in that fchool finds leifure to be wife.
>
> MURPHY.

To hear the debates that frequently occur between
the different purchafers is a fine amufement ; fo that
I have fometimes compared my fhop to a ftage. And
I affure you that a variety of characters, ftrongly
marked, conftantly made their appearance.

> Ye who pufh'd on by noble ardour aim
> In focial life to gain immortal fame,
> Obferve the various paffions of mankind,
> Gen'ral, peculiar, fingle and combin'd ;
> How youth from manhood differ in its views,
> And how old age ftill other paths purfues ;
> How zeal in Prifcus nothing more than heats,
> In Codex burns, and ruins all it meets ;
> How freedom now a lovely face fhall wear,
> Now fhock us in the likenefs of a bear ;
> How jealoufy in fome refembles hate,
> In others feems but love-grown delicate ;
> How modefty is often pride refin'd,
> And virtue but the canker of the mind ;

How love of riches, grandeur, life and fame,
Wear diff'rent fhapes, and yet are ftill the fame.

Effay on Converfation.

Would my health permit my conftant attendance, I fhould prefer it to every thing in life (reading excepted) and you may recollect that for fome years I fought no other amufement whatever. It was at a bookfeller's fhop at Athens, that Zeno, after his great lofs by fhipwreck, found confolation in reading Xenophon : there he foon forgot his lofs : Where (fays he to the bookfeller) do thefe fort of men live ? The philofopher Crates was at the door, whom Zeno followed, and from that hour became his difciple.

Having been long habituated to make remarks on whatever I faw or heard, is another reafon why I have fucceeded fo well in my bufinefs. I have for the laft feven years fucceffively told my acquaintances before the year began, how much money I fhould take in the courfe of it, without once failing of taking the fum mentioned. I formed my judgment by obferving what kind of ftock in trade I had in hand, and by confidering how that ftock was adapted to the different taftes and purfuits of the times ; in doing this I was obliged to be pretty well informed of the ftate of politics in Europe, as I have always found that *book-felling* is much affected by the political ftate of affairs. For as mankind are in fearch of amufement, they often embrace the firft that offers. If there is any thing in the news-papers of confequence, that draws many to the coffee-houfe, where they chat away the evenings, inftead of vifiting the fhops of bookfellers (*as they ought to do, no doubt*) or *reading* at home. The beft time for bookfelling, is when there is no kind of news ftirring ; then many of thofe who for months would have done nothing but talk of war or peace, revolutions, and counter-revolutions, &c. &c. for want of other amufement, will have recourfe to books ; fo that I have often experienced that the report of a war, or the trial of a great man, or indeed any fubject that attracts the public attention, has been fome hundreds of pounds out of my pocket in a few weeks.

Before I conclude this letter, I cannot help observing, that the sale of books in general has increased prodigiously within the last twenty years. According to the best estimation I have been able to make, I suppose that more than four times the number of books are sold now than were sold twenty years since. The poorer sort of farmers, and even the poor country people in general, who before that period spent their winter evenings in relating stories of witches, ghosts, hobgoblins, &c. now shorten the winter nights by hearing their sons and daughters read tales, romances, &c. and on entering their houses, you may see Tom Jones, Roderick Random, and other entertaining books, stuck up on their bacon-racks, &c. If *John* goes to town with a load of hay, he is charged to be sure not to forget to bring home " Peregrine Pickle's Adventures ;" and when *Dolly* is sent to market to sell her eggs, she is commissioned to purchase " The History of Pamela Andrews." In short, all ranks and degrees now READ. But the most rapid increase of the sale of books has been since the termination of the late war.

A number of book-clubs are also formed in every part of England, where each member subscribes a certain sum quarterly to purchase books ; in some of these clubs the books after they have been read by all the subscribers, are sold among them to the highest bidders, and the money produced by such sale, is expended in fresh purchases, by which prudent and judicious mode, each member has it in his power to become possessed of the work of any particular author he may judge deserving a superior degree of attention ; and the members at large enjoy the advantage of a continual succession of different publications, instead of being restricted to a repeated perusal of the same authors ; which must have been the case with many, if so rational a plan had not been adopted.

The *Sunday-Schools* are spreading very fast in most parts of England,

> Millions condemn'd, by earliest error taught,
> To live without the privilege of thought.   MERRY.

which will accelerate the diffusion of knowledge among the lower classes of the community, and in a very few years exceedingly increase the sale of books. —Here permit me earnestly to call on every honest bookseller (I trust my call will not be in vain) as well as on every friend to the extension of knowledge, to unite (as *you* I am confident will) in a hearty —AMEN.

> Perish the illiberal thought which would debase
> The native genius of the *lower* race!
> Perish the proud philosophy, which sought
> To rob them of the pow'rs of equal thought.
>
> MRS. H. MOORE.

Let such as doubt, whether the enlightening of the understandings of the lower orders of society makes them happier, or be of any utility to a state, read the following lines (particularly the last twelve) by Dr. Goldsmith, taken from his Traveller:

> " These are the charms to barren states assign'd,
> " Their wants are few, their wishes all confin'd;
> " Yet let them only share the praises due,
> " If few their wants, their pleasures are but few;
> " Since every want that stimulates the breast,
> " Becomes a source of pleasure when redrest.
> " Hence from such lands each pleasing science flies,
> " That first excites desire, and then supplies.
> " Unknown to them, when sensual pleasures cloy,
> " To fill the languid pause with finer joy;
> " Unknown those powers that raise the soul to flame,
> " Catch every nerve, and vibrates thro' the frame;
> " Their level life is but a mould'ring fire,
> " Nor quench'd by want, nor fann'd by strong desire;
> " Unfit for raptures, or if raptures cheer,
> " On some high festival once a year,
> " In mild excess the vulgar breast takes fire,
> " 'Till buried in debauch, the bliss expire.
>
> " But not their joys alone thus coarsely flow,
> " Their morals, like their pleasures, are but low;
> " For, as refinement stops, from sire to son,
> " Unalter'd, unimprov'd their manners run;
> " And love's and friendship's finely pointed dart
> " Fall blunted from each indurated heart;
> " Some sterner virtues o'er the mountain's breast,
> " May sit like falcon's low'ring on the nest,

  " But all the gentler morals, such as play
  " Thro' life's more cultivated walks, and charm our way;
  " These, far dispers'd, on tim'rous pinions fly,
  " To sport and flutter in the kinder sky."

I must beg leave also to quote a passage from the Abbe Rochan's Voyage to Madagascar and the East Indies, translated from the French by Joseph Trapp, A. M. 8vo. page 31.

" The improvement of reason has on the happiness of man an influence, which the heart of the most subtle sophister cannot invalidate. From that only period knowledge is susceptible of increase; and the amelioration and happiness of a man has no other scale of proportion than that very knowledge; for can there be a system more dangerous, more false, than that which would be founded on an opposite principle."

But to shew you the absurdity and inconsistency of mankind, I must inform you, that a small book, in the French language, was published at the Hague in 1792, entitled, L'Homme Bon, i.e. The Benevolent Man.

In this work the author literally curses all the arts and improvements in civil society; represents the pursuits of science, and the employment of all the noble faculties of man, as the means of plunging us into deeper misery, than can be known to uncultivated savages; who, according to him, are the only beings that are happy, and worthy to inhabit the earth. He concludes his view of human life with this gloomy expression: " If the misery of our fatal condition were duly felt, it would not be necessary to menace us with everlasting fire.—This world is a hell!" *See Monthly Review Enlarged*, vol. ix. page 547, &c.

It is worth remarking that the introducing histories, romances, stories, poems, &c. into schools, has been a very great means of diffusing a general taste for reading among all ranks of people, while in schools, the children only read the Bible, (which was the case in many schools a few years ago) children then did not make so early a progress in reading as they have since they have been pleased and entertained, as well as inftructed; and this relish for books, in many, will laft as long as life.

I am alto informed that literature is making a ftill more rapid progrefs in Germany, and that there are at this time, feven thoufand living authors in that country, and that every body reads.

> At nature's birth, Oh! had the power divine
> Commanded the moral fun to fhine,
> Beam'd on the mind all reafon's influence bright,
> And the full day of *intellectual* light,
> Then the free foul, on truth's ftrong pinion born,
> Had never languifh'd in this fhade forlorn.
>
> J. LANGHORNE.

The great rife of paper falls heavy on bookfellers, particularly publifhers: it will in fome degree retard the progrefs of literature, by preventing the publication of many works, that, but for the great price of paper, would have appeared. All new publications are greatly advanced in price, which muft partly prevent the circulation.

The high price of inferior papers, ufed by grocers, cheefemongers, chandlers, &c. &c. have already caufed many thoufand volumes to be deftroyed, that otherwife would have been preferved, and fold at a low price. The old long-winded folio divines are unmercifully facrificed, as are many of the Greek and Latin fathers, faints, fchoolmen, phyficians, &c. &c.

I am,

Dear Friend,

Yours.

LETTER XI.

First let the muse with generous ardour try
To chase the mist from dark opinion's eye :
Nor mean we here to blame that father's care,
Who guards from learned wives his booby heir ;
Since oft that heir with prudence has been known,
To dread a genius that transcends his own :
The wise themselves should with discretion choose,
Since letter'd nymphs their knowledge may abuse,
And husbands oft experience to their cost
The prudent housewife in the scholar lost :
But those incur deserv'd contempt, who prize.
Their own high talents, and their sex despise,
With haughty mien each social bliss defeat,
And sully all their learning with conceit:
Of such the parent justly warns his son,
And such the muse herself will bid him shun.
But lives there one, whose unassuming mind,
Tho' grac'd by nature, and by art refin'd,
Pleas'd with domestic excellence, can spare
Some hours from studious ease to social care,
And with her pen that time alone employs,
Which others waste in visits, cards, and noise ;
From affectation free, tho' deeply read,
" With wit well natur'd, and with books well bred ?"
With such (and such there are) each happy day
Must fly improving, and improv'd away;
Inconstancy might fix and settle there,
And wisdom's voice approve the chosen fair.

J. Duncombe's Feminead.

DEAR FRIEND,

    I Have been informed, that when circulating libraries were first opened, the booksellers were much alarmed, and their rapid increase added to their fears, had led them to think that the sale of books would be much diminished by such libraries. But experience has proved that the sale of books, so far from being diminished by them, has been greatly promoted, as from those repositories, many thousand families have been cheaply supplied with books, by which the taste for reading has become much more general, and thousands of books are purchased every

M 2

year, by such as have first borrowed them at those libraries, and after reading, approving of them, become purchasers.

Circulating libraries have also greatly contributed towards the amusement and cultivation of the other sex; by far the greatest part of ladies have now a taste for books.

> " —— Learning, once the man's exclusive pride,
> " Seems verging fast towards the female side."

It is true, that I do not, with Miss M. Wolstonecraft, " earnestly wish to see the distinction of sex confounded in society," not even with her exception, " unless where love animates the behaviour." I differ widely, however, from those gentlemen, who would prevent the ladies from acquiring a taste for books; and as yet I have never seen any solid reason advanced, why ladies should not polish their understandings, and render themselves fit companions for men of sense.

> Long o'er the world did Prejudice maintain,
> By sounds like these, her undisputed reign:
> " Woman! (she cry'd) to thee, indulgent heaven
> Has all the charms of outward beauty given:
> Be thine the boast, unrival'd, to enslave
> The great, the wise, the witty, and the brave;
> Deck'd with the Paphian rose s damask glow,
> And the vale-lily's vegetable snow;
> Be thine, to move majestic in the dance,
> To roll the eye, and aim the tender glance;
> Or touch the strings, and breathe the melting song,
> Content to emulate that airy throng,
> Who to the sun their painted plumes display,
> And gaily glitter on the hawthorn spray;
> Or wildly warble in the beechen grove,
> Careless of ought but music, joy, and love.
>
> Female Genius.

I have, indeed, often thought that one great reason, why some gentlemen spend all their leisure hours abroad, is the want of rational companions at home; for if a gentleman happens to marry a fine lady, as justly painted by Miss Wolstonecraft, or the square elbow family drudge, as drawn to the life by the same hand, I must confess that I see no great inducement he can have to desire the company of his wife, as she scarce can be called a rational companion, or one fit to be entrusted with the education of her children. Even Rousseau is obliged to acknowledge that it " is a melancholy thing for a father of a family, who is fond of home, to be obliged to be always wrapt up in himself, and to have nobody about him to whom he can impart his sentiments." Zimmerman, by having a more exalted opinion of the sex, has drawn a fine picture of domestic happiness.

" Of what value are all the babblings and vain boastings of society to that domestic felicity which we experience in the company and conversation of an amiable woman, whose charms awaken all the dormant faculties of the soul, and inspire the mind with finer energies than all our own exertions could attain ; who in the execution of our enterprizes prompts us by her assistance, and encourages us by her approbation, to surmount every difficulty; who impresses us with the greatness of her ideas, and the sublimity of her sentiments ; who weighs and examines with judicious penetration our thoughts, our actions, our whole character; who observes all our foibles, warns us with sincerity of their consequences, and reforms us with gentleness and affection; who, by a tender communication of all her thoughts and observations, conveys new instruction to our minds, and by pouring all the warm and generous feelings of her heart into our bosoms, animates us incessantly to the exercise of every virtue, and completes the polished perfection of our character, by the soft allurements of love, and the delightful concord of her sentiments."

Lord Littelton advises well in the two following lines :

> " Do you, my fair, endeavour to possess
> " An elegance of mind, as well as dress."

The following sketch of the life of a fine lady, well deserves a place here :

> Muscalia dreams of last night's ball till ten,
> Drinks chocolate, stroaks fops, and sleeps again ;.

Perhaps at twelve dares ope her drowfy eyes,
Atks Lucy if 'tis late enough to rife;
By three each curl and feature juftly fet,
She dines, talks fcandal, vifits, plays piquet.
Mean while her babes with fome foul nurfe remain,
For modern dames a mother's cares difdain;
Each fortnight once fhe bears to fee the brats,
" For, oh! they ftun one's ears like fqualling cats!"
Tigers and pards proteft and nurfe their young,
The parent fnake will roll her forked tongue,
The vulture hovers vengeful o'er her neft,
If the rude hand the helplefs brood infeft.
Shall lovely woman, fofteft frame of heav'n,
To whom were tears, and feeling pity giv'n
Moft fafhionably cruel, lefs regard
Her offspring, than the vulture, fnake, and pard?
                        Dr. J. WARTON on Fafhion.

I cannot help thinking, that the reafon why fome
of the eaftern nations treat the ladies with fuch contempt, and look upon them in fuch a degrading point
of view, is owing to their marrying them when mere
children, both as to age and underftanding; which
laft being intirely negleéted, they feldom are capable
of rational converfation, and of courfe are negleéted
and defpifed.

Our Britifh nymphs with happier omens rove,
At freedom's call, thro' wifdom's facred grove;
And, as with lavifh hand, each fifter grace
Shapes the fair form, and regulates the face.
Each fifter mufe, in blifsful union join'd,
Adorns, improves, and beautifies the mind.
Even now fond fancy in our polifh'd land
Affembl'd, fhows a blooming, ftudious band:
With various arts our rev'rence they engage,
Some turn the tuneful, fome the moral page;
Thefe, fed by contemplation, foar on high,
And range the heavens with philofophic eye:
While thofe, furrounded by a vocal choir,
The canvafs tinge, or touch the warbling lyre.
Here, like the ftar's mix'd radiance, they unite
To dazzle and perplex our wand'ring fight:
The mufe each charmer fingly fhall furvey,
And tune to each her tributary lay.
So when, in blendid tints, with fweet furprize,
Affembled beauties ftrike our ravifh'd eyes,
Such as in Lely's melting colours fhine,
Or fpring, great Kneller! from a hand like thine.

On all with pleasing awe at once we gaze,
And, loft in wonder, know not which to praise:
But singly view'd, each nymph delights us more,
Disclosing graces unperceiv'd before.   Female Genius.

Ladies now in general read, not only novels, although many of that class are excellent productions, and tend to polish both the heart and head; but they also read the best books in the English language, and many read the best works in various languages; and there are some thousands of ladies, who frequent my shop, that know as well what books to choose, and are as well acquainted with works of taste and genius, as any gentlemen in the kingdom, notwithstanding they sneer against novel readers, &c.

The rights of women, says a female pen,
Are to do every thing as well as men.
And since the sex at length have been inclin'd
To cultivate that useful part, the mind ;
Since they have larnt to read, to write, to spell ;
Since some of them have wit, and use it well ;
Let us not force them back with brow severe,
Within the pale of ignorance and fear !
Confin'd entirely to domestic arts,
Producing only children, pies, and tarts,   NARES.

I am sorry that Dr. Gregory had some reason for giving the following advice to his daughters: " If you happen (says he) to have any learning, keep it a profound secret, especially from the men, who generally look with a jealous and malignant eye on a woman of great parts."

Upon my life, the men are such odd fellows,
They're even grown of female *learning* jealous ;
These *mighty Lords* came all so learn'd from College,
They grudge poor us our little share of knowledge !
Ladies, since things are thus, take this advice,
Be in your choice of men extremely nice.
                          KEATE's Epilogue to the Wonder.

My God, what sort of men must these be! and what degrading ideas must they have of women.—— Butler, when he wrote this couplet, seems to have been one of that sort:

The souls of women are so small,
That some believe they've none at all.   REMAINS.

The following fine lines of Peter Pindar difcovers more generous fentiments: I will add, that I have often been able to repeat them with fenfations almoft bordering on rapture:

> " Why, yes, it may happen, thou *damfel divine*,
> " To be honeft, I freely declare,
> " That e'en now to thy converfe I fo much incline,
> " I've already forgot thou art fair."

A gentleman of my acquaintance, lately rode fifty miles, for the pleafure of feeing and converfing with a learned woman, but very little known; her name is Elizabeth Ogilvie Benger; when very young, fhe wrote a poem, entitled the Female. She not only underftands Latin, Greek, Italian, Spanifh, and other languages, but is well verfed in various branches of arts and fciences. She is a tide-waiter's daughter, in or near Poatfmouth; it feems fhe learned to read and write, by picking up bits of paper in the ftreet, with which fhe would retire to her garret.

> Shall lordly man, the theme of every lay,
> Ufurp the mufe's tributary bay?
> In kingly ftate on Pindus' fummit fit,
> Tyrant of verfe, and arbiter of wit?
> By falic law the female right deny,
> And view their genius with regardlefs eye?
> Juftice, forbid! and every mufe infpire
> To fing the glories of the fifter-choir!
> Rife, rife, bold fwain; and to the lift'ning grove
> Refound the praifes of the fex you love;
> Tell how, adorn'd with every charm, they fhine,
> In mind and perfon equally divine.
> 'Till man, no more to female merit blind,
> Admire the perfon, but adore the mind.
> To thefe weak ftrains, O thou! the fex's friend
> And conftant patron, Richardfon! attend;
> Thou, who fo oft with pleas'd, but anxious care,
> Haft watch'd the dawning genius of the fair,
> With wonted fmiles wilt hear thy friend difplay
> The various graces of the female lay;
> Studious from folly's yoke their minds to free,
> And aid the generous caufe efpous'd by thee.
>   DUNCOMBE's Epiftle to RICHARDSON.

The polite author of the Letters concerning Tafte, fays, "The frequent converfation with women har-

" monizes the souls of men, and gives them an en-
" chanting grace. I am of opinion, (says he) it was
" this constant idea of delicacy and softness, collected
" from an habitual intercourse with the fair polishers
" of our sex, and united into one complicated form
" of beauty, which playing perpetually in the soul of
" Raphael, diffused itself through his pencil over all
" his works; and through his looks, deportment,
" and tongue, over all his words and actions. Such
" has ever been, and ever will be the power of those
" amiable creatures!—Women are the fountains from
" whence flow the blended streams of taste and plea-
" sure; and the draught of life is more or less sweet
" as they are mingled in the cup."

I have inserted the preceding quotation for the
sake of a class of gentlemen which I have often seen,
(but never wish to see again) who are never easy after
dinner until the ladies are withdrawn. This horrid
custom is very much on the decline: it is a remain
of barbarism, which many sensible gentlemen complain of, and wish to see it quite done away; was
that the case, the ladies would have greater motives
to, and more opportunities of cultivating their understandings. I must give you a quotation from the
production of a poor milk-woman, who is another instance to prove that " the soul is of no sex."

Why boast, O arrogant, imperious man,
Perfections so exclusive! are thy powers
Nearer approaching to the Deity? Canst thou solve
Questions which high Infinity propounds,
Soar nobler flights, or dare immortal deeds,
Unknown to woman, if she greatly dare
To use the pow'rs assign'd her? Active strength,
The boast of animals, is clearly thine:
By this upheld, thou think'st the lesson rare
That female virtue teach, poor the height
Which female wit obtains. The theme unfolds
It's ample maze, for Montague befriends
The puzzled thought, and blazing in the eye
Of bolden'd opposition strait presents
The soul's best energies, her keenest powers,
Clear, vigorous, and enlightened. Mrs. Yearsley.

Notwithftanding my having quoted fo much in this letter already, I muft add the following from the Village Curate:

> I do not wifh to fee the female eye
> Wafte all its luftre at the midnight lamp;
> I do not wifh to fee the female cheek
> Grow pale with application. Let their care
> Be to preferve their beauty; that fecur'd,
> Improve their judgment, that the loving fair
> May have an eye to know the man of worth,
> And keep fecure the jewel of her charms
> From him that ill deferves. Let the fpruce beau,
> That beau, fweet-fcented, and palav'rous fool,
> Who talks of honour and his fword, and plucks
> The man that dares advife him by the nofe:
> That puny thing, that hardly crawls about,
> Reduc'd by wine and women, yet drinks on,
> And vapours loudly o'er his glafs, refolv'd
> To tell a tale of nothing, and out-fwear
> The northern tempeft; let that fool, I fay,
> Look for a wife in vain, and live defpis'd.
>
> I would that all the fair ones of this vile
> Were fuch as one I knew. Peace to her foul,
> She lives no more. And I a genius need
> To paint her as fhe was, almoft like, methinks,
> That amiable maid the poet drew, .
> Stealing a glance from Heav'n, and call'd her Portia.
> Happy the man, and happy fure he was,
> So wedded. Bleft with her, he wand'red not
> To feek for happinefs; 'twas his home.
> How often have I paus'd, and chain'd my tongue,
> To hear the mufic of her fober words!
> How often have I wonder'd at the grace
> Inftruction borrow'd from her eye and cheek!
> Surely that maid is worth a nation's gold,
> Who has fuch rich refourfes in her felf
> For them fhe rears. A mother well inform'd
> Entails a blefling on her infant charge
> Better than riches; an unfailing crufe
> She leaves behind her, which the fafter flows
> The more 'tis drawn; where ev'ry foul may feed,
> And nought diminifh of the public ftock.
>
> Say, man, what more delights than the fair?
> Why fhould we not be patient to endure
> If they command? We rule the noify world,
> But they rule us. Then teach them how to guide,

And hold the rein with judgment. Their applause
May once again reſtore a quiet reign
Of virtue, love, and peace, and yet bring back
The bluſh of folly, and the ſhame of vice. HUDDIS.

I am,

Dear Friend,

Yours.

LETTER XLI.

Happy the man that has each fortune try'd,
To whom ſhe much has given, much deny'd,
With abſtinence all delicates he ſees,
And can regale himſelf with toaſt and cheeſe.

Art of Cookery.

" One ſolid diſh his week-day meals affords,
" And added pudding conſecrates the Lord's."

Your buſineſs ne'er defer from day to day,
Sorrow and poverty attends delay;
But lo! the careful man ſhall always find
Encreaſe of wealth according to his mind.

COOKE's Heſiod.

DEAR FRIEND,

THE public at large, and book-
ſellers in particular, have beheld my encreaſing ſtock
with the utmoſt aſtoniſhment, they being entirely at
a loſs to conceive by what means I have been enabled
to make good all my payments; and for ſeveral years,
in the beginning of my buſineſs, ſome of the trade
repeatedly aſſerted, that it was totally impoſſible that
I could continue to pay for the large numbers of
books which I conſtantly purchaſed; and ten years
ſince, being induced to take a journey into my own
country, with a view to the reſtoration of my health,

M 6

materially injured by intense application to catalogue-making, too much reading, &c. During the six weeks that I retired into the west, Mrs. Lackington was perpetually interrogated respecting the time that I was expected to return. This was done in such a manner as evidently shewed that many pretended to think that I never intended to return at all.

> Ye Gods above !—ye blackguard boys below !
> Oh, splash their stockings, and avenge my woe.
> Heroic Epistle to Twiss.

How great was their surprise, when, as a prelude to my return, I sent home several waggon loads of books which I had purchased in the country.

As I never had any part of the *miser* in my composition, I always proportioned my expences according to my profits; that is, I have for many years expended two thirds of the profits of my trade; which proportion of expenditure I never exceeded.

> " Things to their owners minds, their merit square,
> " Good if well used; if ill, they evils are."

If you will please to refer to Dr. Johnson's " Idler" " for the progress of Ned Drugget," you will see much of the progress of your humble servant depicted.

> Should fortune capriciously cease to be coy,
> And in torrents of plenty descend,
> I doubtless, like others, should clasp her with joy,
> And my wants and my wishes extend.
> W. Whitehead.

Like Ned, in the beginning I opened and shut my own shop, and welcomed a friend by a shake of the hand. About a year after, on such occasions I beckoned across the way for *a pot of good porter*. A few years after that, I sometimes invited my friends to dinner, and provided them a roasted *fillet of veal*: in a progressive course the *ham* was introduced, and a *pudding* was the next addition made to the feast. For some time a glass of *brandy and water* was a luxury; a glass of Mr. Beaufoy's *raisin wine* succeeded; and as soon as *two thirds* of my profits enabled me to afford good *red port*, it immediately appeared: nor was sherry long behind.

> " Wine whets the wit, improves its native force,
> " And gives a pleasing flavour to discourse,
> " By making all our spirits debonair,
> " Throws off the fears, the sediments of care."

> " As April when painting the furrows,
> " Drives winter away to the pole ;
> " Old port, by dispelling life's sorrows,
> " Relaxes the frost of the soul."

It was some years before I discovered that a lodging in the country was very conducive to my health. Gay's lines were then repeated :

> " Long in the noisy town I've been immur'd,
> " Respir'd in smoke, and all its cares endur'd."

The year after, my country *lodging* by regular gradation was transformed into a country *house*; and in another year, the inconveniences attending a *stage coach* were remedied by a *chariot*.

> My precious rib has ventur'd to declare,
> 'Tis vulgar on one's legs to take the air.
> Comforts of Marriage.

For four years, *Upper Holloway* was to me an *elysium*.

> " Fled from the dear, delusive town,
> " From scenes of trade and noise ;
> " Here, undisturb'd, I set me down,
> " And taste serener joys.

> " Here, happiness must ever live,
> " Here, health and peace unite,
> " While art and nature join to give
> " Refreshment with delight."

Surrey next appeared unquestionably the most beautiful county in England, and *Upper Merton* the most rural village in Surrey. So now *Merton* is selected as the seat of occasional philosophical retirement.

> Here on a single plank thrown safe ashore,
> I hear the tumult of the distant throng,
> As that of seas remote or dying storms.
> Here like a shepherd gazing from his hut,
> Touching his reed, or leaning on his staff,
> Eager ambition's fiery chace I see ;

I fee the circling hunt of noify men,
Burft law's inclofure, leap the mounds of right,
Purfuing and purfu'd, each other's prey.   Young.

But I affure you, my dear friend, that in every
ftep of my progrefs, envy and malevolence has pur-
fued me clofe.

When Envy, rifing from the realms below,
Look'd round the world, her vengeance to beftow,
No little fcheme of fupercilious pride,
No mean, malicious arts fhe left untry'd.
                                 Mifs M. Falconer.

When by the advice of that eminent phyfician,
Dr. Letfom, I ;purchafed a horfe, and faved my life
by the exercife it afforded me, the old adage, " *Set
a beggar on horfeback and he'll ride to the Devil*," was
deemed fully verified; but when Mrs. Lackington
mounted another, " they were very forry to fee
people fo young in bufinefs run on at fo great a rate!"
The occafional relaxation which we enjoyed in the
country was cenfured as an abominable piece of pride;
but when the *carriage* and *fervants* in *livery* appeared,
" they would not be the firft to hurt a foolifh tradefman's character; but if (as was but too probable) the
docket was not already ftruck, the Gazette would foon
fettle that point."

Bafe Envy withers at another's joy,
And hates that excellence it cannot reach.   Thomson.

" It is no lefs a proof (fays Dr. Johnfon) of eminence to have many enemies, than many friends."

Thofe envious perfons will appear in a more un-
favourable point of view when I inform you that
they all well knew that I could with propriety adopt
the following lines of Thomfon :

All is the gift of Industry; whatfo'er
Exalts, embellifhes and renders life
Delightful.   Seasons.

But I have been lately informed that thefe *good
natured* and *compaffionate* people have for fome time
found it neceffary to alter their ftory.

No more shall want thy weary hand constrain,
Henceforth good days and plenty shall betide;
The gods will for thy good old age provide;
A glorious change attends thy low estate;
Sudden and mighty riches round thee wait;
Be wise, and use the lucky hour of fate.

ROWE'S LUCAN.

It seems that at last they have discovered the secret springs from whence I drew my wealth; however, they do not quite agree in their accounts, for although some can tell you the very *number* of my fortunate lottery ticket, others are as positive that I found bank-notes in an old book, to the amount of many thousand pounds, and if they please, can even tell you the title of the very fortunate old book that contained this treasure. But you shall receive it from me, which you will deem authority to the full as unexceptionable. I assure you then, upon my honour, that I found the whole of what I am possessed of, in SMALL PROFITS, *bound* by INDUSTRY, and *clasped* by OECONOMY.

Gilt toils for gain at honour's vast expence,
Heaven throws the trifle into innocence,
And fixes happiness in hell's despite,
The necessary consequence of right.

Earl NUGENT to Lord CORNBURY.

Read this, ye covetous wretches, in all trades, who, when you get a good customer, are for making the most of him! But if you have neither honour nor honesty, you should at least possess a little *common sense.* Reflect on the many customers that your over-charges have already driven from your shops! do you think that you can always find a sufficient number of customers, so deficient in penetration as not to discover your characters? no such thing. Your exorbitant charges are a general subject of conversation and dislike: you cannot with confidence look your own customers in the face, as you are conscious of your meanness and imposition, and your sordid disposition is evidently the reason, that some gentlemen are led to look with contempt and disdain on tradesmen. But when men in trade are men of honour, they will in general be treated as such; and were it otherwise,

One self-approving hour whole years outweighs,
Of stupid starers, and of loud huzzas:
And more true joy Marcellus exil'd feels,
Than Cæsar with a senate at his heels.   POPE.

" Self-esteem (says a French author) is one of the
first ingredients of man's happiness."

" From thence such sensations, such high pleasures flow,
" As mean souls ne'er dream of, as bad hearts ne'er know."

I pity from my soul many wretches whom I observe bartering away their constitutions, and what
few liberal sentiments they may possess; rising early
and sitting up late, exerting all the powers of
body and mind, to get what they call a competency,
no matter by what means this is effected.

Silver to gold, we own, should yield the prize;
And gold to virtue; louder folly cries.
Ye sons of care, let money first be sought;
Virtue is only worth a second thought.
My friends get money; get a large estate,
By honest means; but get at any rate.
This maxim echoes still from street to street,
While young and old the pleasing strains repeat.
                                FRANCIS's Horace.

Thousands actually destroy themselves in accom-
plishing their grand design.

—— I see with what grovelling prospects in view,
Human creatures self-interest unceasing pursue.
                                DR. DODD.

Others, live to obtain the long-wished for country
retreat. But, alas! the promised happiness is as far
from them as ever, often farther. The busy bustling
scene of business being over, a vacuity in the mind
takes place, spleen and vapours succeed, which en-
crease bodily infirmities, death stares them in the face.
The mean dirty ways by which much of their wealth
has been obtained make retrospect reflections intolerable. Philosophy stands aloof, nor ever deigns to
visit the sordid soul. Gardens and pleasure grounds
become dreary deserts; the miserable possessors linger
out a wretched existence, or put a period to it with

a halter or pistol: and the world goes on as well without them:

> Sated, loathing, hopeless hear of bliss,
> Some plunge to seek it into death's abyss.
>
> LORD NUGENT.

> " Were this not common would it not be strange?
> " That 'tis so common, this is stranger still."

I cannot omit to quote the following fine lines
from Mr. Soame Jenyns, as they naturally occur to
my recollection:

> Useless in business, yet unfit for ease,
> Nor skill'd to mend mankind, nor form'd to please.
> The mind not taught to think, no useful store
> To fix reflection, dreads the vacant hour;
> Turn'd in itself, its numerous faults are seen,
> And all the mighty void that lies within.
> 'Tis conscious virtue crowns the blest retreat.

" Solitude (says Cowley) can be well fitted and
set aright, but upon very few persons. They
have knowledge enough of the world to see the follies
of it; and virtue enough to despise all vanity."

> Sweet solitude has charms to sooth thy soul;
> To purge thy mind from thoughts that wound thy peace,
> And fill that reason which should be thy guide.
> But let the guilty murderer beware
> He come not near these happy plains of peace;
> Each bush he meets shall make him start amaz'd,
> And each bright star strike horror to his soul!
> Lost as he wanders thro' the mazy grove,
> (Affrighted nature shrinking from his touch)
> The warbling birds, whose notes melodious sound
> On every bush their great Creator's praise,
> And Philomel strike murder to his ears!
> Dagger to the guilty minds; and balm to those,
> Whose conscience, free from guilt, affliction feels.
> O solitude! thou spring of earthly bliss,
> Where honest worth may meet a sure reward,
> And, free from scandal, pride and envy, live
> Content on earth, till it grows ripe for Heaven!
>
> SWAIN.

The profits of my business the present year 1791,
will amount to FOUR THOUSAND POUNDS*. What

---

* Since this was wrote, my business is enlarged; in 1792, my
profits were about 5000l.—in 1793, about the same sum.—I
suppose, had it not been for the war, the profits of 1793,
would have been at least 6000l.

it will increase to I know not ; but if my health will permit me to carry it on a few years longer, there is very great probability, confidering the rapid increase which each fucceeding year has produced, that the profits will be double what they now are; for I here pledge my reputation as a tradefman, never to deviate from my old plan of giving as much for libraries as it is poffible for a tradefman to give, and felling them and *new* publications alfo, for the fame SMALL PROFITS that have been attended with fuch aftonifhing fuccefs for fome years paft.   And I hope that my affiftants will alfo perfevere in that attentive obliging mode of conduct which has fo long diftinguifhed No. 46 and 47 Chifwell-ftreet, Moorfields ; confcious, that fhould I ever be weak enough to adopt an oppofite line of conduct, or permit thofe who act under my direction fo to do, I fhould no longer meet with the very extraordinary enceuragement and fupport which I have hitherto experieneed; neither fhould I have the fmalleft claim to a continuance of it under fuch circumftances.

> But may confufion on the wretch await !
> Be poverty, difgrace, contempt his fate !
> Who the juft end and means can difregard,
> Yet arrogantly hope the juft reward.
> Epiftle to a Barrifter.

I cannot here help addreffing my cuftomers in the following lines :

> Unlike th' iugrate, tho' favours ceafe to flow,
> Never may I forget the debt I owe.
> Still as each circling feafon fhall return,
> May gratitude within my bofom burn.
> Unbid, be mindful of your fmiles before,
> Make it my ftudy to deferve them more.
> ARLEY's Occafional Epilogue.

I am,

Dear Friend,

Yours.

LETTER XLII.

Be mine by prudence to enhance my fame,
And rear o'er fons of gold my deathlefs fame;
From trade, yet great, my competence I bring,
Nor grudge, tho' riches from a courtier fpring.
JUVENAL Imitated.

But by your revenue meafure your expence,
And to your funds and acres join your fenfe.
YOUNG's Love of Fame.

Learn what thou ow'ft thy country and thy friend,
What's requifite to fpare, and what to fpend.
DRYDEN's Perfius.

DEAR FRIEND,

THE open manner of ftating my profits will no doubt appear ftrange to many who are not acquainted with my fingular conduct in that and other refpects. But you, Sir, know that I have for fourteen years paft kept a ftrict account of my profits. Every book in my poffeffion, before it is offered to fale is marked with a private mark, what it coft me, and with a public mark of what it is to be fold for; and every article, whether the price is fixpence or fixty pounds, is entered in a day-book as it is fold, with the price it coft and the money it fold for: and each night the profits of the day are caft up by one of my fhopmen, as every one of them underftands my private marks. Every Saturday night the profits of the week are added together, and mentioned before all my fhopmen, &c. the week's profits, and alfo the expences of the week are then entered one oppofite the other, in a book kept for the purpofe; the whole fum taken in the week is alfo fet down, and the fum that has been paid for books bought. Thefe accounts are kept publicly in my fhop, and ever have been fo, as I never faw any reafon for concealing them, nor was ever jealous of any of my men's profiting by my example and taking away any of my bufinefs; as I always found that fuch of them as did fet up for themfelves came to my shop, and purchased to the amount of ten times more than they hindered me from selling. By keeping an account of my profits, and also of my expences, I have always known how to regulate the latter by the former. " To live above our station, shews a proud heart; and to live under it, discovers a narrow soul." Horace says,

> " A part I will enjoy as well as keep,
> " My heir may sigh and think it want of grace;
> " But sure no stature in his favour says,
> " How free or frugal I shall pass my days.
> " I get and sometimes spend, and at others spare,
> " Divided between carelessness and care."

And I have done that, without the trifling way of setting down a halfpenny-worth of matches, or a penny for a turnpike. I have one person in the shop whose constant employment is to receive all the cash, and discharge all bills that are brought for payment, and if Mrs. Lackington wants money for house-keeping, &c. or if I want money for *bobby-horses*, &c. we take five or ten guineas, pocket it, and set down the sum taken out of trade as expended; when that is gone we repeat our application, but never take the trouble of setting down the *items*. But such of my servants as are entrusted to lay out money are always obliged to give in their accounts, to shew how each sum has been expended.

> Bless'd who with order their affairs dispose,
> But rude confusion is the source of woes.
>
> COOKE's Hesiod.

It may not be improper here to take a little notice of some very late insinuations of my old envious *friends*. It has been suggested that I am now grown *immensely rich*, and that having already more property than I can reasonably expect to live to expend, and no young family to provide for, I for these reasons ought to decline my business, and no longer engross trade to myself that ought to be divided into a number of channels, and thus support many families. In answer to which I will observe, that some of these objectors were in trade before me, and when I first embarked in the profession of a bookseller, despised me for my mean beginning. When afterwards I adopted my plan of selling cheap, and for ready-money only, they made themselves very merry at my expence, for expecting to succeed by so *ridiculous* a project, (as they in their consummate wisdom were pleased to term it) and predestined my ruin, so that no doubt I ought to comply with any thing they desire, however unreasonable it may appear to me.

To deny that I have a competence, would be unpardonable ingratitude to the public, to go no higher;

'Tis one thing madly to despise my store :
Another not to heed to treasure more ;
Glad like a boy to snatch the first good day,
And pleas'd if sordid want be far away.
What is't to me (a passenger, God wot)
Whether the vessel be first rate or not,
The ship itself may make a better figure,
But I that sail, neither less nor bigger ;
I neither strut with ev'ry fav'ring breath,
Nor strive with all the tempest in my teeth ;
In pow'r, wit, figure, virtue, fortune, plac'd,
Behind the foremost, and before the last,
Divided between carelessness and care,
Sometimes I spend, at other times I spare.

FORTESQUE.

But to insinuate that I am getting money for no good purposes, is false and invidious.* The great apostle St. Paul, who was an humble follower of CHRIST, thought he might be permitted to boast of himself a little.

" If a man (says Selden) does not take notice of that excellency and perfection that is in himself, how can he be thankful to God who is the author of it.

* When I wrote my life in 1791, I had no partner. In the summer of 1793, I sold Mr. Robert Allen one fourth share of the profits of my trade. This young gentleman was brought up in my shop, and of course is well acquainted with my method of doing business; and having been a witness to the profitable effects resulting from small profits, is as much in love with that mode of transacting business as I am ; and as the trade is continually increasing, I suppose I shall be obliged to take another quarter partner very soon, as I cannot bear to see even trifles neglected.

Nay, if a man hath too mean an opinion of himself, it will render him unserviceable both to God and man. He adds, pride may be allowed to this or that degree, else a man cannot keep up to his dignity." Montaigne says, "that to speak more of one's self than is really true, is not only presumption but folly; and for a man to speak less of himself than he really is, is folly, not modesty; and to take that for current pay, which is under a man's value, is cowardice and pusillanimity." Aristotle says, "no virtue assists itself with falsehood, and that truth is never subject matter of error." "False modesty (says Bruyere) is the most cunning sort of vanity; by this a man never appears what he is." After which, I suppose it will not be thought very presumptuous in me, if I should state a few facts, merely to justify my conduct in carrying on my trade beyond the time that certain persons would prescribe to me.

And if I should even wish to be praised by my friends, I see no damning sin in that.

> There's nought beneath the welkin's vault,
> So much my spirits can exalt,
> As that applause a mind bestows,
> The bliss for which my bosom glows.
> Pleasure this—I own conveys,
> And what is life devoid of praise?
> The greatest pleasure of the mind,
> True friendship, is but praise refin'd.
>
> Epilogue to J.— T—, Esq.

Take the witty Peter's opinion also on the subject:

> Fair praise is sterling gold—all should desire it—
> Flatt'ry, base coin—a cheat upon the nation;
> And yet, our vanity doth much admire it,
> And really gives it all its circulation.
>
> PETER PINDAR.

It is now about five years since I began to entertain serious thoughts of going out of business, on account of the bad state of health which both Mrs. Lackington and myself have laboured under; and having no desire to be rich, we adopted Swift's prayer:

" Preferve almighty, providence !
" Juft what you gave me, competence,
" Remov'd from all th' ambitious fcene,
" Nor puff'd by pride, nor funk by fpleen."

But it was then fuggefted by feveral of my friends,
that as I had about fifty poor relations, a great number of whom are children, others are old and nearly
helplefs, and that many had juftly formed fome expectations from me: therefore to give up fuch a
grade as I was in poffeffion of, before I was abfolutely
obliged to do it, would be a kind of *injuftice* to thofe
whom by the ties of blood I was in fome meafure
bound to relieve and protect.

Twice five and twenty coufins have implor'd,
That help, his purfe, they cry, can well afford.
                              Comforts of Marriage.

Thefe and other confiderations induced me to wave
the thoughs of precipitating myfelf out of fo extenfive and lucrative a bufinefs; and in the mean time
I apply a part of the profits of it to maintain my good
old mother, who is alive at Wellington in Somerfet-
fhire, her native place. I have two aged men and
one woman, whom I fupport: and I have alfo four
children to maintain and educate; three of thefe children have loft their father, and alfo their mother
(who was my fifter) the other child has both her parents living, but they are poor; many others of my
relations are in the fame circumftances, and ftand in
need of my affiftance, fo that———

" If e'er I've mourn'd my humble, lowly ftate,
" If e'er I've bow'd my knee at fortune's fhrine,
" If e'er a wifh efcap'd me to be great,
" The fervent prayer, humanity, was thine.
" Perifh the man who bears the piteous tale
" Unmov'd, to whom the heart-felt glow's unknown ;
" On whom the widow's plaints could ne'er prevail,
" Nor made the injur'd wretch's caufe his own.
" How little knows he the extatic joy,
" The thrilling blifs of cheering wan defpair !
" How little knows the pleafing warm employ,
" That calls the grateful tribute of a tear,

" The fplendid dome, the vaulted rock to rear,
  " The glare of pride and pomp, be, grandeur, thine !
" To wipe from mifery's eye the wailing tear,
  " And foothe the oppreffed orphan's woe, be mine."

It has alfo been frequently faid, that by felling my
books very cheap, I have materially injured other
bookfellers both in town and country.

For hard fufpicion's anger'd eye,
Deems all it fees unjuft;
And jaundic'd envy, low'ring by,
Supports the foul miftruft.   ARLEY's Complaint.

But I ftill deny the charge: and here I will firft
Obferve, that I have as juft a reafon to complain of
them for giving credit, as they can have for my
felling cheap and giving *no* credit ; as it is well known
that there are many thoufands of people every where
to be found who will decine purchafing at a fhop
where credit is denied, when they can find fhop-
keepers enough who will readily give it ; and as I frequently lofe cuftomers who having always been accuftomed to have credit, they will not take the trouble to pay for every article as fent home ; thefe of
courfe deal at thofe fhops who followed the old mode
of bufinefs ; fo that in fuch cafes, I might fay to the
proprietors of thefe fhops, ' You ought not to give
' any perfon credit : becaufe by fo doing you are
' taking cuftomers from me.' As to my *hurting the
trade* by felling *cheap,* they are, upon the whole,
miftaken ; for although, no doubt, fome inftances will
occur, in which they may obferve that the preference
is given to *my* fhop, and the books purchafed of me
on account of their being cheap ; they never confider
how many books they difpofe of on the very fame account. As, however, this may appear rather paradoxical, I will explain my meaning farther:

I now fell more than one hundred thoufand volumes annually ; many who purchafe part of thefe,
do fo folely on account of their cheapnefs ; many
thoufands of thefe books would have been deftroyed,
as I have before remarked, but for my felling them
on thofe very moderate terms ; now when thoufands
of thefe articles are fold, they become known by being

handed about in various circles of acquaintances, many of whom wishing to be possessed of the same books without enquiring the price of their friends, step into the first bookseller's shop, and give their orders for articles, which they never would have heard of, had not I, by selling them cheap, been the original cause of their being dispersed abroad; thus, by means of the plan pursued in my shop, whole editions of books are sold off, and new editions printed of the works of authors, who, were it not for that circumstance, would have been scarce noticed at all.

But (say they) you not only sell such books cheap, as are but little known, but you even sell a great deal under price the very first rate articles however well they may be known, or however highly they may be thought of by the literary world. I acknowledge the charge, and again repeat that as I do not give any credit, I certainly ought to do so, and I may add, that in some measure I am obliged to do it; for who would come out of their way to Chiswell-street to pay me the same price in ready money, as they might purchase for at the first shop they came to, and have credit also.

And although first rate authors are very well known, yet I am confident that by selling them cheaper than others, many are purchased of me that never would have been bought at the full price; now every book that is sold tends to spread the fame of the author, rapidly extends the sale, and as I before remarked, sends more customers to other shops as well as to my own.

I must also inform you, that besides five or six private catalogues of books in sheets, for booksellers only, I publish two catalogues for the public every year, and of each of those public catalogues I print above three thousand copies, most of those copies are lent about from one to another, so that supposing only four persons see each copy, twenty four thousand persons look over my catalogues annually; no other mode of advertising bears the least proportion to it.

I could enlarge considerably on this subject, but will not unnecessarily take up your time, as I trust

what is here advanced will convey full conviction to
your mind, especially as I believe it is universally
known and allowed, that no man ever promoted the
sale of books in an equal degree, with your old friend;
and as in reading I have experienced many thousand
happy hours, so it still engrosses the largest portion
of my time, and gives me more real pleasure and solid
satisfaction than all other things in the world. You
cannot conceive what agreeable sensations I enjoy,
when I reflect on my having contributed so much towards the pleasures of others, in diffusing through
the world, such an immense number of books, by
which many have been enlightened and taught to
think, and from meer animals have become rational
beings. With a book the poor man in his intervals
from labour forgets his hard lot, or learns to bear it
with pleasure, whilst in intellectual pleasures he can
vie with kings. Books afford comfort to the afflicted,
and consolation to the prisoner; books are our most
constant and most faithful companions and friends, of
which we never are cloyed.

Dr. Zimmermann, in his excellent book on Solitude, says, " Reading is perhaps one of the most
sure and certain remedics against lassitude and discon-
tent."—" Every species of misfortune, however ac-
cumulated, may be overcome by those who possess tranquility at home, who are capable of enjoying the
privacy of study, and the elegant recreation which
books afford."—" The man to whose bosom neither
riches, nor pleasure, nor grandeur, can convey felicity, may, with a book in his hand, learn to forget his
cares under the friendly shade of a tree."

" Petrarch, by being deprived of his books three
days, was thrown into a fever: he was always gloomy
and less spirited, except while he was reading or
writing."—" Pliny the younger, read wherever it
was possible, whether riding, walking, sitting, or
whenever the subject of his employment afforded him
the opportunity."

" Pliny the Elder, had always some person to
read to him during his meals; and he never travelled without a book and a portable writing desk."—

" Alexander was remarkably fond of reading, and amidst his conquests felt himself unhappy in Afia for want of books."—" Brutus, while ferving in the Army under Pompey, employed all the moments he could fpare from the duties of his ftation among books ; while the army was repofing he was reading."—"Plutarch fays, that he entirely lived on hiftory ; and while (fays he) I contemplate the pictures it prefents to my view, my mind enjoys a rich repaft from the reprefentation of great and virtuous characters."—" The ftreams of mental pleafures, thofe which of courfe all men of whatever condition may equally partake, flow from one to another : the ftream of which we have moft frequently tafted, lofes neither its flavour nor its virtues, but frequently acquires new charms, and conveys additional pleafure the oftener it is tafted. The fubjects of thefe pleafures are as unbounded as the reign of truth, as extenfive as the world, as unlimited as the divine perfections. The incorporeal pleafures, therefore, are more durable than all others. They neither difappear with the light of the day, nor change with the eternal form of things. They accompany us under all viciffitudes, fecure us in the darknefs of the night, and compenfate for all the miferies we are doomed to fuffer." " Men of exalted minds therefore have always, amidft the buftle of the world, and even in the brilliant career of heroifm, preferved a tafte for books."

The great Dr. Young, in his letter to Richardfon, fays, " With what a guft do we retire to our difinterefted and immortal friends in our clofet, and find our minds, when applied to fome favourite theme, as naturally, and as eafily quieted, and refrefhed, as a peevifh child, when laid to the breaft."

" I know not of any pleafures more lively (fays Zimmermann) than thofe I experienced in converfing with the dead."

> What heart-felt blifs! what pleafure-winged hours,
> Tranfported are we to Rome's letter'd fons;
> We by their favour Tyber's banks enjoy,
> The temples trace, and fhare their noble games;

Enter the crowded theatre at will ;
March to the Forum, hear the conful plead,
Are prefent in the thundering Capitol
When Tully fpeaks ; at fofter hours attend
Harmonious Virgil to his Mantuan farm,
Or Baia's fhore : how often drink his ftrains,
Rural or epic fweet ! how often rove
With Horace, bard and moralift benign,
With happy Horace rove, in fragrant paths
Of myrtle bowers, by Tifoli's cafcade.
Hail, precious pages ! that amufe and teach,
Exalt the genius, and improve the breaft ;
But chiefly thou, fupreme philofophy,
Shed thy beft influence, with thy train appear
Of graces mild.——————

Tutor of human life ! aufpicious guide
Whofe faithful clue unravels ev'ry maze,
Whofe fkill can difengage the tangled thorn,
And fmooth the rock to down ! whofe magic powers
Controul each ftorm, and bid the roar be ftill.

DR. S. DAVIES.

I am,

Dear Friend,

Yours.

LETTER XLIII.

—This is a traveller, Sir; knows men and manners; and has
plough'd up sea so far, 'till both the poles have knock'd; has
seen the sun take coach, and can diftinguifh the colour of his
horfes, and their kinds, and had a Flanders mare leap'd there.
BEUMONT and FLETCHER's Scornful Lady.

In many an author of renown
 I've read this curious obfervation,
That, by much wand'ring up and down,
Men catch the faults of every nation,
And loofe the virtues of their own.   VER—VERTA.

DEAR FRIEND,

A MONGST the variety of oc-
currences with which I have endeavoured to entertain you, perhaps not all equally interefting (and the
moft material of them, I am duly fenfible, not entitling me to the claim of being efteemed a writer
poffeffed of the very firft abilities this age or nation
has produced,) I recollect my not yet having given
you an account of my principal TRAVELS. Poffibly
you might very readily pardon that omiffion, as from
what has already appeared it muft be evident, the engagements which from time to time have fully en-
groffed my attention, have not furnifhed me with an
opportunity of making the tour of Europe, or tracing
the fource of the river Nile, much lefs circumnavi-
gating the globe. And even fuppofing I had been
poffeffed both of the time and inclination for fuch extenfive undertakings, the difadvantages which I labour under for want of having received a proper education, would have difqualified me from making fuch
remarks and obfervations as naturally prefent themfelves to thofe who have been fortunate enough to
poffefs that advantage, and of courfe are qualified to
prefent the world with a variety of fubjects equally
curious and inftructive : though it is not without reluctance I think it neceffary here to obferve, that

some of these gentlemen, not content with giving a
true account of what actually occurred to them,
and suppofing that plain matter of fact would not be
fufficiently interefting to excite that fuperior degree
of attention and admiration which they were ambitious
as authors to acquire, they have thought proper to
intermix fo much of the *marvel'ous* into their narra-
tions, as has been the occafion of many perfons reading them with fuch diffidence, as to doubt the truth
of many relations, which though really ftrictly confiftent with veracity, yet being novel and uncommon,
they were unwilling to credit, left they fhould incur
the cenfure of being poffeffed of a fuperior degree of
weaknefs and credulity. This I am alfo confident
has induced many a modeft author to omit paffages,
which though really true, he was cautious of publifhing, from a fear of being fubjected to the fame
fevere animadverfions, or what is ftill worfe, being
fufpected of wilfully impofing on his readers. Recent
inftances of which, were it neceffary, I could adduce; but I fhall proceed with cautioning you from
being alarmed left I fhould fall into either of thefe
errors. Nothing *very marvellous* will occur in what I
mean to prefent you with; though I fhall not be intimidated from relating *real facts*, from the apprehenfion of not being credited. As an additional recommendation, (no doubt) the hiftory of my travels
will be interfperfed with fuch remarks on *men* and
manners as have prefented themfelves to me during
my peregrination; and this I previoufly warn you,
will be well done in my " accuftomed defultory manner," from which, as Mr. *Pennant* fays in his *Hiftory of London*, " I am too old to depart," that is, as
Dr. *Johnfon* might poffibly have expained it, " Sir,
you are then too old to MEND." But you, my dear
friend, are not fo faftidious a critic: although you
may find the whole very *dull*, it fhall not be very
long; fo that if it does not act as a cordial to enliven
your fpirits, it may (if read in the evening) prove a
powerful *narcotic* and afford you fome pleafing dreams,
when

" Tir'd nature's sweet restorer, balmy sleep,
" His ready visit pays."

I shall therefore not trouble you with a detail of bad
roads, the impositions of innkeepers, what food I
partook of, how many bottles of wine were drank,
the height of steeples. Nor will I

—— Tell how Richard stray'd from post to post,
What towns he din'd in, and what bridges crost;
How many eagles by the way were seen,
How many asses graz'd along the green.
                              Heroic Epistle to Twiss.

A sufficiency of this, I trust, has already appeared in
different writers. Thus much by way of preparation
for my journies. I now set out.

In *September*, seventeen hundred and eighty seven,
I set off for Edinburgh; and in all the principal towns
through which I passed, was led from a motive of
curiosity, as well as with a view towards obtaining
some valuable purchases, to examine the booksellers
shops for scarce and valuable books; but although I
went by the way of York, Newcastle-upon-Tyne, &c.
and returned through Glasgow, Carlisle, Leeds,
Lancaster, Preston, Manchester, and other confiderable places, I was much surprized, as well as disappointed, at meeting with very few of the works of
the most esteemed authors; and those few consisted
in general of ordinary editions, besides an assemblage
of common trifling books, bound in sheep, and that
too in a very bad manner. It is true, at York and
Leeds there were a few (and but very few) good
books; but in all the other towns between London and
Edinburgh nothing but trash was to be found: in the
latter city indeed, a few capital articles are kept, but
in no other part of Scotland.

In seventeen hundred and ninety, I repeated my
journey, and was much mortified to be under a necessity of confirming my former observations. This
remarkable deficiency in the article of books, is however not peculiar to the northern parts of England:
as I have repeatedly travelled into the western parts,
and found abundant cause for dissatisfaction on the

N 4

same account; so that I may venture without fear of contradiction to assert, that London, as in all other articles of commerce, is likewise the grand emporium of Great-Britain for books, engrossing nearly the whole of what is valuable in that very extensive, beneficial, and I may add lucrative branch of trade. As to Ireland, I shall only observe, that if the booksellers in that part of the empire do not shine in the possession of valuable books, they must certainly be allowed to possess superior industry in reprinting the works of every English author of merit, as soon as published, and *very liberally* endeavouring to disseminate them, in a surreptitious manner through every part of our island, though the attempts now generally proves abortive, to the great loss and injury of the ingenious projectors.

At Newcastle, I passed a day or two in the year 1787, where I was much delighted with viewing a singular phœnomenon in natural history, namely, the celebrated *crow's nest* affixed above the weather-cock, on the upper extremity of the Exchange, in the market-place. In the year 1783, as I was well informed, the crows first built this curious nest, and succeeded in hatching and rearing their young. In the following year they attempted to rebuild it: but a contest ensuing among some of the sable fraternity, after a fierce engagement they were obliged to relinquish it, and the nest was demolished by the victorious party before it was finished. This bad success, however, did not deter the original builders and possessors from returning in the year 1785, when they took quiet possession of their freehold, rebuilt the premises, and reared another family. This they repeated the three following years with equal success, and when I was there in the year 1790, much of the nest remained, but the crows had forsaken it. The above occurrence, though to many it may appear incredible, is an undoubted fact. That *crows* should come into the center of a populous town to build their nests, is of itself remarkable, but much more so, that they should prefer a weathercock to any other situation, where the whole family, and their habitation turned

round with every puff of wind, though they were
perfectly secured from falling, by the spike of iron
which rose above the fane, around which the whole
made their revolutions; and as on one side the nest
was higher than on the other, that part being always
to windward, by this ingenious contrivance of the
feathered architects, the inside of the nest was continually kept in a proper degree of warmth. I never
recollect these various circumstances, without being
lost in admiration at the extraordinary sagacity of these
birds. While I am on the subject of birds, I will
relate another odd circumstance that happened not far
from Moorfields: In the summer of 1781, in a burial-
ground near Peerless-Pool, there was one corner
where human bones were piled up, and in one of the
skulls a blackbird made her nest, and hatched five
young ones, three or four of which, being cocks, were
kept by the neighbours, and turn out fine singers.

In Newcastle however, I met with a greater curiosity, as well as a more amiable subject of it than a
crows nest to excite my astonishment.

In my first journey, Mr. _Fisher_ the bookseller, introduced me to his daughter, a charming young lady,
who being unfortunately born deaf, was consequently
dumb, till a gentleman a few years since taught her
to understand what was said to her by the motion of
the lips. I had the pleasure of conversing with her
several times, and found that she had much of the
Scotch accent, which as Mr. Fisher informed me, she
acquired of the gentleman who taught her not only to
understand the conversation of others but to _speak_, he
being a native of that country : He remarked also,
that she never had spoken the Newcastle dialect. This
young lady, I was also informed, dances exceedingly
well, keeping exact time with the music, whether it
is played slow or quick. When it is considered what
an intense application must have been used, both on
the part of the teacher and his fair pupil, to produce
such a happy effect, it surely reflects great credit on
each of the parties!

In the year 1790, when I again visited Newcastle
with Mrs. Lackington, this young lady became the

N 5

firſt object of inquiry, and we were both introduced to her.

I have lately been informed of a lady now in London, who although ſhe is deaf, takes great *delight in muſic*, and when aſked how ſhe is affected by it, ſhe anſwers that ſhe feels it at her *breaſt* and at *the bottom of her feet.*

Being on the ſubject of *Curioſities*, and having juſt related the pleaſure I experienced on account of a lady acquiring the uſe of ſpeech, permit me now to preſent you with another *rarity* indeed!—ſomewhat connected with the former, no doubt, but intended as an effectual remedy (temporary, at leaſt) for an oppoſite complaint of the ſame organs, viz. too great a *volubility of ſpeech*, with which (as it is ſaid) many females are ſo infected, as ſometimes to lead them to exceed the bounds of due moderation and female decorum, and even diſplay itſelf in the utterance of ſuch harſh (though frequently inarticulate) terms as tend too much to diſgrace the unhappy patient, and violently affect the auditory nerves of all perſons within a conſiderable diſtance.—To quit metaphor.

At the town-hall I was ſhewn a piece of antiquity called a *brank*. It conſiſts of a combination of iron filletts, and is faſtened to the head by a lock fixed to the back part of it; a thin plate of iron goes into the mouth, ſufficiently ſtrong however, to confine the tongue, and thus prevent the wearer from making any uſe of that reſtleſs member. The uſe of this piece of machinery is to puniſh notorious *ſcolds.* I am pleaſed to find that it is now conſidered merely as a matter of curioſity, the females of that town happily having not the ſmalleſt occaſion for the application of ſo harſh an inſtrument: whether it is that all females, apprehenſive of being included in *that* deſcription, have travelled ſouthward, to avoid the danger of ſo degrading an exhibition, or whatever other reaſon is aſſigned, I forgot to enquire. It however affords me pleaſure to reflect, that the ladies of Newcaſtle are left at liberty to adopt a head-dreſs of their own chooſing, confident that they poſſeſs a more refined taſte than to fix upon one by no means calcu-

lated to difplay their lovely countenances to advantage, as I am perfuaded the *brank* would caft fuch a
gloom on the faireft of them, as would tend much to
diminifh the influence of their charms, and give pain
to every beholder. It may be prudent, notwithftanding, ftill to preferve it *in terrorem*, as who knows what
future times may produce ? As I efteem it a very ingenious contrivance, and as there may be parts of the
country ftill to be found, where the application of
fuch a machine may be ufeful in fome chriftian families (I will not fay in *all*, having fufficient grounds
for afferting the contrary) I here prefent you with an
accurate fketch of it,

together with the manner of its application : that if
any ingenious artift fhould be applied to, he may not
be at a lofs how it is to be made. I would however,
advife him to be cautious in offering them to public
fale, and by no means to advertife them, efpecially if
a married man, or having any views towards matrimony.

'Tis thus the nuptial ſtate affords.
  Uninterrupted joy ;
When no diſcordant haſty words
  The huſband's peace deſtroy.

His leiſure ſeeks no gay reſort,
  But to his partner ſteals ;
And thinks the longeſt day too ſhort
  To ſpeak the bliſs he feels.

But when the gales which paſſions blow,
  The boſom's calm remove,
He flies the fair one's angry brow,
  And ſcorn ſucceeds to love.

                    BELL's Britiſh Album.

                I am,

            Dear Friend,

                Yours.

LETTER XLIV.

" O, land of cakes ! how oft my eyes
" Deſire to ſee thy mountains riſe;
" How fancy loves thy ſteeps to climb,
" So wild, ſo ſolemn, ſo ſublime."

" All the ſtage-coaches that travel ſo faſt,
" Muſt get now and then an unfortunate caſt."

DEAR FRIEND,

IN my firſt journey to Scotland I
ſometimes travelled poſt, but often entered the different ſtage-coaches, &c. for a ſtage or two, when I
happened to ſee any ſetting out ſo as to ſuit my time
and inclination : but at laſt I had pretty nearly paid
dear for it, as the driver of the diligence from Darlington to Durham happened to be much inebriated,
and before his quitting Darlington had almoſt over-
ſet us ; not obſerving the man was drunk, we attri-

buted the fault to the horses; we were, however, very
speedily undeceived in that respect by many concur-
rent circumstances, being one minute nearly in the
ditch on the right hand, and the next but just es-
caping that on the left; at other times we experienced
striking proofs of the inability of our conductor against
the number of one-horse *coal-carts*, not to mention
their frequently running foul of us for being on the
wrong side of the road; (for drivers of coaches and
carts can be to the full as savage towards each other
in the country, as in London): however, notwithstanding all these "hair breadth escapes," we retained
our seats, till we arrived within three quarters of a
mile of Durham, when at length the specific gravity
of the driver's head preponderating over all the other
parts of his frame united, precipitated him with violence from the elevated station he had, till then
(though with difficulty) possessed, to his parent earth.
There were three unfortunate passengers in the carriage, left to the discretion of the horses, viz. a gentlemen, an innkeeper's wife, and your humble servant; the lady in strict compliance with the practice
of her sex in similar situations, on seeing the rapid
descent of our charioteer, immediately honoured us
with a loud and shrill shriek; this the *quadrupeds*, not
accustomed to this pretty famale note so much as the
sonorous voice of a coachman, mistook for a signal to
mend their pace, and they, habituated to pay all due
obedience to the commands of their superiors of the
biped creation, when understood by them, and finding no check, instantly proceeded to a full gallop;
and we, however reluctantly, followed them down a
gentle descent, not at a *gentle* rate, but with prodigious velocity. As I was quite calm and collected,
I coolly reconnoitred the road before us, and observing that it was perfectly clear, as for half a mile not
a coal-cart was to be seen, although we had lately
passed several score, I began to reason with my companions, and they speedily became calm enough to
assist in holding a council what was best to be done
in our critical situation. Our debates were quickly
ended, as we were unanimous in opinion that if we

once entered the city of Durham, the carriage muſt inevitably be torn to pieces, owing to the variety of turnings and obſtructions we ſhould have to encounter, we therefore entered into an immediate reſolution, *nem. con.* that to open the doors, and exhibit our agility by leaping out, was, of " two evils chooſing the leaſt :" this we inſtantly did, in as careful a manner as poſſible; we firſt alighted on our feet, and next complimented the ground with our noſes, without receiving much injury. Our female companion indeed, by being rather too precipitate, alighted in a manner which on any other occaſion would not have appeared ſtrictly decent, of which ſhe, poor lady! was ſo ſenſible, that ſhe immediately " hoped *as how* we were both *married* gentlemen;" which was quickly replied to by both in the affirmative; and thus we ſaved our fair one the trouble of exerting herſelf in another ſcream, and ourſelves the puniſhment of hearing it.

Being no longer parties concerned in the danger, it afforded us ſome entertainment to obſerve the progreſs of our vehicle now conſiderably lightened by our eſcape from it, and becoming every moment ſtill lighter by the excluſion of ſmall trunks, boxes, parcels, great coats, &c. they, in imitation of our example, making leaps, ſome from the inſide of the carriage, and others from the boot; whether occaſioned by the *repulſion* of the carriage and its appendages, or the *attraction* of the earth, I am not ſufficiently verſed in philoſophy to decide. Poſterity, when they peruſe my labours, no doubt will determine this *weighty* point, and tranſmit it to the remoteſt period of time, properly digniſied by *F. R. S.* in *Phil. Tranſ.*

The horſes finding themſelves leſs incumbered, and urged on by the noiſe of the doors continually flapping, increaſed their ſpeed: happily, however, the carriage was ſtopped before it entered the city, and no damage was ſuſtained either by the horſes or the carriage. Before we left the inn, our careful *ſon of the whip* arrived, not in the leaſt injured, but rather benefited by his diſaſter, being ſuddenly transformed into a ſtate of perfect ſobriety; after him followed two countrymen laden with the several articles which had been so violently ejected. As I reflected that this unguarded man might not always be equally successful, either to himself or his passengers, as in the present instance, I obtained a promise from the innkeeper never to permit him to drive any carriage in future, in the management of which he had any concern. But I have since learned that the innkeeper did not keep his word, as he soon permitted him to drive the same diligence, and a few months after, being drunk as usual, he fell from the box, and was killed on the spot.

It is astonishing what a number of fatal accidents continually happen from carelessness and want of sobriety in this thoughtless race of beings. I was informed that only two days previous to my arrival at Durham, a coachman quitting his box to step into an adjacent house, in his absence the horses began to move gently, and a lady in the carriage giving a loud scream, the noise occasioned the horses to set off full gallop, in consequence of which a lady of Durham, happening unfortunately at that instant to be crossing the way, was thrown down, and the wheels passing over her, she died on the spot. One of the many melancholy effects resulting from the ridiculous practice of screaming. But I crave pardon of the ladies; when I begin passing censure on them, it is high time to close my epistle, (which if not very long, may perhaps be deemed sufficiently pertinent.)

I am,

Dear Friend,

Yours.

LETTER XLV.

O that the too cenforious world would learn
This wholefome rule, and with each other bear !
But man, as if a foe to his own fpecies,
Takes p'eafure to report his neighbour's faults.
Judging with rigour ev'ry fmall offence,
And prides *himfelf* in fcandal.

HAYWOOD's D. of BRUNSWICK.

a nation fam'd for fong, and beauty's charms ;
Zealous, yet modeft, innocent, though free :
Patient of toil ;' fincere amidft alarms ;-
Inflexible in faith: invincible in arms.

BEATTIE's Minftrel.

DEAR FRIEND,

IT is reported of a very eminent
author, that he never blotted a line of what he had
once written: on which it has been remarked, that it
was a pity he had not blotted a thoufand. Now
though my extreme modefty will not permit me to
put myfelf on a level with that great man as an
author, whatever the impartial world may think of
our comparative merits, I muft confefs I do not like
to blot what I have once written, fearful left when I
begin, (another proof of my modefty) I fhould deface
the major part of my manufcripts, and thus deprive
the public of the great advantages which may refult
from them. What I allude to, is an unfortune flip
of my pen in my laft; however, as " confeffion of a
fault makes fome amends," and I immediately checked
myfelf, craved pardon, abruptly clofed my letter,
and threw the offending pen from me with fome degree of anger, I hope thofe lovely fair ones, who
might think I meant to affront them, will, with their
accuftomed benignity, forgive, and indulge me with a
fmile on my future labours; and, as a convincing
proof how fenfible I am of their kind condefcenfion,
I here engage never more to exprefs my diflike of
their *fcreaming*, except they fhould omit purchafing.

books of me, which I am sure every candid fair (and what fair one is not candid?) will think sufficiently provoking.

But in order to remind them that every great man does not always conduct himself with equal politeness towards the ladies, I beg permission to introduce a very great man to them: no less a personage than Dr. JOHNSON. Of whom indeed so much hath already been sung and said, that the subject may be supposed to be nearly exhausted; which is, however, so far from being the case, that notwithstanding two quarto volumes of his life, by Mr. Boswell, are just published, we are taught to expect another Life by a different hand. Indeed, until some other great man makes his exit (myself out of the question) we are likely to be entertained with fresh anecdotes of him; but when that period once arrives, then farewel *Johnson!*

The Doctor, whose extreme fondness for that agreeable beverage *tea*, is well known, was once in company with a number of ladies, assembled to partake with him of the same refreshment. The lady of the house happened to be one of those particularly attentive to punctilio, and had exhibited her finest set of china for the entertainment of her guests; the Dr. who drank large quantities, and with considerable expedition, could not always wait with becoming patience ceremoniously to ask for and receive in due form the addition of a lump of sugar when necessary; he therefore without permission put his finger and thumb into the sugar-dish, tumbling the contents over, till he met with a piece of the proper size; the lady kept her eye fixed on him the whole time, and deeming his conduct a great breach of decorum, resolved to make him sensible of it, by immediately ordering the servant to change the sugar-dish. The Doctor, tho' apparently attentive only to his tea, noticed it, and as soon as he had emptied the cup, put it together with the saucer under the fire-place, with due care, however, not to break them. This was too severe a trial for the poor lady, who, apprehensive for the fate of her dear china, after a decent scream, with warmth demanded the reason of his treating her in so rude a manner. "Why, my dear madam, (replied "he) I was alarmed with the idea that whatever I "touched was thereby contaminated, and impressed "with anxious desire to contribute towards your "felicity, I removed the object so defiled from your "presence with all possible expedition." This reply, though it extorted a smile from all the company present, did not satisfy the lady to whom it was addressed, who notwithstanding she exerted herself to appear in good humour, was too much offended to forget the affront.—This anecdote has been related to me with some *addenda* which heighten the story, though more to the disadvantage of the Doctor; but I believe, as here related, it may be depended on as the real fact.

During my continuance in Scotland, which was about three weeks the first time, and about a month the last, I often reflected with pain on the illiberal, not to say brutal treatment, the inhabitants received from the Doctor. At Edinburgh I heard various anecdotes related of him, which were perfectly novel to me, and in all probabity will be so to you. I shall therefore give you a specimen:

Being one day at a gentleman's house in Edinburgh, several ladies and gentlemen came in to pay their respects to him; and among others the then Lord Provost went up to the Doctor, bowing repeatedly, and expressing the highest respect for him, to all which the Doctor paid not the least attention. Exceedingly hurt at so flagrant a mark of disrespect, he turned round, and put a shilling into the hand of the gentleman of the house: On being asked what the shilling was intended for, he replied, "Have not I seen your *bear?*"

As the Doctor was one day drinking tea at another gentleman's house, the lady asked him if he did not choose another cup: It seems she had forgot her having before asked him the same question; and on her repeating it he replied, "Woman, have I not already told you that I had done?" On which the lady answered him in his own gruff manner. During his continuance in her house she always talked to him without ceremony, and it was remarked that she had more influence with him than any other perſon in Scotland.

I was much pleaſed with the politeneſs of the gentleman who related me this ſtory of the Doctor, as he appeared anxious to excuſe him for his want of due decorum, and thus to palliate a moſt obvious blemiſh in the character of one of the moſt eminent of my countrymen. I could wiſh the compilers of the biographical department of that truly great and uſeful work, the "*Encyclopoedia Britannica*," would obſerve the ſame politeneſs and impartiality. And I hope that this hint will alſo induce them in ſome ſubſequent edition, when I am gone to

"*That bourne from whence no traveller returns,*"

to do juſtice to my *great and aſtoniſhing merits*, by way of compenſation for having falling ſhort in ſpeaking of other *great men*; and ſhould I happen to be *out of print* by the time the editors of the *Biographia Britannica* arrive at letter *L.* which ſeems extremely probable, according to the very deliberate progreſs of that work, I hope they will not ſlightly paſs *me* over. If they ſhould, let them take the conſequence: as I here give them fair and timely notice, and they have not to plead as an excuſe, the want of materials.

I will give you one anecdote more of the great Doctor, becauſe it relates to a Scotchman very eminent in the literary world. I had it from Mr. Samuel, who was one of the party.

Dr. Johnſon being one afternoon at the houſe of Mr. Samuel's uncle (whoſe name I have forgot) who lived in one of the ſtreets that leads from the Strand to the Thames, a number of gentlemen being preſent, they agreed to croſs the water and make a little excurſion on the other ſide; in ſtepping into the boat one of the company ſaid, Mr. Hume, give me your hand. As ſoon as they were ſeated, our Doctor aſked Mr. Samuel if that was Hume the Deiſt. Mr. Samuel replied, that it was the great Mr. Hume, the deep metaphyſician and famous hiſtorian. Had I known that (ſaid the Doctor) I would not have put a foot in the boat with him. In the evening they had all agreed to sup together at a house near St. Clement's Church in the Strand, and Doctor Johnson coming in after the rest of the company had some time been met, he walked up to Mr. Hume, and taking him by the hand, said, Mr. Hume, I am very glad to see you, and seemed well pleased to find him there; and it appeared to Mr. Samuel that the Doctor had thus chose to atone for his hasty expression before related.

As I do not recollect any thing being recorded respecting the Doctor's *pugilistic* abilities (excepting his knocking down Osborn the bookseller, be considered as such) I shall beg leave to relate another anecdote which I received from the gentleman who favoured me with the preceding one.

Dr. Johnson being at the water side when some ladies had just quitted a boat and were endeavouring to settle the fare with the waterman; this son of the Thames, like too many of his brethren, insisted on much more than his due, accompanying his demand in the usual stile of eloquence, with abusive language, the Doctor kindly interfering, furnished the ladies with the opportunity of retreating, and transferred the whole abuse to himself, who finding that argument made no impression on the waterman, tried what he could effect by the strength of his arm, and gave the refractory fellow a hearty drubbing, which had the desired effect.

One word more concerning our great Lexicographer. It must be allowed by every candid and impartial person, that the extreme contempt and prejudice he entertained towards our friends of *North Britain* reflected a very strong shade on his character, which his warmest admirers cannot justify.

> How fondly partial are our judgments grown,
> We deem all manners odious but our own!
> Look from the frigid to the torrid zone,
> By custom all are led, by nature none.
>
> Dr. WARTON on Fashion

Were I, as a South Britain, called upon to give my fair and unprejudiced opinion respecting the national character of the natives of Scotland and those of England, and I flatter myself I have had ample opportunities of obferving the peculiar traits of both countries; I would fay, that if we in England excel them in fome virtues, they no lefs fhine in others; and if the North Britons poffefs fome peculiar frailties and prejudices, we of the South are not entirely free from ours; fo that were the virtues and vices of a certain number of each country placed in an hydroftatical balance (it muft however be a pretty large one,) I believe it very difficult to prognofticate which of the two would preponderate. It is true, I have met with one very great villain in Scotland, in Mr. S. which only tends to prove there are probably *fcoundrels* to be found every where, and that without taking the trouble which Diogenes did, in fearch of an *honeft man*; and I much afraid, were I to enquire of fome North Britons, they could without any great difficulty point out to me fome of my own countrymen as bad.

> Full many a youth, fit for each horrid fcene,
>   The dark and footy hues of chimnies bear;
> Full many a rogue is born to cheat unfeen,
>   And dies unhang'd for want of proper care.
>
> Let not ambition mock their humble toil,
>   Their vulgar crimes and villainy obfcure;
> Nor rich rogues hear with a difdainful fmile
>   The low and petty knav'ries of the poor.
>
> The titled villain, and the theif in power,
>   The greateft rogue that ever bore a name,
> Await alike th' inevitable hour,
>   The paths of wickednefs but lead to fhame.
>   **Elegy in Covent-Garden Church-yard.**

I deteft all national prejudices, as I think it betrays great weknefs in the parties who are influenced by them. Every nation of the habitable globe, nay, each particular province of thofe countries has certainly fome peculiar traits belonging to it which diftinguifhes it from its neighbours. But if we are difpofed to view one another with the feverity of criticifm, how eafy, nay, how frequent it is to difcover fuperior virtues (as we think) as well as abilities in that particular fpot which gave birth to ourfelves,

and equally divefted of that ftrict impartiality which
alone can enable us to judge properly, difcover pro-
portionable blemifhes in the natives of other countries.

> " But travellers who want the *will*
> " To mark the fhapes of good and ill,
> " With vacant ftare thro' Europe range,
> " And deem all bad, becaufe 'tis ftrange,
> " Thro' varying modes of life, we trace
> " The finer trait, the latent grace,
> " Quite free from fpleen's incumb'ring load
> " At little evils on the road;
> " So while the path of life I tread,
> " A path to me with briars fpread;
> " Let me its tangl'd mazes fpy,
> " Like you, with gay, good humour eye,
> " And be my fpirit light as air,
> " Call life a jeft, and laugh at care."

In faying thus much, I do not mean to infer, that
we ought not to be infpired with a laudable ambition
to excel, nor thofe of other countries only, but even
thofe with whom we are more intimately connected:
but that fhould be done without drawing invidious
comparifons of the merits and demerits of others. In
fhort, let it be the earneft endeavour of each country,
and every individual of that country in particular,
united under our amiable monarch, to ftrive which
fhall have a fuperior claim to the title of being GOOD
MEN, ufeful members of fociety, friends to the whole
human race, and peaceable fubjects of a government,
which though not abfolutely in a ftate of *perfection*——
(and can that man be really deemed *wife* who expects to
meet with perfection in any human eftablifhment?)
is ftill happily fuperior to every other in the known
world.

> Britain now one! thro' all her various parts,
> No diff'rent name fhould know, no diff'ring hearts:
> Strong by connection, like to tougheft cords
> Strain only one, one no defence affords;
> Unite them firm, behold a ftrenuous rope,
> Baffling refiftance, and confirming hope.
> May Britain this refiftlefs ftrength employ,
> Her foes fubdue, and every blifs enjoy.   BRUCIAD

But to return to Edinburgh. The Old Town, fo
called, has not much to boaft of; but the New Town

is by the moft complete and elegant I ever faw. In various towns of England and Scotland, I have indeed feen fome good ftreets, and many good houfes, but in this the whole is uniformly fine; not one houfe, much lefs a whole ftreet that can be termed indifferent in the whole town.

And here let me do juftice to North Britifh hofpitality, and their very polite attention to fuch Englifhmen who happen to travel to the " land of cakes." I can truly fay, that the polite and friendly behaviour of the inhabitants towards Mrs. Lackington and myfelf, claims our warmeft gratitude and fincereft thanks. This the more civilized part of my countrymen will readily believe; and as to thofe of another defcription (happily but a comparatively fmall number, I truft) are welcome to treat my affertion with that contempt ufually attendant on prejudice, which is the refult of ignorance.

The fubject I now mean to enter into being a delicate one, permit me here to clofe my letter; thus affording you a fhort refpite and myfelf a little time for confideration on the propriety of fubmitting my ideas (as you feem determined all thofe I fend you fhall be) to public notice, and I muft confefs,

> " Indeed, my friend, I much delight,
> " That you are pleas'd with what I write."

I am,

Dear Sir,

Yours.

LETTER XLVI.

Set *woman* in his eye, and in his walk,
Among the daughters of men the faireft found,
Many are in each region paffing fair
As the noon fky, more like to goddeffes
Than mortal creatures ; graceful and difcreet,
Expert in amorous arts, enchanting tongues :
Perfuafive, virgin majefty, with mild
And fweet allay'd, yet terrible to approach ;
Skill'd to retire, and in retiring draw
Hearts after them, tangl'd in amorous nets ;
Such objects have the power to foften and tame
Severeft temper, fmooth the rugged'ft brow,
Enerve and with voluptuous hope diffolve ;
Draw out with credulous defire,
At will, the manlieft refoluteft breaft.   MILTON.

DEAR FRIEND,

        I N my laft I expreffed fome diffi-
dence refpecting the propriety of committing to paper
my thoughts on a particular fubject; I have fince
weighed it with due caution, and the confideration
of my having, during the long courfe of my epiftelary
correfpondence, always declared my fentiments freely
on every fubject, foon determined me not to degrafe
myfelf by fhrinking back, now it is fo near drawing to
a conclufion.

    The fubject then is—that bright lovely part of the
creation, WOMAN!—the fource of all our joys, the
affuagers of all our griefs ; deprived of whofe powerful attractive charms, man would be a wretch indeed.
But alas! the utmoft efforts of my abilities are far in-
adequate to do juftice to their merits; happily that
pleafing theme has engaged the attention of the ableft
and worthieft of men, from the remoteft period down
to the prefent time ; and I truft ever will, nay muft,
fo long as a fpark of virtue remains in the human
breaft.

    Weak tho' her frame, not her's to yield
    To fteel, to fire, to dart, or fhield ;

Vain are th' embattl'd warrior's arms—
No proof 'gainst beauty's heav'nly charms ;
Beauty ! whose smiles, with soft controul,
At once—can pierce him to the soul.

FAWKES's Anacreon.

And when I reflect, that

" They are not only FAIR, but JUST as fair."

I have nought to fear.

I therefore proceed with cheerfulness to say, that in Edinburgh, Glasgow, Sterling, &c. there are more real fine women to be found than in any place I ever visited. I do not mean to say that we have not as many handsome women in England ; but the idea I wish to convey is, that we have not so many in proportion : that is, go to any public place where a number of ladies are assembled, in either of the above towns, and then go to any place in England where an equal number are met, and you will notice a greater number of fine women among the former, than among the latter. It must be obvious that in making this declaration, I allude to the genteeler part ; for among the lower classes of women in Scotland, by being more exposed to the inclemency of the weather, the majority are very homely, and the want of the advantages of apparel, (which those in a higher sphere can avail themselves of, and know how to apply) together with their sluttish and negligent appearance, does not tend in the least to heighten their charms.

Having both read and heard much related of the manner of washing their linen, which I must confess I could not credit without having ocular demonstration, during my continuance at Glasgow, curiosity led me to the mead by the river side. For the poor women here instead of the water coming to them, as in London, are obliged to travel loaded with their linen to the water ; where you may daily see great numbers washing, in *their* way ; which if seen by some of our London prudes, would incline them to form very unjust and uncharitable ideas of the modesty of these Scottish lasses. Many of them give a trifle to be accommodated with the use of a large

O

wafh-houfe near the water, where about a hundred may be furnifhed with every convenience for their purpofe. But by far the greateft part make fires, and heat the water in the open air, and as they finifh their linen, they fpread it on the grafs to dry; which is the univerfal mode of drying throughout Scotland. Here the

.‟ Maidens bleach their fummer fmocks.‟

I had walked to and fro feveral times, and began to conclude that the cuftom of getting into the tubs and treading on the linen, either never had been practifed, or was come into difufe; but I had not waited more than half an hour, when many of them jumped into the tubs, without fhoes or ftockings, with their fhift and petticoats drawn up far above the knees, and ftamped away with great compofure in their countenances, and with all their ftrength, no Scotchman taking the leaft notice, or even looking towards them, conftant habit having rendered the fcene perfectly familiar.

On converfing with fome gentlemen of Glafgow on this curious fubject, they affured me that thefe fingular laundreffes (as they appeared to me) were ftrictly modeft women, who only did what others of unblemifhed reputation had been accuftomed to for a long feries of years; and added, that at any other time a purfe of gold would not tempt them to draw the curtain fo high. By way of contraft, let me obferve that many of our London fervant-maids, though not always fo nice in other refpects, would not be feen thus habited *in public* on any terms, leaft their precious characters fhould be called in queftion. A ftriking inftance of the powerful influence of habit! Pomfret fays,

‟ Cuftom's the world's great idol we adore,
‟ And knowing that we feek to know no more.‟

Moft of the female fervants in Edinburgh, Glaf-glow, &c. do all their work, and run about the town the fore part of the day without ftays, fhoes, or ftockings; and on Sundays I faw the country-women

going towards kirk, in the same manner (ftays excepted ;) however, they do not go into kirk, till
they have dreffed their legs and feet; for that purpofe
they feat themfelves on the grafs, fomewhere near,
put on their fhoes and ftockings, and garter up very
deliberately,

" Nor heed the paffenger that looks that way."

Moft of thefe poor young country-women go without any caps or hats; they have in general fine heads
of hair, many plait it, others let it hang loofe down
their backs; and I affure you, my friend, they look
very agreeable.

I returned each time through Buxton, where ftay-
ing a week or two, I vifited Caftleton, and fpent feveral hours in exploring that ftupendous cavern, called
The Devil's A—— in the Peake. I alfo furveyed
Poole's Hole, near Buxton, and purchafed a great
variety of petrifactions. In our way home I faw the
great marble manuafactory at Afton, in the water,
fpent fome days at Matlock, the moft romantic village
that I ever faw, but the fight of it coft me dear; as
we were conveyed there in an old crazy poft-chaife,
in which I caught a violent cold, the lining being
very damp.

I am,

Dear Friend,

Yours.

L E T T E R XLVII.

Good feen expected, evil unforefeen,
Appear by turns as fortune fhifts the fcene:
Some rais'd aloft come tumbling down amain,
Then fall fo hard, they bound and rife again.
                                    DRYDEN's Virgil.

New turns and changes every day
    Are of inconftant chance the conftant arts;
Soon fortune gives, foon takes away.
    She comes, embraces, naufeates you, and parts.
But if fhe ftays or if fhe goes,
    The wife man little joy or little forrow knows:
For over all there hangs a doubtful fate,
    And few there be that're always fortunate.
One gains by what another is bereft :
    The frugal deftinies have only left
A common bank of happinefs below,
    Maintain'd, like nature, by an ebb and flow.
                                    How's Indian Emp.

    " They fay there's a Providence fets up aloft,
    " To keep watch for the life of poor Jack."

DEAR FRIEND,

        I Did not intend to trouble you or
the public with an account of any more of my *wonderful travels*, but being now at Lyme, for want of
other amufements this rainy morning, I thought that
a fhort account of this journey might afford you fome
entertainment.

    My ftate of health being but indifferent, and Mrs.
Lackington's ftill worfe, I was induced to try what
effect a journey would produce;

    " When med'cine fails, amufement fhould be fought,
    " Though but to footh the miferies of thought."

It being immaterial what part I travelled to; and as
I had not for a long time feen my native place, and
perhaps might not be furnifhed with another opportunity, we refolved to vifit it.

And many a year elaps'd, return to view
Where once the cottage stood, the hawthorn grew,
Remembrance wakes with all her busy train,
Swells at my breast——————————————
I still had hopes, for pride attends us still,
Amidst the swains to shew my book-learn'd skill.
Yes, let the rich deride, with proud disdain
The simple blessings of the lowly train ;
To me, more dear, congenial to my heart,
One native charm, than all the glofs of art ;
Spontaneous joys, where nature has its play,
The soul adopts, and owns their first born sway :
Lightly they frolick o'er the vacant mind,
Unenvy'd, unmolested, unconfin'd."

GODDSMITH.

Accordingly in July last, 1791, we set out from Merton, which I now make my chief residence, taking Bath, Bristol, &c. in our way to my native place Wellington.

In Bristol, Exbridge, Bridgewater, Taunton, Wellington, and other places, I amused myself in calling on some of my masters, with whom I had about twenty years before worked as a journeyman shoemaker. I addressed each with, " *Pray, Sir, have you got any occasion?*" which is the term made use of by journeymen in that useful occupation, when seeking employment. Most of those honest men had quite forgot my person, as many of them had not seen me since I worked for them : so that it is not easy for you to conceive with what surprize and astonishment they gazed on me. For you must know that I had the vanity (I call it humour) to do this in my chariot, attended by my servants ; and on telling them who I was, all appeared to be very happy to see me.

" Up springs at every step, to claim a tear,
" Some little friendship form'd and cherish'd here."

And I assure you, my friend, it afforded me much real pleasure to see so many of my old acquaintances alive and well, and tolerably happy. The following lines often occurred to my mind:

" Far from the madding crowds ignoble strife,
  " Their sober wishes never learn'd to stray ;
 " Along the cool sequester'd vale of life
  " They keep the noiseless tenor of their way."

At Taunton and Wellington it seemed to be the unanimous determination of all the poorer fort, that I should by no means be deficient in *old acquaintances.*

> Faithful mem'ry wakes each past delight,
> Each youthful transport bursting on the sight,
> Equal in years when frolic sports display,
> And Phœbus gladdens with a brighter ray.
> GREEN's Appollonius Rhodius.

Some poor souls declared that they had known me for *fifty* years) that is, years before I was born;) others had danced me in their arms a thousand times; nay, better still, some knew my grandmother; but, best of all, one old man claimed acquaintance with me, for having seen me many times on the top of a fix-and-twenty round ladder, balanced on the chin of a merry andrew! The old man was however egregiously mistaken, as I never was so precariously exalted, my ambition, as you well know, taking a very different turn. But that was of no consequence: all the old fellow wanted was *a shilling*—and I gave it him. No matter (as Sterne says) from what motive. I never examine into these things.

> A small gratuity dilates their heart,
> And many a blessing follows as we part.
> J. FITZGERALD.

This I observed, that none of them were common beggars, but poor useful labouring people; (giving to common strollers is but encouraging idleness and every other vice) and as *small matters made many happy,* I was supremely so, to be the means of contributing to their comfort. And indeed who would hesiate at being the means of diffusing happiness on such easy terms, and with so little trouble?

> His faithful kin, though forty times remov'd,
> Will let him hear how tenderly he's lov'd;
> Silence when he harangues will ne'er be broke,
> But ev'ry tongue repeat his poorest joke.
> LORD GARDENSTONE.

The bells rang merrily all the day of my arrival. I was also honoured with the attention of many of the most respectable people in and near Wellington and other parts: Some of whom were pleased to inform me, that the reason of their paying a particular attention to me was their having heard, and now having themselves an opportunity of observing, that I did not so far forget myself, as many proud upstarts had done; that the notice I took of my poor relations and old acquaintance merited the respect and approbation of every real gentleman.

> By dear experience every day we find,
> That riches commonly degrade the mind,
> That he, who train'd through wants instructive school,
> Had prov'd a man of sense, becomes a fool.
> As dirt on all beneath himself looks down,
> Nor feels for any sorrow but his own.
>   LORD GARDENSTON.

They were also pleased to express a wish, that as soon as I could dispose of my business, I would come down and spend the remainder of my days among them. Those ideas were pleasing to me, and perhaps may be realized; I wish it may be soon.

> " There could I trifle carelesly away,
> " The milder evening of life's clouded day,
> " From business, and the world's intrusion free,
> " With books, with love, with friendship, and with thee,
> " No farther want, no wish yet unpossest,
> " Could e'er disturb my unambitious breast.

Tibullus was much of the same mind nearly two thousand years since. Although he had been much better acquainted with state and grandeur, yet when the soldiers of the Triumvirate were rewarded with his possessions, he would not make his court to Augustus, in order to recover them, but in retirement obtained a tranquility of mind not to be found in the gay, or busy world: in his first elegy, he says,

> For treasur'd wealth, for stores of golden wheat,
>   The hoard of frugal fires, I'll never call;
> A little farm be mine, a cottage neat
>   And wonted couch, where balmy sleep may fall.
>
> What joy to hear the tempest howl in vain,
>   And clasp a fearful mistress to my breast;
> Or lull'd to slumber by the beating rain,
>   Secure and happy sink at last to rest.

Content with little, I would rather ftay
 Than fpend long months amid the wat'ry wafte:
In cooling fhade, elude the fcorching ray .
 Befide fome fountain's gliding waters plac'd.

There are that fame, and wounds, and riches prize;
For me, while I poffefs one plenteous year,
 I ll wealth and meagre want alike defpife.

In his fourth elegy is the following ufeful hint:

I've feen the aged oft lament their fate,
That fenfelefs they had learnt to live too late.

In elegy the fixth, he fays,

The fons of opulence are folly's care,
But want's rough child is fenfe, and honour's heir.

GRAINGER.

Often have fuch thoughts as thefe, cheered me
with hopes, and then

——————————— I defcend,
To join the worldly croud: Perchance to talk,
To think, to act as they; then all thefe thoughts,
That left the expanded heart above this fpot
To heavenly mufing; thefe pafs away,
(Even as this goodly profpect from my view)
Hidden by near and earthy-rooted cares.
So paffeth human life; our better mind
Is as a Sunday's garment, then put on
When we have nought to do; but at our work
We wear a worfe for thrift.

CROWE's Lewefdown Hill, a Poem.

The above reception was the more pleafing, as I have
fometimes obferved a contrary conduct practifed by
fome, who have been pleafed to ftile themfelves gen‐
tlemen, and on that fcore think that they have a right
to treat men of bufinefs (however refpectable they
may be) as by much their inferiors; and it too often
happens that one of thofe petty gentry who poffeffes
but a hundred or two per annum, will behave in a
haughty manner to a man in bufinefs who fpends as
many thoufands; but fuch fhould be told, that a real
gentleman in any company will never either by word
or action, attempt to make the meaneft perfon feel his
inferiority, but on the contrary.

They should be informed also how highly impolitic and unjust it is to attempt to fix a stigma on trade and commerce, the very things that have caused England to rise so high in the political scale of Europe.

―――――― Mighty commerce, hail!
By thee the sons of Attic's sterile land,
A scanty number, laws imposed on Greece,
Nor aw'd they Greece alone; vast Asia's king,
Tho' girt by rich arm'd myriads at their frown,
Felt his heart wither on his farthest throne.
Perennial source of population, thou!
While scanty peasants plough the flow'ry plains,
What swarms of useful citizens spring up,
Hatch'd by thy fostering wing.

GRAINGER's Sugar-cane.

Dean Swift was in the right; "If a proud man (says he) makes me keep my distance the comfort is, he keeps his at the same time."

'Tis true that even in England you may see great numbers of very opulent tradesmen who have not an idea but what they have acquired behind the counter, or at their punch-clubs; but you may also find many thousands of the same class of life who are possessed of very liberal sentiments, and who would not commit an action that would disgrace a title.

" In England (says Thicknesse) one may trust the honour of a respectable tradesman; in France and Flanders I never experienced a single instance of it." (He adds) " and an English merch'nt, who has resided many years at Marseilles, assured me that there was not a merchant in that great city, who would not only over-reach him if he could, but would boast also all over the town of having so done." And I think that we may easily account for this very great difference, in the national characters of merchants and tradesmen. On the continent, merchants and tradesmen are looked upon in a degrading point of view, merely for being of that class, nor would the most honourable or respectable behaviour ever raise them in the ideas or estimation of the nobles or gentry, who are taught to treat them with neglect, and even contempt. Thus being deprived of that great motive to noble or liberal actions, the love of honour, rank,

O 5

the notice of the great, &c. &c. their minds become depreſſed and degraded ; whilſt in England the merchants and reſpectable tradeſmen, being held in higher eſtimation, and often admitted to the company, converſation, and honours of higher claſſes, the ſordid mind by degrees imbibes more liberal ſentiments, and the rough manners receive a degree of poliſh. For my part, I will endeavour to adhere to the advice given by Perſius as it is tranſlated :

> " Study thyſelf what rank, or what degree
> " The wiſe Creator has ordain'd for thee :
> " And all the offices of that ſtate
> " Perform ; and with thy prudence guide thy fate."

We are informed that Dr. Johnſon leaped over the ſame poſts which he had often leaped over when a boy. I did much the ſame, and with great pleaſure, viſited moſt of the lanes, gates, hedges, fields, trees, &c. with which I had been acquainted, when a boy : while

> ―――― Faithful memory's friendly hand,
> That waves her all-enliv'ning wand,
>   And brings to fancy's view ;
> What time, when wing'd with gay delight,
> Each thoughtleſs day and eaſy night,
>   On pleaſure's pinions flew.
>
> There, pleas'd I trace the flow'ry mead,
> And round the well-known elm trees tread,
>   Where oft I've careleſs play'd ;
> And ſure my choiceſt days were ſpent,
> Cheer'd with the ſmiles of glad content,
>   Beneath their peaceful ſhade.
>
> The church, the yard, the neighb'ring yew,
> All join to warm my heart anew,
>   And paſtimes paſt recall ;
> 'Twas here I laſh'd the murm'ring top,
> Here drove the tile with eager hop,
>   There ſtruck the bounding ball.
>
> Hail, happy ſtate of infant years !
> There lovely peace her temple rears,
>   And ſmiling ſtands confeſs'd ;
> There virtue holds her chearful court,
> And youthful gay deſires, reſort
>   To charm the tranquil breaſt.

No lawlefs paffions wound the mind,
There pleafures leave no fting behind,
  Sad fource of other's care;
Nor fell remorfe, nor envious ire,
Nor black revenge, with purpofe dire,
  Occafion dark defpair.

Their's is the rofy bloom of health,
The boundlefs tranfport fnatch'd by ftealth,
  The heart devoid of guile;
What riper manhood feldom knows,
The peaceful undifturb'd repofe,
  And undiffembled fmile.

Affliction's load they feldom bear,
'Tis their's to fhed a fhort-liv'd tear,
  Nor forrows foon forgot;
The fweets that from contentment flow,
That health and peace of mind beftow,
  Complete their happy lot.

BELL's Britifh Album.

I alfo with renewed pleafure vifited the delightful
banks of the river Tone, near Taunton: where
formerly I had taken fo many pleafing walks with
Nancy Smith and Hannah Allen, and in imagination
kiffed them over and over again in every old refting
place. "The impreffion (fays Zimmermann) is in-
deliable, the bofom for ever retains a fenfe of that
higheft extacy of love, and of the place where the
firft time that happy difcovery, that fortunate moment, when two lovers perceive their mutual fondnefs." "Precious moments, (fays Rouffeau) fo
much regretted! oh! begin again your delightful
courfe; flow on with longer duration in my remembrance, if poffible, than you did in reality in your
fugitive fucceffion." "Petrarch, fpeaking of the fine
fenfations of a perfon in love, fays, "This is a condition which every young man ought to wifh for,
who wifhes to fly from the mercilefs approaches of a
cold old age."

No fweet folicitude to know
Nor other's blifs, for other's woe.
A frozen apathy to find,
A fad vacuity of mind;

O 6

O, haften back, then, heav'nly boy,
And with thy anguifh bring thy joy !
Return with all thy torments here,
And let me hope, and doubt, and fear.
O rend my heart with ev'ry pain !
But let me, let me love again.   DELLA CRUSCA.

William Jones, Efq. of Foxdowne, near Wellington, informed me of a remarkable *prognoftication*
in my favour; he told me that when I was a boy,
about twelve years of age, Mr. Paul, then a very
confiderable wholefale linen-draper, in Friday-ftreet,
London, (I believe ftill living) paffing by my father's
houfe one day, ftopped at the door and afked various
queftions about fome guinea-pigs which I had in a
box. My anfwers it feems pleafed and furprized him,
and turning towards Mr. Jones, faid, " *Depend upon*
it, Sir, that boy will one day rife far above the fituation
that his prefent mean circumftances feem to promife." So
who knows what a great man I may yet be ?—perhaps

" A double pica in the book of fame."

Give me leave to introduce another prediction,
though not altogether fo pleafing as that juft related.
An Italian gentleman, and if we may judge by appearance, a perfon of rank, was fome years fince
looking at fome books of *palmiftry* in my fhop, and at
the fame time endeavoured to convince me of the
reality of that fcience. In the midft of his difcourfe,
he fuddenly feized my right-hand, and looking for
fome time with great attention on the various lines,
he informed me that I had twice been in danger of
lofing my life, once by water, and once by a wound
in my head; he was certainly right, but I believe by
chance, as I have many other times been in very
great danger. He added, that I had much of the
goddefs *Venus* in me, but much more of *Mars*; and
affured me that I fhould go to the wars, and arrive at
great honour. He likewife informed me, that I
fhould die by *fire-arms* pointed *over a wall.*—How far
the former part of this gentleman's prediction may
be relied on, I will not pretend to decide, but the
laft part of it was lately very near coming to fuch a

decifion as would have proved the infallibility of that
part of his prognoftication, though even in that cafe
he might have pleaded his being pretty near the matter of fact, only fubftituting *gunpowder* inftead of *fire-
arms*, and I fhould not have had it in my power to
contend the point with him. I will endeavour to
render this intelligible: On Tuefday the fifth of
July 1791, I very nearly efcaped being blown up with
the powder-mills belonging to Mr. Bridges, at Ewell,
near Merton in Surry. A quarter of an hour before
that event took place, I was riding out within one
mile of the mills, and having enquired of Mr. Rofe,
at Coombe-Farm, for the way that leads round by the
mills, I actually rode part of the way, with an intent of vifiting them. But fomehow or other, I
fcarce knew why, I turned my horfe about, and a
few minutes after faw the fatal cataftrophe; which
happening by day, refembled a large cloud of fmoke,
of a very light colour, and the report reached my ears
immediately after. I inftantly concluded, it could be
nothing lefs than the powder-mills blown up; and on
my return to my houfe at Merton, I foon learned
that it was the identical powder-mill that in all probability I fhould have been in, or clofe by, at the
time of the explofion. By this accident it feems four
men were killed, fome of whom had large families.
The bodies were fo much mangled by the explofion,
that they could not be diftinguifhed from each other,
and the head of one of them was thrown to a great
diftance.

On the 19th of March, 1794, Dr. Sinclair died
fuddenly in a bookfeller's fhop in Birmingham.
The doctor a few months previous to his death, caft
the nativity of Mr. Hindmarfh the printer, and pro-
phefied that he would die fuddenly within twelve-
months. How came the doctor not to fee, that it
would be his own fate fo to end his life, and within the time that he was pleafed to appoint for Mr. Hindmarfh? I wifh it was made banifhment for any one to
pretend to foretel the death of another.

Horace advifes Leucone to enjoy the prefent hour:
to make no enquiry of fortune-tellers relative to the
future.

Strive not, Leucone, to pry
  Into the secret will of fate,
Nor impious magic vainly try,
  To know our lives' uncertain date;

Whether th' indulgent pow'r divine
  Hath many seasons yet in store,
Or this the latest winter thine
  Which breaks its waves against the shore.

Thy life with wiser arts be crown'd,
  Thy filter'd wines abundant pour;
The lengthen'd hope with prudence bound
  Proportion'd to the flying hour.

Ev'n while we talk in careless ease,
  Our envious minutes wing their flight;
Then swift the fleeting pleasure seize
  Nor trust to-morrow's doubtful light.   FRANCIS.

But to proceed with my journey. I esteem myself
peculiarly happy, on one account in particular, that
I undertook it; and have only to regret it did not
take place sooner, as it tended to undeceive me in a
matter in which I had long been in an error.

How much one good well-natur'd deed
  Exhilerates the mind!
Self-love should prompt each human heart
  To study to be kind!

Remembrance of a little act
  Will always smiling look,
Which, though 'twas useful and humane,
  Small cost and labour took.
                Dr. DODD's Poem to Humanity.

The case was this: I had for seven years past supposed that the parents of my first wife were dead;
and on enquiring after them of Mr. Cash at Bridgewater, he confirmed the report. However, as we
passed through North Petherton, being but a mile
from the place where they formerly lived, I could
not help stopping to find out the time when they died,
and what other particulars I could learn relative to
them; but, to my very great surprise, I was informed that they were both living at Newton, two miles
distant. On this information I gave the coachman
orders to drive us there, but still could scarcely credit

that they really were alive.—But, O my dear friend, it is utterly impoffible for me to defcribe the fenfations of Mrs. Lackington and myfelf, on entering

> ————— " The cobweb'd cottage,
> " With ragged wall of mould'ring mud"

which contained them!

> Then Poverty, grim fpectre, rofe,
> And horror o'er the profpect threw. AMWELL.

There we found—two

> " Poor human ruins, tottering o'er the grave."

The dim light on our entrance feemed a little to flafh in the focket, and every moment threatened to difappear for ever! while their " pale wither'd hands were ftretched out towards me," trembling at once with eagernefs and age. Never before did I feel the full force of Shakfpeare's defcription,

> " ————— Laft fcene of all
> " That ends this ftrange eventful hiftory,
> " Is fecond childifhnefs, and mere oblivion :
> " Sans teeth, fans eyes, fans tafte, fans every thing."

From fuch a ftate of poverty and wretchednefs, good God, deliver every worthy character.

The old man is ninety years of age, and the good old woman eighty. The old man's intellects are much impaired; he for a moment knew me, and then his recollection forfook him. His behaviour brought to my mind, the paffage in the Odyffey, where the good old man meets his long loft fon.

> " He faints, he finks, with mighty joys oppreft,
> " But as returning life regains its feat,
> " And his breath lengthens, and his pulfes beat;
> " Yes, I believe, he cries, almighty Jove!
> " Heav'n rules as yet, and gods there are above."

The old woman retained her fenfes and knowledge during the whole of the time we were with them.

> " They breath'd their prayer, long may fuch goodnefs live !
> " 'Twas all they gave, 'twas all they had to give."

On inquiry I found, that what little property they had poffeffed had been all expended for fome years.

How many once in Fortune's lap high fed,
Solicit the cold hand of Charity !
To fhock us more—folicit it in vain !   Dr. Young.

Amidft this dreary fcene, it was fome alleviation to
learn that their pious fon had given them weekly as
much as he could afford from his own little family,
and I have added enough to render them as comfortable as their great age can poffibly admit of. But for
your fake and my own, I will drop this gloomy fubject; which to me proved one of the moft affecting
fcenes that ever I experienced in the whole courfe of
my life; and I believe that had I not afforded them
relief, the dreary fcene would have followed my
haunted imagination to my grave.

Oh Charity ! our helplefs nature's pride,
Thou friend to him who knows no friend befide,
Is there a morning s breath, or the fweet gale
That fteals o'er the tir'd pilgrim of the vale,
Cheering with fragrance frefh his weary frame,
Aught like the incenfe of the holy flame ?
Is aught in all the beauties that adorn
The azure heaven, or purple light of morn ?
Is aught fo fair in evening's ling'ring gleam,
As from thine eye the meek and penfive beam,
That falls, like faddeft moonlight on the hill
And diftant grove, when the wide world is ftill.
                                        Bowles.

It is a fine fpeech that Metaftafio puts into the mouth
of Titus :

What would'ft thou leave me, friend, if thou deny'ft me
The glorious privilege of doing good ?
Shall I my only joy forego ;
No more my kind protection fhew,
  To thofe by fortune's frown purfu'd ;
No more exalt each virtuous friend,
No more a bounteous hand extend,
  T' enrich the worthy and the good ?   Hoole.

During our continuance at Wellington, I one
morning rode over to Black Down, on purpofe to
infpect an immenfe heap of ftones on the top of the
hill, ftraight before the town, which I remembered
to have feen when a boy. The diftance from Wellington is about two miles. Thefe ftones cover about an

acre of ground, and rise to a great height. The country people informed me with great gravity, that " the devil brought them there in one night in his *leathern apron*." But the name of it, as well as the form, proves what it was. It is called Symmon's *Borough* or *Barrow*; which, you know, signifies a burial-place. I should not have taken any notice of it here, had I ever seen any Barrow of *stones* besides this, and five other smaller Barrows, about half a mile from the large one. The country people informed me that the *devil* brought the five heaps there in his *glove*. I also observed the remains of a large camp near the spot. Camden has taken notice of a large camp at Roach Castle, three or four miles from hence; it is strange that neither he nor Gough should take any notice of so singular a Barrow as this certainly is.

I am,

Dear Friend,

Yours.

LETTER XLVIII.

Ye who amid this feverish world would wear
A body free of pain, of cares the mind,
Fly the rank city; shun its turbid air:
Breathe not the chaos of eternal smoke
And volatile corruption from the dead,
The dying, sickening, and the living world
Exhal'd, te fully heaven's transparent dome
With dim mortality. It is not air
That from a thousand lungs reke back to thine,
Sated with exhalations, rank and fell,
The spoil of dunghills, and the putrid thaw
Of Nature; when from shape and texture she
Relapsed into fighting Elements.
It is not air, but floats a nauseous mass
Of all obscene, corrupt, offensive things,
Much moisture hurts: here a sordid bath,
With daily rancour fraught, relaxes more
The solids than simple moisture can.
ARMSTRONG's Art of Health.

I once in several years am seen,
At Bath or Tunbridge, to careen.   SPLEEN.

Lyme Sep. 4, 1791.

DEAR FRIEND,

BEING now at one of those places usually called *watering places*, that is, a place where invalids resort in great numbers for the real or pretended purpose of drinking the waters for which each particular situation is in repute, and bathing in them with a view to the restoration of their health; I shall trouble you with a few observations which have occurred to me on the subject. I cannot entertain a doubt but that many by this practice have been highly benefited; but at the same time I must observe that such relief is only to be reasonably expected where the parties possess a sufficient share of prudence to conform to such rules as are laid down to them by those who are best acquainted with the nature of the several complaints, the strength or weakness of their constitutions, and the different virtues those several waters possess, so as properly to adapt them to each particular case, by drinking the waters at proper stated periods, as well as in proper doses; besides conforming to such a regimen as shall co-operate with them in producing the desired effect. But where invalids neglect all, or indeed any of those rules, is it not rather an absurdity to expect relief? —I will endeavour to explain myself:

Those waters either possess powerful virtues, or they do not. If they do, is it not obvious that some judgment and caution is necessary in the use of them? which must either produce good or bad effects, according to the prudence with which they are applied. If on the other hand, they are of so insignificant a nature, that they may be used at any time, and in any proportion, without injury; and that too in disorders and constitutions very much varying from each other, then surely the inference must be, that no dependence is to be placed on them, and consequently it matters not if they are never used at all. For what purpose then do such numbers put themselves to the inconvenience, expence, and trouble of travelling (frequently from distant parts of the kingdom) and that too when many of them are in so debilitated a state, that their very removal is attended with extreme danger, and sometimes proves fatal? But that those waters are not inactive, I am well convinced, having seen the bad effects arising from the imprudent use of them, in many instances, as well as the happy consequences attending their being used with due caution.

I was first led into these reflections by having been highly diverted, when I visited Buxton several summers, with the preposterous and absurd conduct of some of the company who resorted thither for the purpose of restoring their health. I remember six or seven gentlemen informing me, that they were violently afflicted with the gout and rheumatism, and had undertaken this journey in hopes of receiving benefit by the waters. These gentlemen often rode or walked about the cold dreary hills, in very damp wet mornings, and afterwards drank claret from three o'clock in the afternoon to three the next morning: But I did not continue there long enough to be a witnefs of the happy effects which muft inevitably be produced by a perfeverance in fuch a judicious regimen.

I alfo vifited Freeftone, near Bofton in Lincoln-fhire: to which place a number of tradefmen and farmers reforted with their wives, in hopes of receiving benefit from the ufe of the falt water, in a variety of complaints; which they had been advifed to do by the faculty, for a month, with particular directions to bathe every other day, and on the intermediate days to drink half a pint of the water in the courfe of that day. But thefe wife people on duly confidering the matter, were fully convinced that this would detain them from their families and bufinefs longer than was altogether convenient; and alfo (which they fuppofed their medical friends never thought of) that they could bathe the full number of times, and drink the prefcribed quantity of the water in a week or a fortnight at fartheft, and thus not only expedite the cure, but likewife enable them to return to their families and bufinefs fo much earlier, as well as fave the neceffary expences attending their continuing for fuch a length of time at the watering place. Thefe united confiderations appeared to them fo confiftent with prudence and œconomy, that they refolved to put them into immediate practice. I remonftrated with feveral of thefe good people on the impropriety of their conduct; but whether they concluded I was a party interefted in detaining them on the fpot, or whether they deemed my judgment inferior to their own, I know not; but I obferved that fome of them bathed feveral times in a day, and drank falt-water by the quart, the confequence of which was, that they left the place, when the time expired which *they* had prefcribed to themfelves, much worfe than they came. Some indeed were fo very weak, that I am perfuaded they could with difficulty reach their homes alive. And in thefe cafes the want of fuccefs, inftead of being attributed to the *folly* of the patients, is generally transferred to the *waters*, and to the want of judgment in those who advised the use of them.

I assure you, my dear friend, this is pretty much the case at Lyme. My rooms commanding a view of the sea, I have this and several other days noticed many decent looking men going down the beach three or four times in as many hours, and drinking a pint of water each time. I have made the same observation at *Margate, Brighton, Hastings, Eastbourne, Seaton, Charmouth,* and other places, so that the observation of Crabshaw's nurse, in the Adventures of Sir Launcelot Greaves, has frequently occurred to me : " Blessed be G— (said she) my patient is in a fair way ! his apozem has had a blessed effect ! five and twenty stools since three o'clock in the morning !"

Relating these particulars to a medical friend, he informed me that such specimens of ignorance and obstinacy were by no means confined to the watering places ; as he had in the course of his practice met with repeated instances, where patients with a view of hastening the cure, and *getting out of the doctor's hands* (whom the vulgar *charitably* suppose wish to retain them there as long as possible) have swallowed a half pint mixture intended for several doses at once, and a whole box of pills in the same manner. The consequences of which have been, that from the violence of the operations they have remained *in his hands* a considerable time, some so long as life (thus foolishly trifled with) lasted.

But here are many of another class ; some of whom, though not *all*, came on purpose to bathe, but during the whole of their continuance, never found time to bathe once. Some hasten to the billiard-room as soon as they are out of their beds in the morning, and there they continue until bed-time again. A few of these are indeed much benefited, being cured of *consumptions in their purses,* while others become proportionably as much emaciated. And a great number, both of ladies and gentlemen, devote the whole of their time to dressing, eating, and playing at whist. Charming *exercise* it must be ! as they frequently sit still in their chairs, for eight or ten hours together.

Where knights, and beaux, and lords, and sharpers run:
Some to undo, but more to be undone.
Of all the plagues that from the birth of time,
Have rang'd by turns this sublunary clime,
And in their various forms the nations curs'd,
The boundless love of play is sure the worst.

Whist, a Poem.

Here are others again, who, like the gentlemen at Buxton, sit drinking (*often red port after salt-water*) until three or four in the morning; making a delightful noise, to *compose* those in the same house who are real *invalids*, and who desirous of obtaining rest, retire early, though frequently to very little purpose.

I have also observed, that all the above places are as healthy for horses, as they are for their masters. For as the innkeepers depend almost entirely on the season, they take great care, and do all they can to make these places comfortable. So that if gentlemen have fat, lazy, prancing horses, and want to reduce them in size and temper, they may be sure to have it done in some of the inns and stables at the various watering places; where such hay is procured as must infallibly answer the purpose even though they be allowed a double portion of corn.

There is yet another very great advantage (which I had like to have forgot) resulting from attending the watering places. Such gentlemen who happen to have servants too honest, too industrious, too attentive, too cleanly, too humble, too sober, &c. by taking them to any of these places, where they have so much leisure time, and where these party-coloured gentry meet together so often, and in such numbers, no one can go away unimproved, except he is a very dull fellow indeed.—This is not merely my own observation : for several gentlemen of my acquaintance assured me that they had always found their servants improved prodigiously after each of these excursions.

We purpose setting out for Weymouth in a day or two : but as I intend that this shall be my last epistle, I will not conclude it until I arrive at Merton.

> " If into diftant parts I vainly roam,
> " And novelty from varied objects try,
> " My bufy thoughts refeek their wonted home,
> " And ficken at the vain variety."

I think Lord Bacon fomewhere fays, that no man is as happy abroad, as he is at home: and I can, without much fcruple of confcience, fubfcribe to the following lines of the poet:

> Happy the man who truly loves his home,
> And never wanders farther from his door
> Than we have gone to-day; who feels his heart
> Still drawing homeward, and delights like us,
> Once more to reft his foot on his own threfhold.
>
> HUDDIS.

Merton, Sept. 11th. We arrived here fafe laft night, being my birth-day.

> " Here, here for ever could I ftay,
> " Here calmly loiter life away,
> " No more thofe vain connections know
> " Which fetter down the free-born mind,
> " The flave of intereft or of fhow."

At Weymouth we had the honour of walking feveral evenings on the Efplanade, with their majefties and the four princeffes. His majefty feems in perfect health and fpirits, and diffufes life and fpirits to all around him. Long, very long may he continue to enjoy the fame degree of health and happinefs! But I could not help pitying Mr. Hughes, the manager of the Theatre there; as the company in general feem to pay but very little attention to plays, while they can partake of the pleafure of walking and breathing the fea air with fo many of the royal family. But his majefty, whofe humanity is by no means the leaft of his many virtues, will no doubt confider Mr. Hughes, who is induftrious to an extreme, as he is fcarce a moment idle. For befides managing his company, performing himfelf fix, fometimes eight characters in a week, he paints all his own fcenes, and attends to many other fubjects; and although he has had a large expenfive family (nine children,) the theatre there, and that alfo at Exeter is his own.

Weymouth theatre he rebuilt about four years fince; every thing is very neat; his fcenes are fine, and his company a very good one. I faw them perform four pieces with a deal of pleafure; notwithftanding I had often feen the fame in London, I remarked here as I had long before done at Bath, that the parts were more equally fupported than they often are at Drury-lane and Covent-garden; for although at thofe places we have many firft-rate actors and actreffes, yet fometimes parts are given to fuch wretched performers as would not grace a barn, which I never faw done at Bath or Weymouth.

In our road home, within half a mile of Dorchefter, we ftopt and fpent half an hour in looking round the famous Roman Amphitheatre. It is clofe to the road, on the right-hand fide, and covers about an acre of ground. It is judged that ten thoufand people might without interruption have beheld fuch exercifes as were exhibited in this fchool of the ancients; it is called Mambury, and is fuppofed to be the compleateft antiquity of the kind in England.

I alfo amufed myfelf, as I travelled through Dorfetfhire and Wiltfhire, in furveying many of the numerous camps, fortifications, and barrows: which lafting monuments of antiquity are to be feen in a-bundance in thefe counties, a great number of them remaining in a perfect ftate.

Nor could I any longer omit the opportunity of feeing that ftupendous piece of antiquity on Salifbury Plain, the famous *Stonehenge*, two miles from Ambrefbury. We fpent near two hours there in aftonifh-ment; and had not night came on, we fhould not have been able to parted from it fo foon. We found a very good inn at Ambrefbury, which proves very convenient to fuch whom curiofity may detain on this wonderful fpot until it is late. It is remarkable, that although fo many able antiquaries have devoted their time and attention to the inveftigation of Stone-henge, it remains ftill a matter undecided when and for what purpofe this amazing pile was formed; nor is there lefs caufe of admiration, how ftones of fuch magnitude were brought hither! I fhall not prefume, either to decide on this curious point, or offer any conjectures of my own.

I have now, Sir, not only given you the most material circumstances of my life, but have also superadded a short sketch of some of my travels. And should the fine air of Merton preserve the stock of health and spirits, which I have acquired in this last excursion, I intend during the summer to spend a few hours in the middle of three or four days in every week in Chiswell-street, devoting the mornings and the remainder of the evenings to my rural retreat,

" Where cheerfulness, triumphant fair,
" Dispels the painful cloud of care,
" O, sweet of language, mild of mien,
" O, Virtue's friend, and pleasure's queen !
" By thee our board with flow'rs is crown'd,
" By thee with songs our walks resound ;
" By thee the sprightly mornings shine,
" And evening hours in peace decline."

As my house at Merton is not far from the churchyard, I was a few evenings since walking in this receptacle of mortality, and recollecting the scene between Sir Lucius O'Trigger and Acres, said to myself, " Here is good snug lying," in this place. So I sat down on one of the graves, and wrote the following lines, which I hope when I am gone to heaven (I am not in haste) my friends will have engraved on my tomb-stone :

LACKINGTON's EPITAPH.

Good passenger, one moment stay,
And contemplate this heap of clay ;
'Tis LACKINGTON that claims a pause,
Who strove with Death, but lost his cause;
A stranger genius ne'er need be,
Than many a merry year was he.
Some faults he had ; some virtues too ;
(The Devil himself should have his due :)
And as Dame Fortune's wheel turn'd round,
Whether at top or bottom found,
He never once forgot his station,
Nor e'er disown'd a poor relation ;

P

In poverty he found content,
Riches ne'er made him insolent.
When poor, he'd rather read than eat ;
When rich, books form'd his highest treat.
His first great wish, to act, with care,
The several parts assign'd him here :
And, as his heart to truth inclin'd,
He study'd hard the truth to find.
Much pride he had, 'twas love of fame,
And slighted gold, to get a name;
But fame herf. If prov'd greatest gain,
For riches follow'd in her train.
Much had he read, and much had thought,
And yet, you fee, he's come to nought ;
Or out of print, as he would fay,
To be revis'd fome future day ;
Free from errata, with addition,
A new, and a complete edition.

In fine weather I never leave this place for London, but with great reluctance. I have a good private library here, and with a book in my hand I wander from field to field ; and during fuch hours feel not a wish unfatisfied. And was my immenfe stock of books turned into money, great as the profits are at No. 46 and 47, Chifwell-ftreet, they would be no temptation to me, ever to fee it more.

——————————— I feel the mind
Expand itfelt in wider liberty.
The diftant found breaks gently on my fenfe,
Soothing to meditation : fo methinks,
Even fo, fequefter'd from the noify world,
Could I wear out this tranfitory being
In peaceful contemplation and calm eafe.

I would not make this life a life of toil
For wealth o'erbalanc'd with a thoufand cares ;
Or power, which bafe compliance muft uphold ;
Or honour lavifh'd moft on courtly flaves ;
Or Fame, vain breath of a misjudging world !
Who for fuch perifhable gaudes would put
A yoke upon his free-unbroken fpirit,
And gall himfelf with trammels and the rubs
Of this world's bufinefs ?

CROWE's Lewesdown Hill, a Poem.

The following lines exprefs the ideas which have often been my own :

Refolv'd the roving, reftlefs mind to cure,
And guide the future different from the paft,
I fought for fweets that might thro' life endure,
And fondly fancied they were found at laft.

British Album.

During the winter I purpofe fpending moft of my
time in town; where I hope again to enjoy the company of you, Sir, and fome others of our old philo-
fophical friends, and when tired of philofophizing,
we will again fing our old verfes:

" What tho' the many wholly bend,
" To things beneath our ftate,
" Some poorly to be rich contend,
" And others meanly great.

" There liv'd a few in ev'ry fpace,
" Since firft our kind began,
" Who ftill maintain'd, with better grace,
" The dignity of man.

In the mean time, I am,

Dear friend, yours.

P. S. I fhould deem myfelf deficient in point of
juftice to the ingenious artift who painted the portrait from whence the engraving affixed as a frontif-
piece to this volume is taken, if I did not embrace
this opportunity of acknowledging the approbation it
has been honoured with by all who have feen it, as a
ftriking likenefs.

The following circumftance, though to many it
may appear in a ludicrous point of view, yet as it is a
fact, which does not depend folely on my affertion, I
fhall not hefitate to mention it.

Before the portrait was finifhed, Mrs. Lackington,
accompanied by another lady, called on the painter to
view it. Being introduced into a room filled with
portraits, her little dog (the faithful Argus) being
with her, immediately ran to that particular portrait,
paying it the fame attention as he is always accuftomed to do the original; which made it neceffary to
remove him from it, left he fhould damage it; though
this was not accomplifhed without expreffions of dif-
fatisfaction on the part of poor Argus.

P 2

He knew his lord, he knew and strove to meet,
And all he could, his tail, his ears, his eyes,
Salute his master, and confess his joys.   Pope's Odyssey

Those who are conversant in history will not doubt the fact; several similar instances being recorded of the sagacity and nice discrimination of these animals.

A PRAYER.

O may my work for ever live!
(Dear friend, this selfish zeal forgive:)
May no vile miscreant saucy cook
Presume to tear my learned book,
To singe his fowl for nicer guest,
Or pin it on the turkey's breast.
Keep it from pastry bak'd, or buying.
From broiling steak, and fritters frying;
From lighting pipes or wrapping snuff,
Or casing up a feather muff;
From all the several ways the grocer
(Who to the learned world's a foe, Sir,)
Has found in twisting, folding, packing,
His brain and ours at once a racking:
And may it never curl the head
Of either living block, or dead.
Thus when all dangers they have past,
My leaves like leaves of brass shall last.
No blast shall from a critic's breath,
By vile infection cause their death,
'Till they in flames at last expire,
And help to set the world on fire.   AMEN.

INDEX.

F I N I S.